DOCTRINE TWISTING

How Core Biblical Truths Are Distorted

H. WAYNE HOUSE
AND GORDON CARLE

IVP Books
An imprint of InterVarsity Press
Downers Grove, Illinois

InterVarsity Press
P.O. Box 1400, Downers Grove, IL 60515-1426
World Wide Web: www.ivpress.com
E-mail: email@ivpress.com

InterVarsity Press® is the book-publishing division of InterVarsity Christian Fellowship/USA®, a movement of students and faculty active on campus at hundreds of universities, colleges and schools of nursing in the United States of America, and a member movement of the International Fellowship of Evangelical Students. For information about local and regional activities, write Public Relations Dept., InterVarsity Christian Fellowship/USA, 6400 Schroeder Rd., P.O. Box 7895, Madison, WI 53707-7895, or visit the IVCF website at <www.intervarsity.org>.

Cover design: Cindy Kiple
Cover and interior image: Hulton Archive/Getty Images

ISBN 978-0-8308-1369-8

Printed in the United States of America ∞

InterVarsity Press is committed to protecting the environment and to the responsible use of natural resources. As a member of the Green Press Initiative we use recycled paper whenever possible. To learn more about the Green Press Initiative, visit <www.greenpressinitiative.org>.

Library of Congress Cataloging-in-Publication Data

House, H. Wayne.
Doctrine twisting / H. Wayne House and Gordon Carle.
p. cm.
Includes bibliographical references and index.
ISBN 0-8308-1369-1 (pbk.: alk. paper)
1. Theology, Doctrinal. 2. Christian sects. 3. Cults. I. Carle, Gordon. II. Title.
BT78.H68 2003
230—dc21

2003008229

P	19	18	17	16	15	14	13	12	11	10	9	8	7	6	5	4	3	2
Y	24	23	22	21	20	19	18	17	16	15	14	13	12	11	10	09		

H. Wayne House

to Gary Bassham,

former pastor, present friend

and eternal brother in Christ

Gordon Carle

to Walter, whose outlandish presentation of the teleological argument on his living room floor led a young Air Force airman to Christ

CONTENTS

1

INTRODUCTION

The title of this book deliberately echoes another title, published by InterVarsity Press in 1980: *Scripture Twisting: Twenty Ways the Cults Misread the Bible* by James W. Sire. Sire's book has had an ongoing influence with its superb exposition of ways the nonorthodox groups have formulated and taught doctrines clearly out of harmony with the teachings of Scripture and orthodox Christianity.

In *Doctrine Twisting: How Core Biblical Truths Are Distorted* we endeavor to set forth the basic doctrines of orthodox Christianity and then compare and contrast the teachings of various nonorthodox religious groups. Though among orthodox believers there certainly are differences of opinion regarding aspects of the doctrines presented, there is unity around the core doctrines that distinguish Christian denominations from heterodox groups and sects.

Orthodox Christians join in their commitment to the following doctrines:

1. There is one God who is eternally existent as three persons, Father, Son and Holy Spirit.
2. The Bible, in whole and in part, is the written Word of God and

thus is fully authoritative and sufficient for the Christian's beliefs and practice.

3. Jesus Christ is the Son of God, born of the virgin Mary, being both fully God and fully man with neither confusion of natures nor division of person.
4. Jesus died as a substitutionary sacrifice for humankind, his death alone being necessary and sufficient for our redemption.
5. Jesus Christ was raised from the dead in the same physical body in which he died, though glorified, now subject to neither death nor decay.
6. Jesus will return again bodily to receive his people and judge the wicked.
7. Justification is by grace through faith alone.

These doctrines serve as the basis to evaluate the religious groups discussed in this volume. The reader should understand that the book does not deal with any of these groups regarding any issue but their aberrant theology. Our concern here is only with their lack of adherence to the Scriptures.

Heterodox groups and individuals may reject a biblical teaching for different reasons. For example, the orthodox doctrine of the Trinity may be denied by some because they believe in many gods, or because they reject the deity of the Son or the Spirit, or because they deny the plurality of the persons of the Godhead, or because they reject the personal nature of God and prefer pantheism. In each chapter we will highlight the biblical view while pointing out differences among the groups and why they reject orthodox theology.

In dealing with such doctrines and the beliefs of other people, we need to be cautious. The fact that some people are not orthodox in their thinking and practices does not mean they are not sincere, honest, diligent or personable. We have had informative and friendly conversations with individuals from groups discussed in this book. Though we believe that they fall short of orthodox understanding of the Word of God, we admire their commitment to their beliefs and their zeal to promulgate them. Unfortunately, they very often put evangelical Christians to shame in their Bible study and evangelism.

Our purpose is threefold. First, we desire to help orthodox believers better understand the core doctrines of the Bible so that they may more faithfully appreciate and worship the God of the Bible and embrace the truths concerning him, his works and the salvation we have through Christ. Second, we hope to equip believers with an understanding of orthodox theology *and* aberrant theology so that they may minister to persons outside biblical Christianity. Finally, we would hope that persons who do not subscribe to orthodoxy may through the arguments of the book embrace the truth of God and Jesus Christ, the Savior of humankind.

But aren't we told to love our neighbor as we love ourselves? If this is what we, as believers in Christ, ought to do, why then should we enter into the realm of heated theological debates that often do not accomplish much at all? Such questions arise in the minds of many believers and unbelievers alike. How could anyone ever dare to call someone "unorthodox" or a "heretic"? This is an issue that deserves attention. It is true that we ought to love our neighbor as ourselves, and we believe this includes helping to clear up erroneous teachings on critical issues that could affect one's very salvation. If someone is going down the path of destruction, led by teachings contrary to the Christian message, then the loving thing to do is to clarify, if possible, where the erring group has gone wrong.

The real issue, then, is not to argue people into the Christian faith but to set the orthodox Christian record straight. We seek not so much to attack the unorthodox as to respond to beliefs that are contrary to biblical teaching. This is precisely what the Bible commands us to do (2 Tim 3:16-17). As we respond to attacks on Christian doctrine by employing good hermeneutics and logic, we will clarify Christian truth.

Pascal says, "Those who do not love truth excuse themselves on the grounds that it is disputed and that very many people deny it."[1] The fact that a doctrine is under dispute certainly does not mean that truth cannot be found. To be sure, certain questions will continue to be debated. Still, in relation to the core Christian message, where the evidence is clear as to what is true, a stand needs to be taken.

Orthodoxy essentially means right belief. As historical theologian Bruce Shelley points out, "In church history, however, orthodox Christianity is something purely denotative—referring simply to the majority opinion."[2] Of course majorities are not always right, but in this case the majority has well-founded reasons—biblical premises—for laying down certain doctrines as essential to Christian faith. These main doctrines were laid out by the early church in order to combat erroneous teachings or heresies espoused by various groups.

Christians do differ on the "nonessentials"—for example, will the church be taken out of the world before or after the great tribulation? Our exploration of "doctrine twisting" is not concerned with such differences, because one's beliefs on eschatological topics such as the tribulation will not affect one's salvation. Augustine exhorts us: "In essentials unity, in nonessentials liberty, but in all things charity."

Controversy just for the sake of conflict and dispute is wrong. But in the words of Walter Martin, "Controversy for the sake of truth is a divine command."[3] We are to contend earnestly for the faith that has been given to believers (Jude 3).

The essential doctrines of orthodox Christianity are virtually all denied and distorted by new religious movements. Why and where do they go wrong? As the following chapters will show, some doctrines are outright rejected, contradicted and compromised. But there is another side to the issue, and that is ignorance. By this we do not mean stupidity. Rather, sometimes there is a lack of accurate information. Ignorance could be the outcome of reading an organization's materials rather than independently studying God's Word. It could also be the consequence of being poorly schooled in biblical truth. Such ignorance opens the door to confusion. This is of course why the Christian should be educated not only in biblical knowledge but also in systematic theology (the systematic study of God and related concepts), apologetics (the branch of theology dealing with the defense of the faith), hermeneutics (the art of interpretation) and logic (correct thinking or reasoning).

When we fail to use proper hermeneutical techniques, the conclusions we draw from Bible study may actually be unscriptural.[4] The Holy Spirit does help us understand God's Word; however, this does not minimize the responsibility of the believer to "rightly divide the word of truth." There are three main principles to be used in biblical interpretation. The first is that Scripture should be used to interpret Scripture: clear Scripture helps us to interpret the unclear Scripture. Second, we need to examine the context of a given passage, for this is key to understanding the meaning the author intended. The third principle is that Scripture should be understood in a plain sense, giving due consideration to grammatical structure, figures of speech, literary genre and cultural-historical background. People may well be vulnerable to unorthodox teachings because they have never learned about hermeneutics.

Another aspect of dangerous ignorance is that many people are comfortable just where they are—or have been led to believe that questioning their group's teachings is wrong. As mentioned earlier, many group members face pressure and threats, and their group's teachings encourage them to constantly question their salvation.

Yet we must not explain away all adherence to unorthodox teachings as based on ignorance. For it is possible to see the truth but respond with willful denial and disobedience. The truth seeker will search the Scriptures daily, with much prayer for the help of the Holy Spirit. As we do so, God will reveal himself. This is a promise if we draw near to him.

2

REVELATION

How Is the Bible the Word of God?

The issue of authority is central to any theological or philosophical discussion. How one understands the nature and function of the Bible will determine, in many instances, the content of one's beliefs. There are three factors that appear to be central to this issue of responding to teachings of alternate religious movements. First, what authority does the Bible claim for its message? Second, is the biblical claim credible? Third, how do these groups handle the biblical claims? But even more basic is the reason the Bible exists: to reveal God.

Christians believe the Bible is revelation from God. Nearly every religion believes in revelation in one form or another. Revelation may be defined as the act of God's self-disclosure to humanity. "If we are authorized to say anything at all about the living God, it is only because of God's initiative and revelation. God's disclosure alone can transform our wavering questions concerning ultimate reality into confident exclamations!"[1] Thus knowledge of God's person and works is communicated from God himself. This knowledge is not merely a personal preference or opinion of the individual; it may claim authority through the act of revelation. Revelation means that we can have an accurate knowledge of God, though it may be incomplete. Thus the idea of revelation is a necessary component for any discussion of theology, especially within Christendom.

But God does not simply insert knowledge of himself into our minds. Reformation theology teaches a notion of divine knowledge that Calvin termed the *divinitas,* our human "sense of divinity." Although our awareness of God has been marred by sin, it has not been erased. This "sense of God" was, according to Calvin, the "seed of religion."[2] The great Calvin notwithstanding, however, we contend that to know God involves a dedicated investigation of the revelation he has supplied, both natural and special. And there is something unique about human investigation of God, as Louis Berkhof notes:

> In the study of all other sciences man places himself *above* the object of his investigation and actively elicits from it his knowledge by whatever method may seem most appropriate; but in theology he does not stand above but rather *under* the object of his knowledge. In other words, man can know God only in so far as the latter actively makes Himself known.[3]

When we examine the self-disclosure of God we must come with a humble attitude.

Christian theology has two classifications for the self-disclosure of God: general revelation and special revelation. Theologians typically define general revelation and special revelation in terms of both the content of the revelation and its recipients. General revelation constitutes general information about the person and nature of God and is available to any human at any time. General revelation is the data from which theists construct their arguments for the existence of God, such as the cosmological and teleological arguments, without which there would be no basis for Christian apologetics. Natural theology is the study of God based on what can be inferred from design in nature, the orderliness of the cosmos and the world. From general revelation all may see that the one true God exists. Certain aspects of his character and the plan of salvation, however, are not specified. This is Paul's point in Romans 1:19-21: all people understand that God exists; however, that knowledge is repugnant to the worldview of those in rebellion against their Creator. They know him from the design evident in nature, but they suppress and contort that revelation to alleviate the guilt of their rebellious hearts.

Special revelation, in contrast, contains very specific information about the person and nature of God.[4] The Bible is an example of special revelation in written form. Here one can find specific and detailed information about God, as well as his loving plan of salvation for humankind.

The Orthodox View of Revelation

The Bible looks as if it is one book. After all, it is nicely bound in a leather cover. However, in reality the Bible is a compilation of many books arranged topically and divided into two main sections: the Old Testament and the New Testament. There has been disagreement about how many books the Bible contains. For the purposes of our discussion, the Bible contains sixty-six books.[5] The generally accepted texts of the Old and New Testament books were composed over a period of approximately fifteen hundred years (1440 B.C.-A.D. 100) by at least forty different authors of diverse backgrounds, such as an expatriate Egyptian prince (Moses), a politician (Daniel), a court servant (Nehemiah), a fisherman (Peter) and a high-ranking Jew (Paul). The books were written in different places (for example, the tabernacle quarters, the temple precincts, caves, prisons), on three different continents (Africa, Asia and Europe) and using three different languages (Hebrew, Aramaic and Greek).[6] Clearly the Bible is an extraordinary example of ancient literature that has been transmitted to us.

What makes the Bible and its inspiration unique among the works of antiquity is its unity. From the book of "beginnings" (Genesis) through the book of "unveilings" (Revelation), the Bible centers on a singular theme: God's plan and accomplishment of redemption for humankind through the person and work of Jesus Christ. Thus the Bible is a christocentric book. Its unparalleled continuity is one reason Christians view the Bible as the very Word of God.

Another reason Christians hold Scripture in such high regard is that the Bible itself claims to be from God. In the Old Testament several Hebrew words or phrases indicate that God himself is speaking. *Neum* means "utterance," God's very own speech, spoken by the mouth of the prophet. Prophets use this word in its various inflections 360 times to call attention to the direct origin and authority of declarations made by God himself (Gen 22:16; 1 Sam 2:30; Jer 31:31-33; Zech 12:1-2, 4).[7] Another word, *amar,* can be translated "say," "said" or "says." Charles Feinberg notes, "The word *amar* is used repeatedly by God to introduce revelation. One would suppose that this usage emphasizes that God's revelation is a spoken, transmissible, propositional, definite matter. . . . God gives the revelation to persons as one person imparts knowledge to another—by spoken word."[8] In the several hundred times this word appears in the Old Testament, it is often used to describe an action by God (Gen 32:9, 12; Ex 4:19, 21; Is 54:6, 8). There is also *dabar,* meaning speech or the spoken word. It is used 242 times in the Old Testament to signify that a specific message has been communicated from God to his people (Is 1:10; Jer 10:1; Ezek 13:1).

The New Testament carries on the same thought. Paul's declaration in 2 Timothy 3:16 is perhaps the most familiar passage declaring the divine origin of all Scripture. He uses *theopneustos* to express the idea that Scripture is "God-breathed." As Eduard Schweizer notes, "It is thus evident that the author is differentiating the writings ordained by God's authority from other, secular works."[9] Paul testifies in 1 Corinthians 2:13 that he spoke words that were taught by the Spirit. Paul also refers to portions of the Gospels as being authored by God (1 Tim 5:18), as he quotes Christ's words from Luke 10:7. The apostle Peter considers Paul's words to be from God: "His letters contain some things that are hard to understand, which ignorant and unstable people distort, as they do the other Scriptures, to their own destruction" (2 Pet 3:16). Peter makes a similar comment about the rest of Scripture (2 Pet 1:20-21). Other passages indicating that the New Testament is from God are 2 Corinthians 4:2, Ephesians 3:5, Hebrews 4:12, and Revelation 1:2 and 22:18. The authors of the New Testament seem to have been aware that they were writing the very Word of God.

Some object to using biblical statements to support the source and authority of the Bible. They point out that using the Bible to support the Bible is circular reasoning that "proves" only what the Bible says about itself. (A circular argument assumes an argument to be true prior to its being demonstrated as true.) Christians' statements about the Bible would indeed be circular if there were no external, objective sources of evidence for the Bible's divine origin. Three sources of evidence lend support, however, to the divine origin of the Bible. First is the testimony of the early church. The writings of the church fathers, some of whom were disciples of the apostles themselves, are marked by a uniform conviction regarding the divine origin of the Bible. Second is the witness of history and archaeology. Volumes of works provide evidence of the historical accuracy of the Old and New

Testaments, so powerful that there are poignant stories of scholars who traveled the road from antagonism to acceptance of the divine origin of the Scriptures.[10] Third is the evidence throughout the centuries of changed lives of those confronted with the biblical witness.[11]

The greatest attestation to the divine authority and origin of the Bible, however, is the testimony and stamp of approval of Jesus Christ himself. Since he is God's only Son, who proved his unique divine essence and origin through his miracles and resurrection, it may be logically inferred that whatever he says about *anything else* must be true. Jesus unqualifiedly attests to the divine authority of the Jewish Scriptures in numerous places in the Gospel accounts. His authority was demonstrated through his reliance on the Old Testament as God's own Word. Likewise for the New Testament: Jesus promised his disciples that he would cause them to remember everything he wanted them to remember in order to pass on his words to future generations of believers who would believe because of their testimony (Jn 16:12-13).

Opinions vary concerning how the Bible is a divinely authored book. A number of people believe that God dictated each word to the writers—a view known as the dictation theory. Others argue that the Bible is God's Word only in the sense that he gave its writers some general ideas to put in their own words. Others contend that the biblical authors merely recount in their own words various acts of God that they witnessed. Then there are those who hold that the Bible is not inspired at all but is merely inspiring—like Shakespeare or the *Iliad*. Norman Geisler and William Nix articulate the dangers at either extreme:

> If the human nature of the Bible is emphasized on the one hand, the divine may be compromised on the other. If the divine is emphasized, the human is in danger of being relegated to the

> hypothetical. In one case, the divine nature is taken seriously and the human is viewed incidentally. In the other extreme, the human is so prominent that the divine is obscured.[12]

Some might be tempted to think that acceptance of biblical inspiration is merely a blind leap of faith, but it is not. Rather, as John Gerstner points out:

> Man was made in the divine image so that God could communicate with him not confuse him. . . . It calls for no crucifying of the intellect or believing something demonstrably absurd. It merely requires an intelligent use of the intelligence; a reasonable use of reason. The way to the heart is only through the door of the understanding.[13]

So while the process of inspiration is a mystery, belief in inspiration is not contrary to reason or a violation of any principle of logic.

We take what evangelicals call the verbal-plenary view of the inspiration of Scripture. All this means is that the very words themselves (verbal) in every part of the Bible (plenary) are ultimately authored by God. In this view God, rather than merely dictating the words, inspired the biblical authors to perfectly express through their own vocabularies, personalities and writing styles the message he wanted to convey: "On the one hand God spoke, deciding himself what he intended to say, yet not in such a way as to distort the personality of the human authors. On the other hand men spoke, using their faculties freely, yet not in such a way as to distort the message of the divine author."[14]

A corollary to the verbal-plenary view of Scripture is the belief that the Bible's original manuscripts were inerrant and infallible. This means that the words of the Bible in the original manuscripts are entirely true and never false in all they affirm, whether in relation to doctrine, ethics, or the social, physical or life sciences.[15] Christians differ in their beliefs regarding inerrancy, but we are convinced that the Bible's inspiration, inerrancy and authority stand or fall together.

It is understandable, then, that Christians look to the Bible as their final authority in all matters of doctrine and ethics. The Bible contains information on many subjects, yet one would perform a disservice to the Scriptures if one did not relate them all to the primary focus of the Bible—the person and work of Jesus Christ.

God's plan for humankind. The Bible is not primarily about human actions or thoughts, although these are certainly present. Scripture is actually God's revelation of himself and his world. It portrays his actions in the world throughout history. Karl Barth, a neo-orthodox theologian, rightly understood the intent of Scripture even though he did not accept verbal-plenary inspiration:

> It is not the right human thoughts about God, which form the content of the Bible, but the right divine thoughts about men. The Bible tells us not how we should talk with God but what he says to us; not how we find him, but how he has sought and found the way to us; not the right relation in which we must place ourselves to him, but the covenant which he has made with all who are Abraham's spiritual children and which he has sealed once and for all in Jesus Christ.[16]

As Barth asserts, the main purpose of the Bible is to set forth what God has done by sending his Son Jesus to redeem humankind and to restore a proper relationship with those redeemed. As John says, "But these are written that you may believe that Jesus is the Christ, the Son of God" (Jn 20:31).

Textual transmission. The transmission, or history of copying, of the books that the biblical authors wrote has been a truly remarkable process. Although Scripture's transmission has been highly accurate, it has not been entirely perfect. The original manuscripts (known as autographs) of the sixty-six books, to our knowledge, are no longer in existence, but thousands of ancient copies of them have been found. The thought of not possessing the autographs may be troublesome to some, but R. Laird Harris's understanding is apt:

> It is not our contention that the copyists made no mistakes. They did. . . . There are, furthermore, abundant and clear evidences for believing that God in His providence saw to it that the sacred text was preserved *free from any error of consequence* so that we may with confidence declare that we have the text in substantially the form in which it left the hand of the author.[17]

While there have been errors in copying the Scriptures over time, there has not been corruption to the point of distorting their message. Those who contend that there has been such corruption do not understand the situation as it really exists and seem to be asserting what they *hope* to be the case.

The Bible is by far the most reliable ancient document. First, there are nearly 5,500 manuscripts or manuscript fragments that can be compared to one another in order to provide an incredibly accurate picture of how the original texts must have read. No other ancient work has come down to us in such volume; in fact, many of the ancient writings we possess have been transmitted by way of only a handful of surviving manuscripts. The New Testament has about 20,000 lines of text of which some 40 might be questioned; the *Iliad,* by contrast, has 15,600 lines, of which 764 are questioned.[18] So in terms of overall textual purity, the biblical text stands alone. Simply stated, there is no comparison.

Second, we possess biblical manuscripts dating back very near to the time of the original autographs. This literary fact is unprecedented. The following list represents only a small sampling of what has survived the centuries:

- John Rylands Fragment (c. A.D. 117-138, perhaps even earlier) contains portions of five verses from John's Gospel (Jn 18:31-33, 37-38).
- Chester Beatty Papyri (c. A.D. 250) contains most of the New Testament.
- Bodmer Papyri (second-third century A.D.) contains several portions of the New Testament.
- Codex Vaticanus (c. A.D. 325-350) contains the entire Bible.
- Codex Sinaiticus (c. A.D. 340) contains more than half the Old Testament and nearly all of the New Testament.[19]

Not long ago scholars found in the vaults of Oxford's Magdalen College what may be the oldest surviving fragment of a New Testament manuscript. Some believe the Magdalen Fragment, as it is now called, may actually be an eyewitness account of Jesus' life. If accurate, it contains verses from Matthew 26 and includes the oldest written reference to Mary Magdalene and the betrayal of Christ by Judas. It may date to A.D. 40-70.[20]

The closer a written source is to the event it describes, the more likely it is to be reliable, all other things being equal. As F. F. Bruce comments: "The evidence for our New Testament writings is ever so much greater than the evidence for many writings of classical authors, the authenticity of which no one dreams of questioning."[21]

When all of the New Testament manuscripts are compared and contrasted, they show only slight variances. One example of how an error can be resolved as our knowledge grows involves Acts 17:6, 8, where Luke calls the city rulers *politarchs*, a word that occurs nowhere else in Scripture. For many years it was claimed that such a word appeared nowhere else in Greek literature. "Earlier critical scholars accused Luke of either ignorance or carelessness. But since then a number of inscriptions have been found, dating from the second and third centuries A.D., several in Thessalonica itself, which have vindicated Luke's use of the title."[22]

When all the evidence is assembled, it becomes evident that the New Testament is 99.5 percent pure[23]—that is, 99.5 percent of it has come down to us uncorrupted throughout all the years of copying and transmission.

Biblical interpretation. Scripture gives us some marvelous promises regarding God's desire and willingness to reveal himself: "He guides the humble in what is right and teaches them his way" (Ps 25:9). Jesus assured his disciples that the Holy Spirit would be sent to personally teach and guide God's followers (Jn 16:13-15). When it comes to the Bible, God will help us understand it. The Spirit will provide wisdom and illumination so that we may be enlightened by God's truth in Scripture (1 Cor 2:12; Eph 1:17-18). "Illumination refers to the ministry of the Spirit by which the meaning of Scripture is made clear to the believer."[24] As we read Scripture and yield to the Spirit, we can trust that the Lord will impart understanding to our minds.

Passages such as 1 Corinthians 12—14 make no mention of a select person or group with unique or authoritative insight into the truths of Scripture. The noticeable absence of such gifts of unique biblical insight suggests that they have never existed. *Every believer* is to handle the "word of truth" correctly (2 Tim 2:15). This admonition, although originally written to Timothy, suggests that it is the responsibility of all serious disciples to be diligent in study of the Scriptures, as they alone are the standard of truth. Even Paul was examined by the Scriptures (Acts 17:11). The Bible declares that it alone is the benchmark to determine truth.

When we say that the Bible has authority as God's Word, we are referring to the canon as it has come down to us. We believe in a closed canon—that is, no further revelations have been or will be given through divinely inspired messengers, like the prophets or the apostles. Jesus implicitly gave his approval to the accepted canon held by the Jews to be the authoritative Word of God; he promised his apostles that they too would be receptacles of the Word of God as the Holy Spirit led them to remember everything spoken by Jesus for posterity (Jn 16:12-13). Our present Bible of the Old and New Testaments is sufficient for our salvation and our life in Christ.

The Bible and New Religious Movements

As Paul in Romans 1 indicts the Gentiles for their suppression of God's *general* revelation, so many of the movements stand indicted for their suppression of *special* revelation by twisting it to support their preconceived notions.[25] Many religious groups suggest that the Bible has not been transmitted accurately down through the centuries. Some denigrate the Bible, calling it a document full of contradictions, mistranslations and spurious additions, merely a collection of printed words on pages, or a compilation of myths and legends that at best offers only some good advice.

Many groups claim that they have an extra source of knowledge about the person or plan of God. They may state that their new revelations explain what the Bible actually says. These new revelations, whether they are verbal or written, supersede the Bible and often contradict it. Yet these groups that claim to have new revelation also continue to stress their regard for Scripture as a true source of knowledge about God.

Whenever an element of extrabiblical revelation plays a role in the formation or continuation of a new religious movement, there is almost always one person who rises to a position of unquestioned leadership and receives the new revelations. Often this person claims to be a prophet of God.

Church of Jesus Christ of Latter-day Saints (LDS). Members of the LDS church often quote Scripture while conducting missionary forays in people's living rooms or during evangelistic campaigns. They quote the Bible prolifically over the airwaves, sell the Bible in their church-owned bookstores and boast of their reliance on the classic King James Version. This makes it seem that the Mormon Church is just another Protestant denomination.

Here is the official Mormon position on the Bible, from the LDS Articles of Faith: "Article 8: We believe the Bible to be the Word of God as far as it is translated correctly, we also believe the Book of Mormon to be the word of God."[26] Bruce McConkie, Mormon "apostle," amplifies this statement: "The Church uses the King James Version of the Bible, but acceptance of the Bible is coupled with a reservation that it is true only insofar as translated correctly."[27] Thus biblical authority as understood within the greater Christian tradition dies the death of a thousand qualifications every time LDS theology is advanced.

How correctly *is* the Bible translated? The writings of LDS leaders indicate that the answer is, not very well at all. McConkie writes, "As all informed persons know, the various versions of the Bible do not accurately record or perfectly preserve the words, thoughts, and intents of the original inspired authors."[28] An early LDS apostle, Orson Pratt (1811-1881), asks, "What shall we say then, concerning the Bible's being a sufficient guide? Can we rely upon it in its present known corrupted state, as being a faithful record of God's Word?"[29] Pratt answers his own questions thus:

> We all know that but a few of the inspired writings have descended to our times. What few have come down to our day, have been mutilated, changed, and corrupted, in such a shameful manner that no two manuscripts agree. . . . Who, in his right mind, could, for one moment, suppose the Bible in its present form to be a perfect guide? Who knows that even one verse of the whole Bible has escaped pollution so as to convey the same sense now that it did in the original?[30]

Joseph Fielding Smith (1876-1972), tenth president of the Mormon Church, takes the same position: "We are well aware that there are errors in the Bible due to faulty translations and ignorance on the part of translators."[31]

Yet such statements are inconsistent with the way Mormons talk about and use the Bible in more public forums and when dealing with non-Mormons. For example, in a fifteen-page evangelistic tract titled *Apostasy and Restoration,* thirty-nine Bible verses are quoted as having divine authority.[32] The author of another booklet published by the LDS church states, "I believe the Bible to be the Word of God to the Jews and also to the Gentiles."[33]

In the Mormon Church four "Standard Works" are authoritative and considered Scripture: the Bible, the Book of Mormon, Doctrine and Covenants, and Pearl of Great Price.[34] Speeches and writings of current presidents are also authoritative, since the Mormon Church views them as modern-day "prophets." The Book of Mormon, Doctrine and Covenants, and the Pearl of Great Price cover a wide range of subjects and contain, according to Mormons, the very words of God, a restoration of truths that were ignored or wrongly translated throughout church history.[35] A Mormon doctrinal writing defines the Book of Mormon thus: "an account of God's dealings with the people of the American continents from about 2200 [B.C.] . . . to [A.D.] 421. . . . It was translated from gold plates by Joseph Smith and contains the fulness of the gospel."[36] The Book of Mormon itself claims that the Bible is incomplete: "Because of the many plain and precious things which have been taken out of the book, which were plain to the understanding of the children of men, according to the plainness which is the Lamb of God—because of these things which are taken away out of the gospel of the Lamb, an exceeding great many do stumble, yea, insomuch that Satan hath great power over them" (1 Nephi 13:29).

Mormons claim to believe the Bible in its entirety. However, actually they believe the Bible only where it does not conflict with their extrabiblical books, which were produced by their founder/prophet, Joseph Smith Jr. McConkie asserts, "Acceptance of the Bible is coupled with a reservation that it is true only insofar as translated correctly. The other three, having been revealed in modern times in English, are accepted without qualification."[37]

The place of importance given to Smith's writings in comparison to the Bible is perhaps best seen in Ezra Taft Benson's (1899-1994), thirteenth president of the LDS church, quote of McConkie: "Men can get nearer to the Lord . . . through the Book of Mormon than through the Bible. . . . There will be more people saved in the Kingdom of God ten thousand times over because of the Book of Mormon than there will be because of the Bible."[38] Smith's books and statements are thought to interpret the Bible as it should be understood: "When the Bible is read under the guidance of the Spirit, and in harmony with the many latter-day revelations which interpret and make plain its more mysterious parts, it becomes one of the most priceless volumes known to man."[39] For Mormons, then, the Old and New Testaments are inadequate in communicating God's message; other "revelations of God" are required to clarify what God meant.

Jehovah's Witnesses. Not every unorthodox group gives the Bible so little regard. Some groups believe very strongly in the authority and reliability of Scripture. Consider the position of the Jehovah's Witnesses:

> Facts testify to the *integrity* of the Bible. The Bible narrative is inseparably interwoven with the history of the times. It gives straightforward truthful instruction in the simplest manner. The guileless earnestness and fidelity of the writers, their burning zeal for truth, their painstaking effort to attain accuracy in details recommend the Bible for what it is, God's Word of Truth.[40]

The Witnesses' view of the authority of the Bible is commendably orthodox. However, a major problem arises in this and other groups when the interpretation of God's Word is left up to a few persons who form a spiritually elite hierarchy. This practice actually works against, and may contradict, their orthodox views.

Only the Watchtower Society can correctly interpret the Bible; it cannot be properly understood by a mere individual:

> The Bible is an organizational book and belongs to the Christian congregation, not to individuals, regardless of how sincerely they may believe that they can interpret the Bible. . . . The Bible cannot be properly understood without Jehovah's visible organization in mind.[41]

> God has not arranged for that Word to speak independently or to shine forth life-giving truths by itself. . . . It is through his organization God provides this light.[42]

> Unless we are in touch with this channel of communication that God is using, we will not progress along the road to life, no matter how much Bible reading we do.[43]

Not only does the Watchtower proclaim its own interpretations over and against those of all other people, but it has its own Bible translation. The New World translation is the best Scripture version, according to the Watchtower, and should be used when there is disagreement between translations. "The endeavor of the New World Bible Translation committee has been to avoid this snare of religious traditionalism."[44]

The Witnesses have claimed that anyone who seeks to understand the Bible through a course of personal study will soon find himself or herself in spiritual darkness. The Bible, according to the Witnesses, was never intended for the individual, but for an organization.[45] The Bible can be correctly interpreted only by God's "faithful slave," the Watchtower Bible and Tract Society.[46] The scriptural interpretation the organization puts forth should be viewed as the truth.[47] The Witnesses receive their spiritual nourishment from books published by their organization,[48] and the primary source of truth is *The Watchtower,* a bimonthly magazine that has been in print since 1879. All teachings in *The Watchtower*, or other organizational publications, are to be believed by Witnesses.[49]

Other Unorthodox Groups. The claim that God has revealed other "scripture" is not unique to Mormons; it is also found in Christian Science. And Elizabeth Clare Prophet, leader of the Church Universal and Triumphant, announces in the subtitle of a book that *Many of Jesus' Teachings Were Altered, Deleted or Never Recorded.*[50] She avers, "Apart from intentional deletions by the authors, we know that the Gospels have been edited, interpolated, subjected to scribal errors, garnished by additions and plagued by subtractions."[51] These assertions are made without any attempt to substantiate them.

Still others make similar comments concerning Scripture. Note the words of Roy Masters, founder/director of the Foundation for

Human Understanding: "The Bible to me is not holy. . . . I can if you pardon my expression take that Bible to the toilet with me and use it the same way as anything else . . . I wouldn't feel guilty for that."[52]

Many unorthodox groups claim that the average attendee cannot understand the Bible without special help. Various reasons are given—for example, that Scripture is too complex or holds hidden meanings.

Exactly how rank-and-file group members receive the proper interpretations of the Bible varies. Some use taped messages by their leaders. Others use a particular study book. A number of unorthodox groups have a lengthy series of pamphlets or magazines.

RESPONDING TO THE NEW RELIGIOUS MOVEMENTS

Church of Jesus Christ of Latter-day Saints. Concern over the accuracy of biblical translations is legitimate, but Pratt and modern Mormon writers overstate their case. The credentials of the members of the various biblical translation teams in the past and today reveal a cadre of highly qualified experts who span a variety of theological viewpoints. Most translators' interest in the translation of the biblical text is professional, not theological. Any translation that is skewed is readily recognized as such by scholars and laity alike. As already noted, the history of biblical transmission over the centuries is truly remarkable. There is an amazing consistency between the modern and original renderings of biblical texts. The translation of the Bible has a very high degree of reliability.

When exclusivism is practiced in biblical interpretation, the authority of the Bible is diminished. The individual or organization that tells others what the Bible teaches has the authority, not the Bible. Furthermore, the illuminating ministry of the Spirit becomes unnecessary, if it is held to exist at all.

If God were to give further revelations, they would have to be consistent with any prior revelations. This principle alone would eliminate most Mormon theological writings, since they stand in direct opposition to the divine revelation that has already been given by God in the Bible.

The Mormons claim it is impossible to correctly interpret without outside revelation—from them, of course. Acceptance of the Bible is conditioned with the caveat that it be correctly translated. But what is the standard? For all practical purposes, the Mormon statement implies that the Bible is always wrong whenever and wherever it conflicts with established Mormon doctrine. This effectively places all Mormon writings in a position above Scripture.

The Book of Mormon, which is said to have been translated from gold plates, has been investigated by scholars in linguistics. It has been discovered that the supposed Reformed Egyptian characters that Joseph Smith copied from the Book of Mormon plates are gibberish. There is no existing evidence of a "Reformed Egyptian" language. Nor is there any evidence that the following terms are Egyptian or Semitic: Shazar (1 Nephi 16:13-14), Irreantum (1 Nephi 17:5), deseret (for "bee," Ether 2:3), Liahona (Alma 37:38).

Moreover, although the Book of Mormon was written in the middle of the nineteenth century, it is written in Elizabethan English of the early sixteenth century, the language of the King James Version of the Bible. One wonders why God would use language three centuries old instead of the ordinary English of Smith's day.

The archaeological evidence for the Bible's historical and geographical statements is so prolific as to be eminently impressive.[53] In contrast, there is literally *no* archaeological support for the historical and geographical statements made the Book of Mormon regarding the North American continent. Although the LDS church does claim archaeological support for the Book of Mormon, none of these claims have been verified by physical evidence. Some scholars have left the Mormon Church because they found discrepancies between Mormon claims and the historical record.

For example, 1 Nephi 1:2 and Mosiah 1:4 say that the native Hebrew language from 691-600 B.C. was Egyptian, and Mormon 9:32 says it was Reformed Egyptian by A.D. 400. Both assertions are, of course, incorrect. According to well-established history, the Hebrews spoke Hebrew in 600 B.C. Then, as a result of the Babylonian captivity (560-538 B.C.), the Hebrew language came to be spoken only by scribes, priests and rabbis while the rest of the populace adopted the lingua franca of that period, Aramaic. After A.D. 70, when Titus forced the Jews from Judea and Samaria, they adopted the languages of the nations to which they scattered.

Arabia is described as "bountiful because of its much fruit and also wild honey" (1 Nephi 17:5) and is said to have contained ample timber (1 Nephi 18:1). Yet Arabia has never, in recorded history, had ample or bountiful supplies of timber, fruit or honey. Its land is plentiful only in petroleum, sand and sunshine. Another geographical error: 1 Nephi 2:6-9 speaks of a river named Laman flowing continually to the Red Sea. Recorded history provides no instance of any name of a river in Arabia.

In 1 Nephi 18:25 we read that North America had cows, oxen, asses, horses and goats "for the use of man" in 600 B.C. The fact is that there were no such animals in North America until the Europeans brought them many hundreds of years later, beginning in the seventeenth century. Similarly, 2 Nephi 21:6-8 lifts Isaiah 11:6-8 from the King James Bible and applies it to North America (see also 2 Nephi 30:12-14). But North America had no sheep, lions, leopards, asps or cockatrices at the time that the Book of Mormon indicates.

Jehovah's Witnesses. The Jehovah's Witnesses claim that only "God's organization on earth" has the ability to interpret the Bible means that no Christians in any age had access to scriptural truth until the Watchtower Society began its work. It also relegates the Holy Spirit to a minor or nonexistent role in illuminating Scripture.

Biblical scholars have *never* considered the New World translation one of the better Scripture translations. It is crowded with special pleadings and mistranslations. "It must be viewed as a radically biased piece of work. At some points, it is actually dishonest. At others, it is neither modern nor scholarly."[54] According to Greek scholar Bruce Metzger, "The Jehovah's Witnesses have incorporated in their translation of the New Testament several quite erroneous renderings of the Greek."[55] Possibly in response to such criticisms, in recent years Jehovah's Witnesses have retreated from insistence on the New World translation.

Conclusion

Unfortunately, when the prophecies of a modern-day prophet fail, an excuse is swift in coming. For example, since their inception the Jehovah's Witnesses have claimed to be a corporate prophet of God.[56] The Watchtower prophesied early on that the end of the world would occur in 1914.[57] When the expected apocalypse failed to materialize, the explanation was that the end of human rule began to occur *invisibly* in the heavens with the return of Christ.[58]

Another helpful test for prophecy is to apply a principle of logic known as "the law of noncontradiction." This means simply that *A* cannot be non-*A* at the same time and in the same sense. That is, truth cannot contradict itself. For example, consider attempting to draw a picture of a square circle. It can't be done! This notion violates the law of noncontradiction. While one could draw a picture of a square or a circle, one cannot draw both in the same space at the same time.

Any "new revelation" from God must not contradict what God has already given in Scripture. But at some point each "new revelation" of a religious group inevitably teaches the opposite of what the Bible teaches. When this occurs, the believer is safe in asserting that the "new revelation" is simply human words, not God's.

Jesus is the Way, the Truth and the Life (Jn 14:6)—not simply *a* way, truth or life but *the* way. We do well to heed Jesus' words in Matthew 7:15, where he exhorts us to watch out for false prophets: "they come to you in sheep's clothing, but inwardly they are ferocious wolves."

The only way we can know God is for God to reveal himself to us. God has chosen to do so through special revelation, the Bible. The Bible claims to be the very Word of God. God has given us the Holy Spirit to illumine our application of the Bible and guide each of us daily. And God has promised us that his Word will stand forever (Is 40:8). As Jesus said, Scripture cannot be broken, or proved to be in error (Jn 10:35).

Whether God can reveal further truths to humankind is not the issue. God can do anything consistent with his nature. But has God revealed another gospel to human beings? Not one alternative religious movement has produced new revelations compatible with Scripture. In fact, these new revelations have contradicted every essential doctrine contained in God's revelation.

3

WHO OR WHAT IS GOD?

It has been said that most, if not all, deviations from orthodox doctrine begin with a wrong view of God. If this is correct, then we need to understand carefully God's nature and attributes in order to have sound doctrine. This chapter will examine three things the Scriptures tell us about God. First, God possesses the attributes of personhood. Second, God possesses certain qualities that set him apart from any other being. Third, there is but one God, yet there are three Persons who are called "God." Theologians call this concept "the Trinity."

THE ORTHODOX UNDERSTANDING OF GOD'S NATURE

God is personal. "Over against any abstract neutral metaphysical concept, the God of Scripture is first and foremost a personal being."[1] What does personhood entail? "Self-awareness and especially rationality have figured in most philosophical characterizations of personhood."[2] We normally reserve the word *person* for human beings, and more specifically the metaphysical nature of a human. The nature of a person, as observed in human beings, comprises at least three things—mind, will and emotion.[3] The best comparison of perfect human nature to that of God is expressed in the Word of God, Jesus Christ.

The Bible clearly presents God as having personal qualities. As a being who possesses a *mind*, God can formulate plans and designs for his creation. Scripture emphasizes that God had plans for the salvation of people before the creation of the earth (Eph 1:4). History is moving toward the conclusion of a plan that originates in God (Dan 2:20-45). The Scriptures provide many examples of God's *will*, especially in the ministry of Jesus. Our Lord repeatedly says that he is not doing his own will but "the will of him who sent me" (Jn 6:38). Paul and Peter use the phrase "will of God" many times in their epistles. The *emotion* of God can be found throughout the Scriptures and can be characterized with the same words that describe human emotion.[4] Scripture contains many examples of emotions exhibited by Jesus and the Father, though the Father did not "feel" the kinds of emotions his Son felt while in his humanity. Many more qualities of personhood in the nature of God could be examined and illustrated, but these are sufficient for now to demonstrate that God is personal.

The attributes of God. God possesses certain qualities that separate him from any other personal being in the universe, whether angelic or human. Such qualities are called *attributes.* Louis Berkhof explains that "the incommunicable attributes emphasize the absolute Being of God," while those we call "communicable attributes stress the fact that He enters into various relationships with His creatures."[5] The incommunicable attributes of God are shared within the Trinity alone: eternality, omniscience and omnipotence; the communicable attributes are those God shares with human beings. Here we will consider three incommunicable attributes—self-existence, immutability and infinitude.

God's own being is the basis of his existence. Humans cannot cause their own existence; we must have parents whose union causes us to exist. The same is true for any other living thing, and even the inanimate objects in the universe are dependent on God for their existence. All creation is *contingent* or dependent on something or someone else for its existence.

Often children ask, "Who created God?" The answer is no one, for God is not a contingent being. "For as the Father has life in himself, so he has granted the Son to have life in himself" (Jn 5:26). God said to Moses, "I AM WHO I AM" (Ex 3:14). God needed nothing in order to exist!

The immutability of God means he is unchanging in his nature and purposes.[6] God does not grow, change or develop in any way. This contrasts to our experience of growth and development. Any living thing starts out immature and becomes mature, and the earth around us goes through changes. The God presented in the pages of the Scriptures is the only exception to that rule. "There is change round about Him, change in the relations of men to Him, but there is no change in His Being."[7] The fact that humans change in their relationship to God makes it appear at times that God himself changes. Rather, his treatment of humans relates to their response to his unchanging standards. When a person moves from rebellion to repentance, God may move from justice to mercy in response, thus appearing to change, but God did not change internally. He was *always* merciful and just. This stability enables us to have confidence in an unchanging God.[8]

This concept of God is clearly taught in such passages as James 1:17: "Every good and perfect gift is from above, coming down from the Father of the heavenly lights, who does not change like shifting shadows." Also Malachi 3:6: "I the LORD do not change." The same is true of Jesus, as we are told in Hebrews 13:8: "Jesus Christ is the same yesterday and today and forever."

The infinitude of God should be considered as freedom from all limitations in all aspects of his being, including power, knowledge, spatial existence, time existence. He is infinite in power *(omnipotent)*. God's power is more than strength; it is also authority to accomplish what God desires. What God has planned he has the strength and the authority to accomplish.

God's *omniscience* means that God knows all things: past, present and future, both contingent and actual. Some may be tempted to think that God's knowledge is qualitatively different from ours and thus God's truth may be contradictory to our truth. But God *is* truth, and he made us in his image to think his thoughts after him. Thus truth is universal, and what is true for God is true for us.

God's freedom from spatial limitations is known as *omnipresence:* God transcends all limitations of space, yet he fills all parts of space with his entire being.[9] This does not mean that God is some kind of expansive being with part of him in one part of the universe and part in another. He is not spatial. Rather, God in his totality of being is at every place that space is, without himself being in space or confined by it. God is present in all of creation (as David tells us in Psalm 139), but he is not the creation.

God exists separate from time; he is *eternal.* God created time and does act within time. But God is not merely a being who exists forever; he is above time and its ongoing sequence of motion and events. God can observe the passage of time and interact with us in time. This is communicated in Psalm 90:2, "Before the mountains were born or you brought forth the earth and the world, from everlasting to everlasting you are God." And in Deuteronomy 33:27, "The eternal God is your refuge."

God is a triune being. Christianity, like Judaism and Islam, is a monotheistic religion. Monotheism is defined as belief that there is only one God. The most well known passage that declares this idea is Deuteronomy 6:4: "Hear, O Israel: The LORD our God, the LORD is one." The Hebrew word for "one" signifies a unity of being and purpose.[10] There are many other passages in both the Old and New Testaments that echo this teaching.

The belief in the triune being of God is known as the doctrine of the Trinity: there is only one true God, who within his eternal nature exists as three distinct persons (or three centers of consciousness), the Father, the Son and the Holy Spirit. Although these coequal and coeternal Persons are distinct in function, position and relationship, they all share the same nature or essence. "[Trinity] signifies that within one essence of the Godhead we have to distinguish three 'persons' who are neither three gods on the one side, nor three parts or modes of God on the other, but coequally and coeternally God."[11]

The idea of the Trinity is more clearly developed in the New Testament (for example, Mt 28:19; Jn 1:1), but there are some hints of a plurality within the Godhead in the Old Testament. The first hint of such an idea can be found in Genesis 1:26: "Let us make man in our image, in our likeness."[12] The second is in Genesis 11:7: "Let us go down and confuse their language." A well-known messianic passage that is viewed as a good trinitarian text is Psalm 45:6-7:

> Your throne, O God, will last for ever and ever;
> a scepter of justice will be the scepter of your kingdom.
> You love righteousness and hate wickedness;
> therefore God, your God, has set you above your companions
> by anointing you with the oil of joy.

In the New Testament it is clearer that there are three distinct Persons who are called "God." For example, the Father is called God in 1 Thessalonians 1:1: "To the church of the Thessalonians in God the Father." The Son is called God in Titus 2:13: "the glorious appearing of our great God and Savior, Jesus Christ." Finally, the Spirit is called God in Acts 5:3-4: "Then Peter said, 'Ananias, how is it that Satan has so filled your heart that you have lied to the Holy Spirit and have kept for yourself some of the money you received for the land? . . . You have not lied to men but to God.'"

Two warnings should be sounded concerning one's understanding of the Trinity and the biblical teaching of God. First, as we are finite beings attempting to comprehend an infinite being, there are limits to our understanding. We must not try to force biblical texts to conform to our understanding. Second, we can trust God's self-revelation in the Bible. The doctrine of the Trinity, though difficult, is not logically incoherent. God can communicate exactly what we need to know about his personhood, nature and purposes. If our understanding falters, we must depend on Scripture. Berkhof gives words of guidance for our thinking: "The doctrine of the Trinity is very decidedly a doctrine of revelation. . . . It is a doctrine which we would not have known, nor have been able to maintain with any degree of confidence, on the basis of experience alone, and which is brought to our knowledge only by God's special revelation."[13] As we seek to understand not only the Trinity but the whole doctrine of God, the only infallible source of information on the qualities and character of God is Scripture.

The doctrine of the Trinity was not formally set forth until the Athanasian Creed was drawn up in the first half of the fifth century. Before that, however, trinitarian thought had already been expressed at the Council of Nicaea (A.D. 325). This council was called by Emperor Constantine to deal with a heresy termed Arianism (similar to what Jehovah's Witnesses believe about Jesus). This council, it is generally believed, produced the core of the Nicene Creed, further elaborated on and confirmed in A.D. 381 at Constantinople, what is often called Nicaea II.[14]

God is like human beings in some ways and very different from us in other ways. The word *immanence* refers to God's involvement and relationship with his creation.[15] He is not some distant being who is aloof to our condition; he is greatly concerned about and involved with all aspects of his creation. The word *transcendence* refers to God's existence and rule outside and above creation.[16] God is independent of, and far greater than, his creation.

THE GOD OF THE NEW RELIGIOUS MOVEMENTS

The theology of God within new religious movements deviates from the orthodox view in three primary ways. First, because of a misunderstanding of the immanence and transcendence of God, some unorthodox groups teach *monism*,[17] the philosophical idea that everything in reality is one, not many. Any plurality that we perceive is illusory. Second, some movements fail to understand the relationship of the Persons within the Godhead, so they may teach *modalism*—one God expressed in three different manifestations. Third, they may overstress the plurality of God, effectively denying that God is one in essence.

Mind Science groups. Some of the Mind Science groups portray God as an all-pervasive force, so that everything that exists is one, and all is God. This concept may be presented as a belief in a mind or intelligence that is one. It may be stated using terms that signify "person," yet the result is that it effectively denies that God is a person. Consider the following statement from Christian Science:

> There is no life, truth, intelligence, nor substance in matter. All is infinite Mind and its infinite manifestation, for God is All-in-all. Spirit is immortal Truth; matter is mortal error. Spirit is the real and eternal; matter is the unreal and temporal. Spirit is God, and man is His image and likeness. Therefore man is not material; he is spiritual.[18]

The universe, in this theory, is dualistic in nature, divided between spirit and matter. The world around us communicates error; thus when looking for truth the Christian Scientist must concentrate on the spiritual concept of God. Matter is evil and temporal, not "real" when compared to eternal spirit. Instead of saying "God is Spirit," Christian Science says, "Spirit is God." And since human beings are created in God's image and likeness, they are not material but entirely spiritual—despite the fact that we all must interact with one another as beings limited to a physical reality of time and space.

The Christian Scientist explicitly denies that God is personal in the ordinary sense of the term, as John De Witt states:

> It is true that Scientists do not think of God as a person in the ordinary sense of the word, as it is used in referring to a physical form or a finite personality. But they do think of Him as individual conscious Mind, the all-knowing, all-wise, supreme Intelligence. They think of Him as the Ego, or infinite I AM, the creator to whom we can always turn for comfort, inspiration, and guidance. All of this is indicated when a Christian Scientist speaks of God as Mind.[19]

All of the Mind Science groups redefine the triune God as a trinity of "attributes" or roles. For example, Mary Baker Eddy's *Science and Health* says:

> Life, Truth, and Love constitute the Triune Person called God—that is, the triply divine Principle, Love. They represent a trinity in unity, three in one—the same in essence, though multi-form in office: God the Father-Mother; Christ the spiritual idea of sonship; divine Science or the Holy Comforter. These three express in divine Science the threefold, essential nature of the infinite. They also indicate the divine Principle of scientific being, the intelligent relation of God to man and the universe.[20]

Here is another example: "The Father is Principle, the Son is that Principle revealed in the creative plan, the Holy Spirit is the executive power of both the Father and Son carrying out the plan."[21]

"A Course in Miracles." A popular work that has gained some acceptance within the church, *A Course in Miracles* is not a religious organization. Rather, individuals gather to discuss the work's meaning and how *A Course in Miracles* has affected them. The gatherings may resemble a Bible study group; in fact, this is the way some Christians encounter this text. Christians must be aware of what *A Course in Miracles* teaches, since it uses basic Christian terms yet redefines them in a manner that is not orthodox.

For example, *A Course in Miracles* explicitly teaches monism:

> In my own mind, behind all my insane thoughts of separation and attack, is the knowledge that all is one forever. I have not lost the knowledge of who I am because I have forgotten it. It has kept me in the Mind of God, Who had not left His Thoughts. And I, who am among them, am one with them and one with Him.[22]

> Whenever you question your value, say: "God Himself is incomplete without me."[23]

> God is still everywhere and in everything forever. And we are a part of Him.[24]

Like all monistic faiths, *A Course in Miracles* supports the ancient notion of pantheism, that God is in all. "The recognition of God is the recognition of yourself. There is no separation of God and His creation."[25]

The Church Universal and Triumphant. The Church Universal and Triumphant (CUT) also teaches monism but has more to say about God:

> You have all of the shining qualities of God, of the Creator of a living soul which has the real potential—the *real*ized potential—of the Spirit. *Qualitatively* you can become God. But *quantitatively* you will always be the all within the all. And this monadic self is made in the *real* Christ image, in whose name it, too, has been slain from the foundation of the world.[26]

In CUT theology we are all one with God and originate from the same spirit substance. "We are one with the Word as the Word is one with us. We can be separated neither from the creative Sound nor from the creative Source. So we contain all our beginnings and our endings—and even the Origin of our origin."[27]

Church of Jesus Christ of Latter-day Saints. Perhaps no other religious group in America and the world does more in redefining Christian doctrine than the Mormons. The Mormons believe there are many gods that inhabit the universe. "How many Gods there are, I do no know. But there never was a time when there were not Gods."[28] The Trinity is composed of three separate "gods." "Many men say there is one God; the Father, the Son, and the Holy Ghost are only one God! I say that is a strange God anyhow—three in one and one in three. . . . It would make the biggest God in all the world.

He would be a wonderfully big God—he would be a giant or a monster."[29] Instead, Mormon founder Joseph Smith says, "I have always declared God to be a distinct personage, Jesus Christ a separate personage and distinct personage from God the Father, and the Holy Ghost was a distinct personage and a Spirit: and these three constitute three distinct personages and three Gods."[30]

In Mormon theology God the Father is an exalted man, one who "progressed" to godhood with a body of flesh and bone. This amazing transformation from contingent to necessary being is never explained. Further, Mormons deny that God is omnipresent (everywhere existing at the same time). Gods are "localized" according to their spirit bodies. "The Holy Ghost as a personage of Spirit can no more be omnipresent in person than can the Father or the Son."[31]

How did God the Father became a god?

> God undoubtedly took advantage of every opportunity to learn the laws of truth and as He became acquainted with each new verity He righteously obeyed it. . . . As He gained more knowledge through persistent effort and continuous industry, as well as through absolute obedience, His understanding of the universal laws continued to become more complete . . . until He attained the status of Godhood. . . . He became God by absolute obedience to all the eternal laws of the Gospel.[32]

The God of Mormonism is not a uniquely eternal being: rather, all spirit beings are self-existent eternal matter. Such "matter" (or "intelligences") sometimes becomes "organized" into a spirit being through birth to celestial parents. Then that spirit is born through human parents on earth.

> Abraham used the name *intelligences* to apply to the spirit children of the Eternal Father. . . . Use of this name designates both

> the primal element from which the spirit offspring were created and also their inherited capacity to grow in grace . . . until such intelligences . . . become like their Father, the Supreme Intelligence.[33]

Interestingly, the God of Mormonism would stop being "God" if the other eternal intelligences stopped supporting him as God.

> The universe is filled with vast numbers of intelligences. . . . Ehohim (the Father) is God simply because all of these intelligences honor and sustain Him as such. . . . If [God] should ever do anything to violate the confidence or "sense of justice" of these intelligences, they would promptly withdraw their support, and the "power" of God would disintegrate.[34]

Although they may claim to believe in the one true God, Mormons are actually polytheists. They observe that the Hebrew word *Elohim* is plural, thus there must be multiple gods.

> In the very beginning the Bible shows there is a plurality of Gods beyond the power of refutation. . . . The word *Elohim* is found to be in the plural all the way through—Gods. The heads of the Gods appointed one God for us; and when you take view of the subject, it sets one free to see all the beauty, holiness, and perfection of the Gods.[35]

It would appear that the gods known in the church as Father, Son and Holy Spirit supervise our local planet or universe. "As pertaining to this universe, there are three Gods: the Father, Son, and Holy Ghost."[36] However, Mormon apostle Orson Pratt taught, "If we should take a million of worlds like this and number their particles, we should find that there are more Gods than there are particles of matter in those worlds."[37] The scenario is very logical, according to

Mormon apostle Bruce McConkie: "If Jesus was the Son of God, and John discovered that God the Father of Jesus Christ had a Father, you may suppose that he had a Father also. Where was there ever a son without a father? And where was there ever a father without first being a son?"[38]

According to Mormonism, there is hope for all of us: if we learn and obey, we too will become gods. McConkie observes that this has been a perennial human pursuit: "That exaltation which the saints of all ages have so devoutly sought is godhood itself."[39] This helps us understand why many people have become enamored with the Latter-day Saints. For many, such a tantalizing reward is irresistible. Adam and Eve thought so as well.

United Pentecostal Church. Modalism involves confusion regarding the relationship of persons within the Godhead. This ancient heresy found its greatest expression in a man named Sabellius. In the third century A.D. he put forth the idea that God is a divine entity that manifests itself in various modes or forms—first as the Father, then as the Son and finally as the Holy Spirit.

Modern modalists maintain that God is not three distinct persons but only appears to be in order to reveal different aspects of his character. Interestingly, this heretical view is built on two true doctrines: (1) there is only one God, and (2) Jesus is God. Gregory Boyd, who once subscribed to this view, explains: "For, these . . . groups argue, only their position is consistent with these two foundational truths. Only if Jesus is himself Father, Son, and Holy Spirit can the unity of God and the full deity of Christ be acknowledged with consistency."[40]

A publication for the United Pentecostal Church declares:

> [God's] eternal nature contains no essential distinctions or divisions. All names and title of the Deity such as God, Jehovah,

Lord, Father, Word, and Holy Spirit refer to one and the same being. Any plurality associated with God is only a plurality of attributes, titles, roles, manifestations, modes of activity, or relationships to man.[41]

RESPONDING TO THE NEW RELIGIOUS MOVEMENTS

Mind Science groups. The God of the Bible is clearly described as a personal being, never an impersonal principle. God the Father manifests a subject-object relationship with his Son Jesus Christ (as in Mt 3:17) and with us (as in Ex 3:14). He manifests traits of personality (Gen 6:6; 1 Sam 15:29). He claims to be a personal Spirit and is described with personal pronouns (Jn 4:24; Heb 11:6). The one God of the Bible is described as three eternal, distinct Persons manifesting themselves as Father (Phil 2:11), Son (Col 2:9) and Holy Spirit (Gen 1:2), all with one and the same divine nature. Scripture speaks of Christ performing the work of creation as God (Jn 1:1-3; Col 1:16-17; Heb 1:2). To claim that the God of the Bible is impersonal is to read a false meaning into the text. The only way the Mind Sciences can create a God so foreign to the Bible is to resort to other so-called authorities.

Contrary to monism, the Bible teaches that God is distinct from his creation; reality is plural, not "one." At the beginning of creation God divided light from darkness, the sea from the dry land and humankind from all other creatures (Gen 1). Repeatedly God affirms that he is holy (Lev 11:44; 19:2; Is 6:3), which means not just morally pure and supremely good but also separate in nature and unique in being. God is unlike humankind ethically (Ps 50:21); he absolutely distinguishes sin from righteousness (Is 5:20; Ezek 3:20).

"A Course in Miracles." Contrary to pantheism, though the Bible teaches that God is omnipresent, meaning that his being and Spirit are accessible at all points of the universe (Ps 139:8), his being is not the physical universe. He is never seen to be a part of it nor it a part of him (Neh 9:6; Ps 19:1-2; Acts 17:24, 26; Rev 4:11; 14:7). The Creator is not identified with the creation (Rom 1:20-23), and worship of any created thing is considered idolatry (Ex 20:2-5).

God did not make the universe out of himself or preexistent matter but out of nothing (see Ps 33:6, 9; 148:5; Jer 51:15; Heb 11:3 for biblical illustrations of this concept). Although God is not far from us (Acts 17:27), our sins have caused a spiritual separation from him (Is 59:1-2).

God is infinite, whereas humans are finite and limited. That is, they are contingent, whereas God is necessary; he is self-sufficient and needed no cause for his existence. He was necessary for the existence of every being in the universe—indeed the universe itself.

Church of Jesus Christ of Latter-day Saints. In response to Mormon teaching, while the plurality of the Hebrew word *Elohim* might seem to suggest that there might be more than one God, Hebrew grammar does not support such a conclusion. In Scripture *Elohim* is used with a singular verb in reference to the one God, but in reference to false gods it takes a plural verb. Why then would a plural noun be used for God? The Hebrew language uses plurals for reasons other than numerical plurality. *Elohim* is used to express a plurality of majesty or a sense of the plenitude of God's greatness. "*Elohim* is simply a plural expressing majesty, magnitude, fullness, richness."[42]

The Mormon doctrine of God also betrays the fallacy of infinite regression. The argument goes like this: If God created the universe that exists, who created God? There must be something more powerful than God, and somewhere the chain of being must stop with a being's creating himself, which is a contradiction.[43] The assumption is that all beings that exist are contingent (they need a cause to exist).

The biblical answer is that God is self-existent, and as a self-existent being, he does not need a cause. He is a "necessary" being; he must exist from all eternity before any "contingent" being can exist. This is the orthodox position.

God exists as the sovereign Master of the universe (Deut 33:27; 1 Tim 2:5). While there are similarities between God and man, God points out that he is not a man (Num 23:19; 1 Sam 15:29; Hos 11:9). The incarnation was a unique event when the second person of the Godhead assumed human nature and became flesh.

There are no other gods beside the one true God (Deut 4:35, 39; 32:39; 2 Sam 7:22; 2 Kings 19:19; Ps 86:10; Is 45:5, 22). If there were more than one god, there would really be no sovereign God. If there were two or more gods, one would possess power and knowledge not held by the other (or others). God by necessity must be all-powerful (omnipotent), all-knowing (omniscient) and in complete control of the universe.

Mormons rely heavily on extrabiblical revelations to substantiate their concept of God. For example, *Mormon Doctrine*'s statement that Abraham spoke of spirit children and eternal spirit matter called "intelligences" does not quote the Bible but Mormon writings (specifically the Book of Abraham, which has been demonstrated to be a forgery)—"restored truths" that had been either lost or intentionally removed from the Bible. Such assertions undermining the authority of Scripture have no basis in fact and cannot be proved.

United Pentecostal Church. In regard to modalism, to say that the Father is the Son ignores the personal subject-object relationship between them. Scripture tells us that the Father "loves the Son" (Jn 3:35; 5:20) and that the Son was "sent" by the Father (Jn 3:16; 5:30; 17:8). In fact, Jesus said that he was sent by the Father in the same way that believers are sent by Jesus (Jn 20:21) and that after his resurrection he would return to the Father (Jn 14:12; 16:27-28). The

Son speaks to the Father (Jn 17:1-26) and relates to him as one person relates to another (Mt 10:32-33; Jn 10:14-15).

Modalists also fail to take into account Jesus' defense of the testimony he gave about himself. Our Lord appealed to the Old Testament standard for judging whether a testimony was true: "In your own Law it is written that the testimony of two men is valid." This must mean that he and the Father are distinct persons: "I am one who testifies for myself; my other witness is the Father, who sent me" (Jn 8:17-18). If Jesus and the Father were not distinct persons, Jesus could not have appealed to the Old Testament law requiring at least two witnesses before a testimony could be taken as valid (Deut 17:6, 19:15).

Scripture leaves no room for doubt when it comes to whether Jesus is distinct from the Father. The first letter of John states: "The antichrist . . . denies the Father *and* the Son" (1 Jn 2:22). A number of passages also describe Jesus and the Holy Spirit as distinct Persons. In John 15:26 Jesus promises that he will "send" the Holy Spirit. How could he "send" the Spirit if he *is* the Holy Spirit? Why not say that he would later manifest himself as the Holy Spirit?

Matthew 3:16-17 gives a dramatic picture of the distinction between the Father, Son and Holy Spirit. After being baptized, Jesus came up out of the water and the heavens were opened to reveal the Spirit of God descending like a dove while at the same time the Father spoke: "This is my Son, whom I love; with him I am well pleased."

Another problem arises for modalists in 1 Peter 1:12, which mentions "the Holy Spirit sent from heaven." Sent by whom? If the Father is really Jesus, who in turn became the Holy Spirit, then there seems to be no one left to send the Holy Spirit. Demons certainly do not have the authority to command God. Neither do angels or human beings who have died. Only one equal to or greater than another can "send" that person. The only alternative is what Jesus said in John

15:26—he sent the Holy Spirit. In doing so, it is clear that he also cannot be the Holy Spirit.

A problem at the other extreme from modalism is some groups' definition of the "persons" within the Godhead as entirely separate from each other, the way humans are separate. The Persons of the Trinity must be understood as a unique category. *Person* is simply the most descriptive word available in English to identify God's three distinct centers of consciousness, which, while sharing the same essence, can interact with each other, share emotions with one another, cooperate with each other and function separately from one another.

Responding to Antitrinitarian Arguments

A few more points need to be made to respond to antitrinitarian arguments frequently marshaled by leaders of alternative religious movements, including not only the groups surveyed but also Jehovah's Witnesses, the Way International, the Christadelphians and others.

The Trinity is rejected because the word is not in the Bible. Some people object to the doctrine of the Trinity because the word itself does not appear in Scripture.[44] This point may appear compelling at first, but the objection has no merit. The term *trinity* simply summarizes certain aspects of the biblical teaching about God's nature. One will not find the words *omniscient, omnipresent* or *immensity* in the Bible either, but this absence does not detract from the truth the words represent. We often appropriately use a single word to represent a complex theoretical idea.

The Trinity is viewed as contradictory. Other groups reject the doctrine of the Trinity because they see it as contradictory, incomprehensible and unscriptural. Christian theologians agree that the Trinity is impossible to fully understand, but it is hardly beyond our ability to contemplate and to appreciate with wonder and awe. Holding to a truth while being unable to fully comprehend exactly how that truth can be does not involve contradiction. One does not have to understand everything in order to understand *something*. For example, while we understand that the earth is revolving at a speed of several thousands of miles per hour, it's not easy to comprehend how that can be. The chair I sit in is composed of trillions of molecules moving so fast that they are forming what only appears to be a solid object; I believe this but find it impossible to understand fully. If we are willing to accept facts like these without full comprehension, we can certainly hold to the doctrine of the Trinity despite our inability to fully comprehend it. Moreover, God has told us that certain aspects of his nature are unsearchable (Ps 145:3; Is 40:28; Rom 11:33).

Often analogies are used to illustrate the Trinity, such as the states of water at differing temperatures or the parts of an egg. Unfortunately such illustrations usually lead us toward modalism or tritheism rather than the biblical concept of God. God is Spirit, a Being like no other, and the fact that his triune nature is inscrutable to us is testament to his utter uniqueness. A Being with such an inscrutable nature could not have sprung from human imagination.

There does seem to be one ontological illustration, however, that may help us understand God's nature. Consider time. First, it consists of three distinct things: past, present and future. These three correspond well to the Persons of the Trinity—Father, Son and Holy Spirit. In both cases the three aspects are entirely distinct from one another. Second, all three aspects of time, although distinct, share the same nature of that which they comprise. Past, present and future can each be referred to individually as "time" just as the Father, Son and Holy Spirit can each be referred to as God. (Please note that we are *not* suggesting that the Father represents "past," the Son "present" and the Holy Spirit "future.") Third, if any of the three elements of time were removed, time as we understand it would no longer exist. In this dimension of reality there is no such thing as time without a past, a present *and* a future. Similarly, God would not be God without a Father, a Son and a Holy Spirit. All three Persons are God, just as all three aspects of time are time. All three Persons are indispensable and necessary for God's Being.

The Trinity is supposedly absent from early church history. Another common objection to the Trinity involves its appearance in church history. A comment by Victor Paul Wierwille (1916–1985), founder of the Way International, typifies this accusation: "The trinity was not a part of Christian dogma and formal documents of the first three centuries after Christ."[45]

This is true; however, the notion of a triune God actually began with the apostles, although it was certainly not fully articulated in the first century. The idea of the Trinity was already understood by Irenaeus (c. 130–c. 200), who contributed to the growing development of the doctrine from his study of Scripture. Tertullian (fl. c. 196–c. 212) is largely famous for his early formulation of the trinitarian formula and his Latin designation for it as *trinitas*. It became formalized in creedal language only later, after aggressive heretical challenges to God's nature forced the church to come up with a defense of an already accepted Christian doctrine. Church leaders' understanding of what the Scriptures teach about the nature of God compelled them to formulate these creedal statements.

The Trinity is too close to pagan beliefs. Some movements' denials of the Trinity point to its apparent similarity to descriptions of ancient pagan deities:

> Long before the founding of Christianity the idea of a triune god or a god-in-three-persons was a common belief in ancient reli-

> gions. Although many of these religions had many minor deities, they distinctly acknowledged that there was one supreme God who consisted of three persons or essences. The Babylonians used an equilateral triangle to represent this three-in-one god.[46]

First, the logic of this argument is flawed. All religions have a number of similarities. For example, Christianity teaches that murder is wrong. But so does Buddhism. Does this mean that the Christian stand against murder is wrong? Some pagans believe in the existence of at least one god. Does this mean that anyone else who also believes a God exists is borrowing from pagan teachings? Such a conclusion does not follow.

Further there is a vast difference between the many pagan "triads" and the Christian Trinity. First, all pagan triads consist of three separate gods rather than one God. Second, such triads are "always or nearly always merely the three gods at the top of the hierarchy of many gods worshipped in polytheistic religions."[47] Third, pagan deities are not thought of as being coequal in nature. One of the deities always has greater attributes than the others.

The idea that Christianity borrowed theologically from pagan religions does not square with how the early Christians thought about the truth of their faith. And many have sought to prove that Christians borrowed from pagan religions to form the Trinity doctrine, but no one has presented actual evidence for such a borrowing.

On examination, it is clear that objections against the Trinity, or other aspects of God's nature or personality, are built on little more than poor reasoning, misrepresentations of history and faulty biblical hermeneutics. The choice is very clear: either there is a God who exists as the sovereign Lord of the universe—as revealed in nature and the Scriptures—or there exists no god at all.

4

JESUS CHRIST
Man, Myth or More?

Perhaps no other doctrine, except for the doctrine of the Trinity, has been so persistently and consistently attacked throughout the history of the church as the person of Christ. The incarnation is, historically, the pivotal act of God's redemptive plan. Corrupt, alter or delete this doctrine in any way and the whole edifice of Christianity must collapse. The church fought tenaciously for the purity of this essential doctrine—that Jesus Christ is the Word of God who became flesh—from its inception.

The Christian church has consistently taught that Jesus is both God and man. "In the beginning was the Word, and the Word was with God, and the Word was God" (Jn 1:1). This is the stunning proclamation of those who had actually lived with Jesus for over three years.

Was Jesus half God and half human? Was he a mixture of both? Was he mostly God and a little bit human, or the other way around? Was he just a man with an unusually deep connection with the God-consciousness? Does it even matter what we believe about his nature?

The Orthodox View of the Person of Christ

Jesus Christ is God and man. This teaching is based on Christ's claims about himself and was passed down by the apostles to the church. The same God who conversed with Moses in the Sinai Desert out of the burning bush stood before a hostile crowd of skeptical Jews fifteen hundred years later, now in the flesh, and made stunning revelations about his identity:

> The Jews answered him, "Aren't we right in saying that you are a Samaritan and demon-possessed?"
>
> "I am not possessed by a demon," said Jesus, "but I honor my Father and you dishonor me. I am not seeking glory for myself; but there is one who seeks it, and he is the judge. I tell you the truth, if anyone keeps my word, he will never see death."
>
> At this the Jews exclaimed, "Now we know that you are demon-possessed! Abraham died and so did the prophets, yet you say that if anyone keeps your word, he will never taste death. Are you greater than our father Abraham? He died, and so did the prophets. Who do you think you are?"
>
> Jesus replied, "If I glorify myself, my glory means nothing. My Father, whom you claim as your God, is the one who glorifies me. Though you do not know him, I know him. If I said I did not, I would be a liar like you, but I do know him and keep his word. Your father Abraham rejoiced at the thought of seeing my day; he saw it and was glad."
>
> "You are not yet fifty years old," the Jews said to him, "and you have seen Abraham!"
>
> "I tell you the truth," Jesus answered, "before Abraham was born, I am!" At this, they picked up stones to stone him, but Jesus hid himself, slipping away from the temple grounds. (Jn 8:48-59)

The horrified Jewish leaders concluded that Jesus had committed blasphemy by using God's holy name in relation to himself. Blasphemy it would be, of course, if his claim were false. Later in John's Gospel, Jesus claims that "I and the Father are one" (Jn 10:30).

Christ's deity. Millard Erickson has observed, "We should note that Jesus did not make an explicit and overt claim to deity. He did not say, 'I am God.' What we do find, however, are claims which would be inappropriate if made by someone who is less than God."[1] Wayne Grudem notes, "When Jesus used the divine name, 'I Am,' he was repeating the very words God used of himself when he identified himself to Moses as 'I Am Who I Am.' . . . Jesus was claiming for himself the title, 'I Am,' by which God designates himself as the eternal existing One, the God who is the source of his own existence, and who always has been and always will be."[2]

> In the beginning was the Word, and the Word was toward God [the Father], and the Word was God by nature. He was with God [the Father] in the beginning. Through him all things were made; without him nothing was made that has been made. In him was life, and that life was the light of men. (Jn 1:1-4, personal expanded translation)

Here John refers to Jesus not only as "God" but also as "the Word" *(logos)*. John's Greek readers would have immediately recognized this word, for it already occupied a venerable place in Greek philosophy. To the Greek mind, *logos* referred to the organizing principle of the universe, the thing that held it all together and allowed it to make sense.[3] To John's Jewish readers the word would have meant the creative, powerful word of God by which the heavens and the earth were created (Ps 33:6). John is deliberately identifying Jesus with both of these concepts: Jesus is the creative and powerful word of God (Hebrew concept) and the organizing or unifying force of the universe (Greek concept) who became man.[4]

John's Gospel also makes it clear that we can have real knowledge of God. "Anyone who has seen me has seen the Father" (Jn 14:9). Jesus, as God's Son, shows us what his Father's power, compassion and holiness look like. Moreover, because Christ is God, his redemption is sufficient for all our sins, for all who are called and believe.[5]

After his resurrection, Jesus on numerous occasions presented himself to his disciples as proof of his claim to deity and that he had defeated death. Thomas was skeptical of the others' report: "Unless I see the nail marks in his hands and put my finger where the nails were, and put my hand into his side, I will not believe it." But when Jesus appeared and urged him to touch the scars of crucifixion, Thomas's response was unequivocal: "My Lord and my God!" (Jn 20:24-29).

This was a Jew addressing a man standing in front of him as his God. If Thomas was guilty of blasphemy, why didn't Jesus rebuke or correct him? Instead Jesus commended Thomas for finally believing.

Around A.D. 60, before the Gospels were disseminated, Paul wrote the following concerning the deity of Christ:

> He is the image of the invisible God, the firstborn over all creation. For by him all things were created: things in heaven and on earth, visible and invisible, whether thrones or powers or rulers or authorities; all things were created by him and for him. He is before all things, and in him all things hold together. And he is the head of the body, the church; he is the beginning and the firstborn from among the dead, so that in everything he might have the supremacy. For God was pleased to have all his fullness dwell in him, and through him to reconcile to himself

> all things, whether things on earth or things in heaven, by making peace through his blood, shed on the cross. (Col 1:15-20)

No one in the Old Testament, not even the most godly of men, was referred to in this way. The early church knew that Jesus was no mere man but the eternal Son of God.

As noted above, Jesus shares his Father's nature. When Jesus became human, he assumed a second nature along with his divine nature. This brings us to a Christian doctrine called *the hypostatic union.* It explores the two natures of Christ—the humanity and deity that came together in the one person, Jesus Christ, without confusion or diminishment of the two natures.

Christ's humanity. You might expect that the humanity of Christ might not generate quite the attention and controversy that his deity does, since his humanity seems self-evident. Yet historically Christ's humanity has been in the forefront of theological intrigue, particularly in the early years of the church.[6] Grudem suggests, "In practical terms, it has in some ways posed a greater danger to orthodox theology."[7]

The issue of Christ's humanity, then, is paramount: it pertains directly to our salvation. It is impossible for human beings to elevate themselves to the level of God in a moral effort to expiate their own sin. Any genuine, lasting fellowship between the two requires some radical means of uniting them. Traditionally, this has been understood as having been accomplished by the incarnation, the union of deity and humanity in Christ. The sufficiency and validity of Christ's death as a human on our behalf depend on the genuineness of his deity.[8]

If Christ was genuinely human as we are, then he is able to understand and empathize with our struggles. But if he was not fully human, or was human in an incomplete sense, then he cannot intercede for us as a priest before God.[9]

Scriptural references to Christ's humanity abound. Jesus' virgin birth is abundantly documented in Scripture. But why a virgin birth? Couldn't God have brought his Son into the world without using a human mother?

Jesus needed to be a real human, integrally connected to humanity. His birth from a human woman united both deity and humanity into one person. God could have created Jesus as a complete human being in heaven and then sent him down to us without the need for a human parent, but then Jesus would not have been one blood with the race of Adam. And we would have found it very difficult to identify him as fully human like us.[10]

The eternal Son of God became one with us through the power of the Holy Spirit in his birth from the Virgin Mary. Jesus, as the eternal Son of God, retained his divine nature, and he assumed a human nature through his mother. The angel who announced Jesus' coming to Mary explained that sin would not be transferred to Jesus from her: "The Holy Spirit will come upon you . . . so the holy one to be born will be called the Son of God" (Lk 1:35).

The hypostatic union. The early church struggled to understand the relationship of Christ's deity and his humanity. How could Jesus be omnipotent and yet weak? How could he live in the world and yet be present everywhere? How could he learn things and yet be omniscient? The Chalcedonian Definition addressed the problem, acknowledging two distinct natures in Christ that retain their own properties yet remain together in one person.[11] This is the hypostatic union. Far from being the product of Greek philosophical or speculative thought, the Chalcedonian Definition is a theological definition that the Bible itself demands.

Everything that is true of Christ's human and divine natures is integral to his person. Jesus said, "Before Abraham was born, I am" (Jn

8:58); he did not say, "Before Abraham was, my divine nature existed." He is free to talk about anything that either his divine or his human nature does as something that *he* did. Whatever can be said of one nature or the other can be said of the *person* of Christ.[12]

This helps us understand Mark 13:32, where Jesus says that no one knows the hour of his return, not even the angels in heaven, *nor the Son,* but only the Father. The term "the Son" is used in relation to Jesus' divine nature, and generally of him as a person, *not* to affirm something that is true only of his human nature.[13] There is some sense in which Jesus' human limitation is exercised in reference to this knowledge, differentiated from his divine omnicapacity.

As a human he grew in knowledge and wisdom, even as he grew in physical strength. While Jesus remained what he was, fully divine, he also *became* what he previously had not been, fully human. In the incarnation Jesus did not give up any of the attributes of deity; he did, however, take on new attributes—a humanity that was not his before.[14]

But in the early church as now, Jesus' unique nature was frequently misunderstood.

ANCIENT HERESIES REGARDING JESUS' DIVINE-HUMAN NATURE

Gnosticism. The Gnostics were followers of a variety of religious movements teaching that the way of salvation was provided by the learning of and implementation of secret knowledge, or *gnosis.*[15] A dualistic structure was central to Gnosticism. The transcendent God was pure spirit and therefore good; the god of this world—the Old Testament God—created the universe of matter and was therefore evil.

This dualism of matter and spirit is fundamental to Gnostic beliefs and myths. Within the bodies of the more spiritual individuals in the world are sparks of divinity that await salvation through secret knowledge given by the redeemer Christ. Once awakened, the Gnostics fly from their prison bodies at death, bypassing hostile demons along the way, to be reunited with God. In Gnostic teaching Christ only *appeared* to be human.[16]

Gnostic groups and their leaders taught that the essential secret knowledge was passed on to a few faithful individuals who were worthy of it, not to the original twelve apostles. Gnostic teachings, with their emphasis on aesthetics and philosophy, appealed to the vanity of many people and caused serious divisions in many Christian churches.

Patripassianism. This heresy, also known as Sabellianism, arose during the third century, associated with such writers as Praxeas, Noetus and Sabellius. It focused on the belief that the Father suffered as the Son.[17] The suffering of Jesus on the cross is to be regarded as the suffering of the Father.

Never one to refuse a challenge, particularly one hurled by heretics, church father Tertullian wrote in response:

> The devil is opposed to the truth in many ways. He has sometimes even attempted to destroy it by defending it. He declares that there is only one God, the omnipotent creator of the world, only to make a heresy out of that uniqueness. He says that the Father himself descended into the virgin, was himself born of her, himself suffered; in fact, that he himself was Jesus Christ. . . . It was [Praxis], a restless foreigner, who first brought this kind of perversity from Asia to Rome. . . . He put the Holy Spirit to flight and crucified the Father.[18]

The danger of this heresy was that it minimized the importance of Jesus' person and ministry, replacing his redemptive act with that of the one God, the Father.

Against Sabellianism, the church taught that Jesus is the only name under heaven by which sinful human beings can be saved. One is saved through belief that Jesus was God's own Son, sent for the purpose of making the Father known.

Arianism. More than any other theological viewpoint, Arianism threatened to become the official theological position of the early church.[19] Arius, a presbyter from the church of Alexandria, Egypt, wrote to Eusebius of Nicomedia, around 321, detailing his conviction that Christ definitely had a beginning:

> The Son is not unbegotten, nor part of the unbegotten in any way; nor is he derived from any substance. . . . And before he was begotten or created or appointed or established, he did not exist; for he was not unbegotten. We are persecuted because we say, "the Son has a beginning, but God is without beginning." . . . And this we say because he is neither part of God nor derived from any substance.[20]

This view bid to become the prevailing theological definition of Christ's Person in relation to his deity for the better part of the fourth century. Many Christian bishops and Roman emperors adopted it or the diluted "semi-Arian" view, which described Christ as being *similar* in nature *(homoiousios)* but not the *same* in nature *(homoousios)* as the Father.

The doctrine of Christ's deity is essential to Christianity. Only a person who is eternally God could redeem a lost race from sin and its eternal consequence; no mere finite being could bear such a burden. Only someone who was truly God and truly human could bridge the gap between God and man and reveal God most fully to us (Jn 14:9).[21]

Docetism. Church father Irenaeus, in the latter half of the second century, compiled a list of different christological heresies influenced by Gnosticism.[22] Of particular interest is his reference to the Docetic view that Jesus Christ was a human being in appearance only:

> Among these, Saturninus came from Antioch. . . . Like Menander, he taught that there is one Father *[unum patrem incognitum]*, who made angels, archangels, virtues, powers; and that the world, and everything in it, was made by seven angels. Humanity was also created by these angels. . . . He also declared that the Saviour was unborn, incorporeal and without form, asserting that he was seen as a human being in appearance only. The God of the Jews, he declares, was one of the angels; and because the Father wished to destroy all the rulers *[Principes]*, Christ came to destroy the God of the Jews.[23]

Another important witness to the Docetic heresy was Ignatius of Antioch. Writing around the beginning of the second century, he responds to a Docetic teaching that Christ did not actually suffer in reality but only in appearance, and was thus not truly human.[24] Ignatius writes:

> So do not pay attention when anyone speaks to you apart from Jesus Christ, who was of the Family of David, the Child of Mary, who was truly born, who ate and drank, who was truly persecuted under Pontius Pilate, was truly crucified and truly died, in full view of heaven, earth and hell, and who was truly raised from the dead. It was him who raised him again, and it is him [i.e., the Father] who will likewise raise us in Jesus Christ, we who believe in him, apart from whom we have no true life. But if, as some godless people *[atheoi]*, that is, unbelievers, say, he suffered in mere appearance *[to dokein peponthenai]* being themselves mere appearances—why am I in bonds?[25]

Apollinarianism. For many years a pillar of orthodoxy as well as friend of the irrepressible Athanasius, Apollinarius (c. A.D. 310-c. 390) came to be known chiefly for a heresy that is now commonly referred to as Apollinarianism. Most of his works, now lost, were staunch defenses of orthodox Christianity.[26]

Apollinarius and his followers found the orthodox view of Jesus too vulgar and believed they had come upon the perfect solution: Jesus possessed a human body and a divine soul, a composite of one part humanity (a body) and one part deity (a soul).[27] In a letter to the bishops of Diocaesarea, Apollinarius asserts that the Word did not assume a "changeable" human mind in the incarnation; this would have led, in his view, to the Word's being trapped in human sin. This was his great concern and undoubtedly the motivation for his heretical view. He decided that the Word retained "an immutable and heavenly divine mind." Here lies the rub: Christ could not be said then to be *totally human,* since Christ now had a human body and a divine mind; the mind and spirit of Christ were from the divine nature of the Son of God.[28]

Perhaps the idea that Jesus struggled with the same filthy thoughts that Apollinarius did was unthinkable for him. This is only conjecture, of course, but we can sympathize with such a concern.

How the Unorthodox Interpret Jesus

Jehovah's Witnesses. The ancient Arian heresy that taxed the resources of the fourth-century church resurged in the last century in the Watchtower Bible and Tract Society, commonly known as Jehovah's Witnesses. The Jesus of the Jehovah's Witnesses, like the Jesus of Arius, is a created being. In their literature he is referred to as a lesser god, inferior to Jehovah God. "Christ was the first of God's creations [Col. 1:15; Rev. 3:14]."[29] "[The Word] was created before all the other spirit sons of God, and . . . he is the only one who was directly created by God."[30] The Jehovah's Witnesses go for the heart of Christianity: "When God sent Jesus to earth as the ransom, he made Jesus to be what would satisfy justice, not an incarnation, not a godman, but a perfect man."[31]

In Witness theology, Jesus was originally Michael the archangel, the first and greatest creation of Jehovah God.[32] Before his birth, Jesus, as Michael, was a spokesman for God.[33] While on earth, Jesus was a simple man, not Almighty God. After he died, he was resurrected with his original identity: "Read carefully the following Bible account: 'War broke out in heaven: Michael [who is the resurrected Jesus Christ] and his angels battled with the dragon.'"[34]

> Well, did Jesus ever say that he was God? No, he never did. Rather, in the Bible he is called "God's Son." And he said: "The Father is greater than I am" (John 10:34-36; 14:28). Also, Jesus explained that there were some things that neither he nor the angels knew but that only God knew (Mark 13:32). Further, on one occasion Jesus prayed to God, saying: "Let not *my* will, but *yours* take place" (Luke 22:42). If Jesus were the Almighty God, he would not have prayed to himself, would he? In fact, following Jesus' death, the Scripture says: "This Jesus God resurrected" (Acts 2:32). Thus the Almighty God and Jesus are clearly two separate persons. Even after his death and resurrection and ascension to heaven, Jesus was still not equal to his Father.—1 Corinthians 11:3; 15:28.[35]

Instead of being Almighty God, the Jesus of the Watchtower Bible and Tract Society is "a god":

> At John 1:1, which refers to Jesus as "the Word," some Bible translations say: "In the beginning was the Word, and the Word

> was with God, and the Word was God." But notice, verse 2 says that the Word was "In the beginning *with* God." And while men have seen Jesus, verse 18 says that "no man hath seen God at any time." (*Authorized* or *King James Version*). So we find that some translations of verse 1 give the correct idea of the original language when they read: "The Word was with God, and the Word was divine," or was "a god," that is the Word was a powerful godlike one (An American Translation). Clearly, Jesus is not Almighty God. In fact, Jesus spoke of his Father as "my God" and as "the only true God."—John 20:17; 17:3.[36]

Jesus' humanity does not fare any better. In Witness theology, "Jesus was the equal of the perfect man Adam."[37] He did not become the Christ until he was baptized.[38] Being a mere man of course meant that he was not immortal before he was resurrected.[39]

Church of Jesus Christ of Latter-day Saints. Mormonism also teaches that Jesus is "a god" or a godlike being. Here it is important to note that Mormonism has no "systematic theology" per se. Mormons actually pride themselves in the fact that there is much disparity of doctrine within their belief system.[40] The teachings of founder Joseph Smith differed greatly from the theological opinions of his successor, Brigham Young. Modern Mormons simply maintain that their presiding president speaks for God to their generation of Mormon believers, and it is *his* teachings that must be believed. Earlier theological opinions or teachings may be readily discredited or buried.[41]

Mormons insist that they are "Christians" because they follow Jesus Christ. Yet Jesus' deity is understood to mean that he is but one god among literally *millions*. "Christ is *Jehovah;* they are one and the same Person."[42] Elohim, on the other hand, is the name the Old Testament gives to God the Father.[43]

Mormonism teaches that Jesus Christ once existed as a spirit child of God the Father, the eldest of many spirit children born to God the Father through sexual intercourse with his plethora of goddess wives: Jesus "was the most intelligent, the most faithful, and the most God-like of all the sons and daughters of our Heavenly Father in the spirit world."[44] "Among the spirit children of Elohim the firstborn was and is Jehovah or Jesus Christ."[45] Jesus is the spirit brother of Lucifer, from the same heavenly parentage, but was chosen in eternity past to save humankind. Though Jesus is Lucifer's brother in the historical sense, he is opposed morally to everything Lucifer represents.

While on earth, the Mormons' Jesus was a polygamist who enjoyed conjugal relations with at least Mary Magdalene, Mary the sister of Lazarus, and Martha. This doctrine is not taught in Mormonism today; but it has never been denied, and it was openly preached by some early Mormon leaders: "There was a marriage in Cana of Galilee; and on careful reading of that transaction, it will be discovered that no less a person than Jesus Christ was married on that occasion. . . . Object not, therefore, too strongly against the marriage of Christ."[46] Another example: "I said, in my lecture on Marriage, at our last Conference, that Jesus Christ was married at Cana of Galilee, that Mary, Martha and others were his wives, and that he begat children."[47]

Christadelphians. Christadelphianism had its origins in America, in the writings and musings of John Thomas, who, on arriving to America from England in 1832, became associated with Alexander and Thomas Campbell, founders of the Disciples of Christ. Soon thereafter Thomas opposed the Campbells' teachings regarding the immortality of the soul and hell as a place of eternal conscious punishment. He came to the conclusion that Christianity as expressed in orthodox circles was not founded on genuine biblical teaching. Although he met with considerable opposition, he continued with his studies and proclamation of what he believed to be the truths of Christianity, and eventually he gained a following. In 1864 Thomas named his little band "Christadelphians" by compounding two words, *Christ* and *adelphos* (Greek for "brother"). After his death in 1871 Christadelphian congregations became autonomous, tied to one another only loosely by common beliefs.

The Christadelphian denies Christ's preexistence. He is not co-eternal with the Father and did not exist until he was miraculously begotten of the Virgin Mary by the Holy Ghost.[48] "We reject the doctrine—that the Son of God was co-eternal with the Father."[49] Christadelphians reason that John 1:1 does not prove that Jesus pre-existed:

> The Greek term translated "word" is *Logos*. It signifies the outward form of inward thought or reason. . . . In the very beginning, God's purpose, wisdom or revelation had been in evidence. It was "with God" in that it emanated from him; it "was God" in that it represented Him to mankind. . . . A similar expression is used by Christ in Matthew 26:28: "This is my blood"—that is, this represents my blood.[50]

The Jesus of the Christadelphians is not God, although he is "divine" by virtue of having been begotten of the Holy Ghost. Through this miraculous act Jesus received the very pattern of God's nature and character. God the Father was in him, and this makes it appropriate to speak of Christ as God manifested in the flesh, so long as it is understood that this does not mean Jesus was God in and of himself: "Jesus Christ . . . must be considered from two points of view, one *Deity*, and the other *Man*. The man was the Son, whose existence dates from the birth of Jesus; the Deity dwelling in him was the Father."[51] "From his mother, he [Jesus] derived the nature common to all mankind, but from his Father he inherited latent spiritual proclivities that strengthened him to conquer the flesh, and manifest divine qualities."[52]

In Christadelphian theology Jesus' humanity is vitiated more subtly. In their theology, Jesus was born of the Virgin Mary by the power of the Holy Spirit. "Jesus of Nazareth was the Son of God, begotten of the Virgin Mary by the Holy Spirit."[53] The only thing that separated him from others was his divine conception and predilection for spirituality.[54] His human nature included the same sinful desires common to all human beings. But since the Father's nature and character indwelled him, he was able to live a sinless life and become an example for us. By dying sinless, he redeemed himself from his own sinful nature. "Jesus, as a representative man, who bore in his nature the same flesh-promptings as all other men but conquered them (1 Pet. 2:21-24), was in need of redemption from that nature (not from actual sin for he never committed any) as are all mankind. He obtained this by his own offering."[55]

> There is only one man who has never sinned: he is the Lord Jesus Christ. . . . From whence did Jesus derive the strength to accomplish that which no other person had done: render perfect obedience unto God? He received it from God Who tabernacled in him by His spirit. . . . Jesus' nature was the same as our own.[56]

Jesus did not exist until his miraculous conception by the "Holy Ghost."

Mind Science groups. The Theosophical Society has its doctrinal basis in the writings of early Gnostics as well as other Eastern sources. In common with other Mind Science groups such as Christian Science and Unity, Theosophy defines Jesus as just another divine man. It declares that all people are innately divine: "In time all men become Christs."[57] One Theosophical writer sums up his group's view of Jesus thus:

> Most readers will probably agree that a world teacher known as the Christ did come, and that he founded a religion nearly 2,000 years ago. Why do they think so? They reply that God so loved the world that he sent his son the Christ to bring it light and life. If that is true, how can we avoid the conclusion that he, or his predecessors, must have come many times before. . . . World teachers, the christs and saviours of the age, have been appearing at propitious times since humanity began existence.[58]

Christian Science declares that Jesus and Christ are not the same person: "Jesus is the human man, and Christ is the divine idea, hence the duality of Jesus the Christ."[59] Religious Science, the fastest-growing wing of the Mind Sciences, teaches similarly: "JESUS—the name of a man. Distinguished from the Christ. The man Jesus became the embodiment of the Christ, as the human gave way to the Divine idea of Sonship."[60] "Christ is not limited to any person, nor does he appear in only one age. He is as eternal as God. He is God's idea of Himself, His own Selfknowingness."[61] The Unity School of Christianity, another Mind Science group, reasons thus:

> The Bible says that God so loved the world that He gave His only begotten Son, but the Bible does not here refer to Jesus of Nazareth the outer man; it refers to the Christ, the spiritual identity of Jesus, whom he acknowledged in all his ways, and brought forth into his outer, until even the flesh of his body was lifted up, purified, spiritualized, and redeemed. Thus he became Jesus Christ, the Word made flesh. And we are to follow in this perfect state and become like him, in each of us is the Christ, the only

> begotten Son. We can through Jesus Christ, our Redeemer and example, bring forth the Christ within us, the true self of all men, to be made perfect even as our Father in Heaven is perfect as Jesus Christ commandeth His followers to be.[62]

In the Mind Science groups, Jesus is an example for us, a trail-blazer whose purpose was to show us the way to obtain the nature of "Christ": "Jesus demonstrated Christ; he proved that Christ is the divine idea of God the Holy Ghost, or Comforter, revealing the divine Principle, Love, and leading into all truth."[63] From the writings of Religious Science: "To think of Jesus as being different from other men is to misunderstand His mission and purpose in life. He was a way-shower and proved His way to be a correct one."[64] From the Unity School of Christianity: "The difference between Jesus and us is not one of inherent spiritual capacity, but in difference of demonstration of it. Jesus was potentially perfect, we have not yet expressed it."[65]

Jesus is the man, while Christ is the spiritual idea or element of God. In Christian Science this is understood as the "duality" of Jesus the Christ, that the human Jesus was not eternal but the divine idea of Christ was and is. Jesus was one with the Father, but not as a person; instead the spiritual idea Christ dwells forever in the "bosom of the Father." The Mind Science position is based on the ancient Gnostic heresy of the first century that tried to vitiate the identity of Jesus Christ as the unique God-man that he claimed and proved himself to be.

United Pentecostal Church. A modern equivalent to the Sabellian modalistic idea of the Trinity and the person of Christ is the United Pentecostal Church. This group teaches that Jesus Christ is truly God manifested in the flesh and truly man: "Jesus is God with us, the eternally blessed God, the image of the invisible God, God manifested in the flesh, our God and Savior, and the express image of God's substance."[66] However, like the Sabellians, United Pentecostals hold that Jesus is both the Son and the Father:

> If there is one God and that God is the Father (Malachi 2:10), and if Jesus is God, then it logically follows that Jesus is the Father.[67]
>
> Jesus is the Father incarnate. "His name shall be called. . . . The Mighty God, The Everlasting Father" (Isaiah 9:6). . . . "I and my Father are one" (John 10:30). . . . "He that hath seen me hath seen the Father" (John 14:9).[68]

The United Pentecostal Church is generally orthodox otherwise and is zealous in its evangelization and missions projects. In every way they appear to be Christians who love God. The sobering truth, however, is that it *does* matter what we believe about Jesus Christ. For every man and woman who encounters Jesus, the question is still pertinent: "Who do you say I am?" (Lk 9:20).

RESPONDING TO THE NEW RELIGIOUS MOVEMENTS

Jehovah's Witnesses. We have already learned from the Chalcedonian Definition that Jesus possessed two natures, one divine and one human, united perfectly in the one person. The only perfect man was Jesus, the second Person of the Trinity in human flesh. No mere man born of the sinful Adamic line could be perfect. The only human being who claimed human perfection and made it stick was Jesus of Nazareth, Son of God.

Beyond being the archangel Michael and the first and greatest creation of Jehovah God, in Scripture Jesus is afforded the highest accolades of honor and worship. In the Greek text of Colossians 1:15-17, Jesus is referred to as an heir, first in rank, prior to all of creation and therefore superior to it, its noncreated Lord. This passage uses *proto-*

tokos (firstborn or first-bearer) rather than *protoktistos* (first-created). *Prototokos* can also mean "preeminent." In Jeremiah 31:9, for example, Ephraim is referred to as God's "firstborn son." However, Genesis 41:51-52 tells us that Manasseh, not Ephraim, was the literal firstborn in their family. *Firstborn* does not always indicate actual birth order. It can be a bestowed honor, as it was to Ephraim over and against his elder brother, Manasseh.

In the New World Translation (the Jehovah's Witness version of the Bible) of Colossians, the word *other* appears four times. There is absolutely no basis for this in the Greek text or in the balance of the translation.

Nowhere in the Bible is Jesus called a creation of God. He is, rather, described as the Creator of all that exists (Jn 1:3; Col 1:16).

In John 10:34-36 Jesus was actually making himself equal to God by saying he was the Son of God (see also Jn 5:17-18), intimating that he had the same nature as God in heaven, as any human son would share his father's nature. When Jesus said, "No one knows about that day or hour, not even the angels in heaven, nor the Son, but only the Father" (Mk 13:32), he voluntarily functioned in his humanity, suspending his attribute of omniscience for that purpose. Furthermore, the Greek text of John 1:1 ("the Word was God") does not yield the translation "the Word was a god."[69]

The angel announcing Jesus' birth proclaimed, "A Savior has been born to you; he is Christ [Messiah] the Lord" (Lk 2:11). And in Luke 2:25-32 the old temple priest Simeon, who had been eagerly awaiting the Messiah, declares that the child Jesus is the Messiah ("your salvation"). So Jesus was certainly the Messiah before he was baptized by John.

Jesus in his divine nature is immortal, but in his humanity he was subject to death. Romans 6:9, used by Jehovah's Witnesses to suggest that Jesus did not possess immortality before his resurrection, merely states that Jesus died and was resurrected never to die again. John 5:26 indicates that Jesus had life within his very nature just as the Father has life within himself.

Church of Jesus Christ of Latter-day Saints. Christians familiar with scriptural teachings can readily respond to Mormon claims about Jesus: Christ has existed for all eternity as God the Son, with God the Father and God the Holy Spirit. He did not come into existence after the Father (Ps 90:2; Mic 5:2; Jn 1:1; Col 1:17). Neither is he the spirit brother of Lucifer, since, as God the Son, he is Lucifer's creator. If Jesus was the agent of creation, then he could not be Lucifer's peer. Lucifer is a creature, created by God the Son. Jesus was miraculously begotten in Mary by the Holy Spirit, not through sexual relations. Mary was a virgin at the time and remained a virgin until after Jesus was born (Mt 1:18-25; Lk 1:26-38).

The Scriptures never suggest that Jesus was married, much less that he was a polygamist. In John 2:2 it reads that Jesus was *invited* to the wedding feast. A bridegroom is not invited to his own wedding. Jesus' relationship with Mary Magdalene was a result of his forgiveness of her sin. She was involved in worshiping and ministering to him. His relationship with Mary the sister of Lazarus reflected his friendship with the entire family.

Christadelphians. To argue that "with God" in John 1:1 means only "emanation from God," as the Christadelphians do, betrays a careless reading of the preposition *pros* (Greek meaning "with" or "toward"). It speaks of movement toward God in relationship, not movement from God as an impersonal emanation. Moreover, John 1:1 speaks of an eternal relationship, not Christ's relationship to humans in time to represent God. There were preincarnate revelations of Christ, called christophanies (Ex 23:20; 32:34; Is 63:9), and he was finally revealed in the incarnation (Jn 1:14, 18), but John 1:1 speaks of a time before the world began. Seeking to use "is" in John 1:1 with the same meaning as in Matthew 26:28 is faulty because John 1:1 has straightforward language of Christ's person and is not trying to communicate some other truth to the disciples by means of a physical symbol.

Trying to distinguish between Christ as deity and Christ as divine leads to mere trifling with words. Either Christ was God of very God or he was no God at all. The use of "divine" to speak of persons with "sparks" of divinity falls terribly short of the biblical teaching about Christ's being the same essence as the Father (Heb 1:3) and being in very nature God (Phil 2:6-7). If God's indwelling in human beings imparts divinity, then each Christian is as divine as Christ except for not being indwelt by the Spirit from birth.

Jesus was indeed sinless (1 Pet 1:19), but this is only one way in which he differed from other humans. The second person of the Trinity did not begin with Jesus' birth. Rather, he joined deity and humanity as one person who is fully God and fully man in his incarnation. Jesus possessed our human nature (1 Tim 2:5), but he also possessed his own divine nature (Jn 20:28). Further, he had no sinful nature or propensities as we do. We are born with a sinful tendency, the guilt of Adam, and we commit personal sins. Not only did Christ not sin, but he *had* no sin, neither nature nor guilt (Heb 7:26; 1 Pet 1:19; 3:18).

Mind Science groups. The first epistle of John was written to refute Gnostic notions of Christ, and does so soundly. Jesus claimed on many occasions to be the Christ (Mt 26:63-65; Mk 14:61-64; 15:2; Lk 4:21).[70]

Scripture teaches that in order to be saved one must acknowledge Jesus as the Christ:

> Jesus said to [Martha], "I am the resurrection and the life. He who believes in me will live, even though he dies; and whoever lives and believes in me will never die. Do you believe this?"
>
> "Yes, Lord," she told him, "I believe that you are the Christ, the Son of God, who was to come into the world." (Jn 11:25-27)

In the Bible there are many instances where Christ is doing things that a "divine idea" could never do—for example, being born as a baby: "Today in the town of David a Savior has been born to you; he is Christ the Lord" (Lk 2:11, see also Acts 3:18; 26:23; Rom 7:4; 1 Cor 1:23; 10:16). The Mind Science view betrays ignorance of the fact that Jesus is the personal name of the Christ (Mt 1:21), while Christ is his title or office (Mt 16:16). *Christ* is the Greek equivalent of the Hebrew word *mashiach,* which means "Anointed One" or "Messiah." Messiah and Christ, then, are titles that refer to the same person, Jesus.

Rather than being merely a trailblazer, an example we can follow to obtain the divine nature, Jesus was fully human but claimed to be fully God (Col 2:9) at the same time, being one person with two natures (Phil 2:6-11). Scripture and the creeds reveal a Jesus who was far more than a "way-shower." It is inconsistent to accept some of Jesus' claims and not others. Jesus claimed to be "the way" (Jn 14:6). There is a huge gulf separating a "way-shower" from one who is "the way."

United Pentecostal Church. In their doctrine of Christ, United Pentecostals confuse *being* (or essence) with *person.* To hold to the position that the "deity of Jesus is none other than the Father Himself,"[71] one would be hard put to account for Christ's prayers to his Father, or the statements made by God the Father about his Son in the hearing of human beings. To *whom* (person), not *what* (divine nature), was Jesus praying fervently in the Garden of Gethsemane that the cup before him would pass?

Part of the United Pentecostal error arises from a misunderstanding of orthodox assertions regarding the nature of the Trinity. A United Pentecostal author argues, "Jesus is not just a part of God, but *all* of God is resident in Him."[72] Yet orthodoxy does not paint Jesus as a part of God. According to the Nicene Creed, Jesus is "Light of Light, true God of true God." According to the Chalcedonian Definition, "we, then, . . . teach men to confess one and the same Son, our Lord Jesus Christ, the same perfect in Godhead and also perfect in manhood; truly God and truly man."

What about Isaiah 9:6, where the coming Messiah is prophesied to be called "Everlasting Father" (or more accurately, "Father of eternity")? According to ancient thinking, one who owned a property could be called the "father" of it; thus Christ would be the Father of eternity or the Creator of the ages, as Hebrews 1:2 and 11:3 point out.

In John 1:1-5 the Word was "toward God" (as a careful reading of the Greek preposition *pros* would suggest) yet also "was God." The doctrine of the Trinity is the only logical conclusion one can come to from this passage.

Why We Must Know the Real Jesus

The word *orthodoxy* is derived from two Greek words meaning "right" and "honor." To be orthodox is to be in right relationship with God through right doctrine. To be a heretic is to oppose not only right doctrine but God himself.

In 2 Corinthians 11:4 Paul confesses his fear that his Corinthian sisters and brothers will be led away to a "Jesus other than the Jesus we preached." And in Galatians Paul hurls the divine "anathema," a condemnation or curse, at anyone who would teach a different gospel and thereby pervert the true gospel of Christ. The end result is damnation—and meanwhile the earthly life of one opposed to orthodoxy is slavery, for he or she has no release from the chains of sin and guilt.

The gospel of Christ faithfully communicates the true essence of Christ's person and mission. Pervert his person and you have destroyed our only hope for salvation in this life and the next.

5

JESUS' RESURRECTION
Was It His Actual Body?

Often we regard the church fathers as a cadre of infallible guides, sages of theological authority and acumen. They are never wrong, we suppose. Consider, then, the following piece from one of the early church fathers:

> Now we ask how can anyone imagine that our animal body is to be changed by the grace of the resurrection and become spiritual? . . . It is clearly absurd to say that it will be involved in the passions of flesh and blood. . . . By the command of God the body which was earthly and animal will be replaced by a spiritual body, such as may be able to dwell in heaven; even on those who have been of lower worth, even of contemptible, almost negligible merit, the glory and worth of the body will be bestowed in proportion to the deserts of the life and soul of each. But even for those destined for eternal fire or for punishment there will be an incorruptible body through the change of the resurrection.[1]

The author, Origen, was often subject to theological flights of fancy, for which he got into hot water with other ecclesiastical authorities. He was condemned at the Fifth Ecumenical Council in Constantinople (A.D. 553) for his teachings on the preexistence of the soul and universal salvation, and for his denial of the physical nature of the resurrection.[2] Various groups have found Origen very helpful in their challenges to orthodox Christianity.

Origen's theological bane, and perhaps his most enduring influence on subsequent church practice, was his biblical hermeneutic.[3] Because Scripture is inspired by the Holy Spirit, he taught, every scriptural word has a "spiritual" meaning whether it has a literal meaning or not. Believers, indwelt by the same Spirit, are to interpret the text and discern its real meaning. Nonliteral or "allegorical" interpretations were justified by Origen with the argument that since Scripture is spiritual, it must have a meaning worthy of God and be inerrant despite apparent difficulties. "Controls on the nonliteral interpretation were provided by the history of salvation and the articles of faith, but the understanding of the nature of man and God allowed philosophical ideas to influence the interpretation. The allegorical (spiritual) interpretation was elevated to prominence by Origen's followers, who thereby lost the control exercised by the moral purpose."[4]

A problem with Origen's allegorical method was that it often led to a hermeneutical circle that neglected the objective and literal meaning of a text in favor of a subjective interpretation justified by the interpreter's experience. Predisposed toward Neo-Platonism, Origen was reading meaning *into* the text (eisegesis) rather than *out of* the text (exegesis). The result: his theology of the resurrection was based not on what Scripture clearly teaches but on what Origen *presumed* it teaches.

Did Jesus rise from the dead bodily or spiritually? What has been the Christian church's teaching on this doctrine? What significance does the resurrection of Jesus have for his claims of deity? We will examine how alternative religious movements have distorted this doctrine, followed by a refutation of their heretical teachings.

Jesus' Resurrection in Orthodox Theology

In one of the earliest Christian writings, 1 Corinthians 15, Paul reminds his readers of the gospel he first preached to them, by which they will be saved if they persevere and hold firmly to it. He emphasizes that faith in anything else is vain, or of no value, in salvation:

> For what I received I passed on to you as of first importance: that Christ died for our sins according to the Scriptures, that he was buried, that he was raised on the third day according to the Scriptures, and that he appeared to Peter, and then to the Twelve. After that, he appeared to more than five hundred of the brothers at the same time, most of whom are still living, though some have fallen asleep. Then he appeared to James, then to all the apostles, and last of all he appeared to me also, as to one abnormally born. (1 Cor 15:3-8)

The content of the gospel, according to Paul, is the resurrection victory of Christ over death and the guarantee of our salvation and future resurrection with him. If Jesus was not raised bodily from the grave, then the Corinthians' faith in him was in vain and they were still dead in trespasses and sin. If Jesus was not raised from the dead, then his life, ministry, miracles and atoning death on a Roman cross meant *nothing*.

Paul's overarching ambition was "to know Christ and the power of his resurrection and the fellowship of sharing in his sufferings, becoming like him in his death, and so, somehow, to attain to the resurrection from the dead" (Phil 3:10-11). Paul desired to share in the same transformation from mortality to immortality as his Master, Jesus, the "firstfruits" from the dead (1 Cor 15:20).

The New Testament epistles depend entirely on the assumption that Jesus Christ is reigning as living Savior over the church and will one day return as King over the earth in power and exceeding great glory. Indeed the epistles would not make any sense whatsoever without this underlying conviction.

After the resurrection Jesus had a corporeal body that could be touched and handled. The disciples on the road to Emmaus thought him to be a typical traveler (Lk 24:15-18, 28-29); he took bread and broke it (Lk 24:30); he ate a piece of fish to prove that he was not a spirit or ghost (Lk 24:41-43); Mary thought him to be a gardener (Jn 20:15); he showed the disciples his scarred hands and side (Jn 20:20); he prepared breakfast for some of them (Jn 21:12-13). He urged them, "Look at my hands and my feet. It is I myself! Touch me and see; a ghost does not have flesh and bones, as you see I have" (Lk 24:39). The Gospels and the Epistles are adamant that the body Jesus had after his resurrection was a glorified *physical* body.[5]

Jesus' resurrection was prophesied in the Old Testament (Ps 16:10). He appeared to more than five hundred witnesses, including Paul. Jesus is proclaimed to be at the right hand of the Father interceding for us. Christ's resurrection, not just his crucifixion, secured our justification as a sign of God's approval of Christ's sacrifice for our sins on our behalf. As the "firstfruits" of those who have fallen asleep (1 Cor 15:20-26; compare Ex 23:16-19), Christ serves as an example and a guarantee of what we can expect: our dead physical body will likewise be raised to immortality (1 Cor 15:42). We will be both material and immaterial beings, our soul reunited with our resurrected body. The power behind this tremendous, mysterious event is Jesus, who declared himself to be the "resurrection and the life" (Jn 11:25). Like him, we will have a body that has been altered and prepared for the new life to come, capable of undreamed-of supernatural abilities (Lk 24:31, 36, 51). Our resurrection, and hence our final redemption, will take place at Christ's return for his church (1 Thess 4:13-18).[6]

Jesus' resurrection ensures our regeneration. "He has given us new birth into a living hope through the resurrection of Jesus Christ from the dead" (1 Pet 1:3). Though for now our bodies remain subject to all the vicissitudes of mortal weakness, aging and death, in our spirits we vibrate with the power that raised Jesus from the dead.

Paul connects this regenerative power of the resurrection to the spiritual power at work within us when he writes to the Ephesians of God's "incomparably great power for us who believe. That power is like the working of his mighty strength, which he exerted in Christ when he raised him from the dead and seated him at his right hand in the heavenly realms" (Eph 1:19-20). The power that raised Jesus from the dead in glory is the very same power at work in us through the Holy Spirit. Because of this, Paul urges us to follow not after the lusts of the flesh of our "dead" corrupted bodies. "We were therefore buried with him through baptism into death in order that, just as Christ was raised from the dead through the glory of the Father, we too may live a new life. . . . In the same way, count yourselves dead to sin but alive to God in Christ Jesus" (Rom 6:4, 11).

This line of argument would have no meaning unless Christ's bodily resurrection from the dead were a fact taken for granted in the New Testament. We are not exhorted to live the ethereal life of "a spirit" but the resurrected life of a new being who is no longer dead in trespasses and sins. Death is a consequence of sin. Our parents in the Garden in the beginning were undoubtedly "physical" (no one doubts this), created for a physical realm of existence in eternity. This was the original pristine state that Christ redeemed for us, continuing on with God's original plan.

Jesus' resurrection also secures our justification, our receiving a declaration of innocence before God. In Romans 4:25 Paul writes, "He was delivered over to death for our sins and was raised to life for our justification." God's raising of Jesus from the dead showed God's approval of Jesus' sacrificial death for our sins and declared that his work was completed ("it is finished") and that he need not remain dead.[7]

After being raised from the dead, Jesus entered into a whole new category of existence, being "glorified" and becoming life-giving spirit (see 1 Cor 15:45). "Life-giving spirit" has been misunderstood by many in regard to Christ's postresurrection state. The phrase in Greek *(pneuma zōopoioun)* denotes "the spirit that gives life" or "the spirit that makes alive."[8] Jesus did not become the Spirit or "a spirit"; the second Person of the Trinity did not become the third Person. Instead Jesus' mortal existence and form were altered into that which is spiritual, as Paul says in the preceding verse: "So it will be with the resurrection of the dead. The body that is sown is perishable, it is raised imperishable; it is sown in dishonor, it is raised in glory; it is sown in weakness, it is raised in power; it is sown a natural body, it is raised a *spiritual body*" (1 Cor 15:42-44). Now united with the Spirit in a "glorified" body, Christ is no longer subject to his mortal body. He is now alive in the Spirit (1 Pet 3:18), giving life to all who believe. This is the reason Paul refers to the Spirit of life in Christ Jesus (Rom 8:2).

Jesus' resurrection ensures that we too will receive perfect resurrection bodies. In several New Testament passages our resurrection bodies are connected with Christ's in kind. "By his power God raised the Lord from the dead, and he will raise us also" (1 Cor 6:14). Similarly, "we know that the one who raised the Lord Jesus from the dead will also raise us with Jesus and present us with you in his presence" (2 Cor 4:14).

After Jesus' resurrection he still retained the nail and spear scars received during his crucifixion (Jn 20:25-27). They are an eternal reminder of the sacrifice he made for our salvation. The scars of crucifixion are testimony of his great love for us.

Jesus used his resurrection prophetically as a means of validating his earthly ministry, claim to deity, and identity as Messiah of Israel and Savior of the world. He answered Jewish teachers' insolent demand for a sign from him with a prediction of his death and burial:

> A wicked and adulterous generation asks for a miraculous sign! But none will be given it except the sign of the prophet Jonah. For as Jonah was three days and three nights in the belly of a huge fish, so the Son of Man will be three days and three nights in the heart of the earth. (Mt 12:39-40)

In John's Gospel, Jesus uses imagery of the temple for his next prediction:

> Then the Jews demanded of him, "What miraculous sign can you show us to prove your authority to do all this?"
>
> Jesus answered them, "Destroy this temple, and I will raise it again in three days."
>
> The Jews replied, "It has taken forty-six years to build this temple, and you are going to raise it in three days?" But the temple he had spoken of was his body. After he was raised from the dead, his disciples recalled what he had said. Then they believed the Scripture and the words that Jesus had spoken. (Jn 2:18-22)

When Jesus rose from the dead after three days, just as he had said he would, the early church regarded this as vindication from God that Jesus was who he said he was, the Logos of God, God's very own Son.

The significance of the prediction was not lost on the Jewish leaders:

> The next day [after Christ's crucifixion], the one after Preparation Day, the chief priests and the Pharisees went to Pilate. "Sir," they said, "we remember that while he was still alive that deceiver said, 'After three days I will rise again.' So give the order for the tomb to be made secure until the third day. Otherwise, his disciples may come and steal the body and tell the people that he has been raised from the dead." (Mt 27:62-64)

Any suggestion of an attempted theft of Jesus' body from the tomb by his disciples, however, is entirely implausible. Roman soldiers of this period were highly disciplined and expertly trained, not likely to take any soldierly assignment lightly, even the guarding of an obscure tomb. Strict autocratic rule demanded immediate execution of any soldier found to be derelict in his duties. Moreover, the disciples themselves certainly were in no mental condition to plot, much less attempt, to steal their dead master's body from a sealed tomb guarded by soldiers bristling with weapons. The charge later offered by the Jewish authorities that the disciples stole the body while the guards were asleep is ludicrous; the guards could not have possibly known it was the disciples who had taken the body if in fact they were asleep.[9]

William Lane Craig, in his masterfully written *Reasonable Faith,* summarizes a most forceful argument for the historicity of the resurrection of Christ and its significance for Christian faith:

> The Christian apologists also refurbished the old argument from the origin of the church. Suppose, Vernet [eighteenth-century French apologist] suggests, that no resurrection or miracles occurred: how then could a dozen men, poor, coarse, and apprehensive, turn the world upside down? If Jesus did not rise from the dead, declares Ditton [eighteenth-century English apologist], then either we must believe that a small, unlearned band of deceivers overcame the powers of the world and preached an incredible doctrine over the face of the whole earth, which in turn received this fiction as the sacred truth of God; or else, if they were not deceivers, but enthusiasts, we must believe that these extremists, carried along by the impetus of extravagant fancy, managed to spread a falsity that not only common folk, but statesmen and philosophers as well, embraced as the sober truth. Because such a scenario is simply unbelievable, the message of the apostles, which gave birth to Christianity, must be true.[10]

The proclamation of the apostles was that a most astounding miracle had occurred: the man Jesus Christ was the Son of God in human flesh, who vindicated his claims by defeating death and rising from the dead. In the face of an incredulous and religiously skeptical world they preached this message; by the power of their testimony and on the strength of the historical evidence they convinced the great and the lowly. They suffered horrible persecution, torture and ultimately, for all of them save one (John the beloved apostle), death. Not one of them recanted their original assertion that they were eyewitnesses to the entrance, ministry, death and resurrection of the second Person of the eternal Trinity, Jesus Christ. Because of that historical incident, our eternal destiny has been altered forever.

JESUS' RESURRECTION AND THE NEW RELIGIOUS MOVEMENTS

Church of Jesus Christ of Latter-day Saints. In the Mormon view, Jesus rose from the dead with an immortalized body. "The facts of Christ's resurrection from the dead are attested by such an array of scriptural proofs that no doubt of the reality finds place in the mind of any believer in the inspired records."[11] But his resurrection did not destroy death and sin. The resurrection ensures that *all* people will ultimately be resurrected—that is, be brought back to life with a permanently joined body and soul. Christ's resurrection brings about a general resurrection by addressing Adam's sin, not the sins of each person who trusts in Christ for salvation.

Mormons do not hold to the orthodox Christian view of salvation by grace through faith, nor do they believe that Christ's death on the cross put an end to death and sin. For them his resurrection has no bearing on our eternal salvation, since no one will suffer eternal death except for radically evil and recalcitrant persons. Christ's resurrection merely ensures that *all* humanity will rise from the dead.[12]

Jehovah's Witnesses. Perhaps no other religious group denies the bodily resurrection of Jesus Christ more vehemently than the Watchtower Bible and Tract Society, or Jehovah's Witnesses. This group maintains that Jesus was resurrected in a spirit form. "Jesus Christ . . . was the first to be raised as a spirit person (1 Peter 3:18)."[13] Jehovah's Witnesses teach that Jesus was not resurrected in the same physical body in which he died. "Jesus thus gave up his fleshly body in sacrifice for humankind. . . . Having given up his flesh for the life of the world, Christ could never take it again and become a man once more. For that basic reason his return could never be in the human body that he sacrificed once for all time."[14] How are Jesus' numerous appearances to over five hundred persons explained? "Usually they could not at first tell it was Jesus, for he appeared in different bodies. He appeared and disappeared just as angels had done, because he was resurrected as a spirit creature. Only because Thomas would not believe did Jesus appear in a body like that in which he had died."[15] "Jehovah God raised him from the dead, not as a human Son, but as a mighty immortal spirit Son. . . . For forty days after he materialized, as angels before him had done, to show himself alive to his disciples."[16] Thus when Jesus appeared bodily to his disciples and others, it was a demonstration that he was still "alive"—not as a physical man but as a spirit creature. After the resurrection, Jesus was reborn from God's memory and remade into his original spirit-creature form, Michael the archangel.

Jehovah's Witnesses believe that retaining a physical body would have been shameful for Christ: "Jesus did not take his human body to heaven to be forever a man in heaven. Had he done so, that would have left him even lower than the angels. . . . God did not purpose for Jesus to be humiliated thus forever by being a fleshly man forever. No, but after he had sacrificed his perfect manhood, God raised him to deathless life as a glorious spirit creature."[17]

Christian Science. For Christian Scientists, the resurrection of Jesus Christ, and that of all people, has to do with the spiritualization of consciousness, the transformation of a person from this realm to another, more spiritual one. "RESURRECTION. Spiritualization of thought; a new and higher idea of immortality, or spiritual existence; material belief yielding to spiritual understanding."[18] Mary Baker Eddy declares, "His disciples believed Jesus to be dead while he was hidden in the sepulchre, whereas he was alive."[19] Believing neither that Jesus died on the cross for our sins nor that he was raised from the dead for our justification, Eddy writes, "Jesus' students . . . did not perform many wonderful works until they saw him after his crucifixion and learned that he had not died."[20] She spiritualizes the accounts of Jesus' physical resurrection, as well as his crucifixion and ascension into heaven. "[The disciples'] dear Master would rise again in the spiritual realm of reality, and ascend far above their apprehension. As the reward for his faithfulness, he would disappear to material sense in that change which has since been called the ascension."[21]

Word Faith movement. The Word Faith movement is a new Christian tradition born from the teachings of Kenneth E. Hagin, who based his doctrines on those of E. W. Kenyon. Kenyon had been influenced greatly by the metaphysical Mind Science groups such as Christian Science, Unity School of Christianity and Church of Religious Science.[22]

Kenneth Hagin, Kenneth Copeland and other followers in the Word Faith movement put a new spin on the doctrine of Christ's resurrection:

> In order to redeem humanity, Jesus had to die spiritually as well as physically. When He died spiritually, He died in the same way that Adam died. In other words, He lost His divine nature and was given the nature of Satan. Jesus' death on the cross and His shed blood did not atone for our sins. The atonement took place in hell through the devil's torturing of Jesus' spirit for three days and three nights. Unfortunately for Satan, Jesus was taken to hell "illegally" because He had never sinned. This "technicality" enabled God to use His "force of faith" to revive Jesus' spirit, restore Jesus' divine nature, and resurrect Jesus' body. Through the resurrection process Jesus was "born again."[23]

According to Copeland, when a person is born again, he or she experiences in the *exact manner* the same thing that happened to Jesus: the person's Satanic nature is replaced with God's divine nature, a transformation so complete and identical to Christ's that Christians become little gods and are as much an incarnation of God as was Jesus.[24]

According to Word Faith theology, Jesus died spiritually on the cross as well as physically. His shed blood *did not* atone for our sins.

> Jesus went into hell to free mankind. . . . When His blood poured out it did not atone. In Hell, he [Jesus] suffered death for you and me. . . . Satan was holding the Son of God illegally. God could not go into hell as it was not His domain. [That] Word of the Living God went down into that pit of destruction and charged the spirit of Jesus with resurrection power! Suddenly His twisted, death-wracked spirit began to fill out and come back to life. . . . He was literally being reborn before the devil's very eyes. He began to flex His spiritual muscles. . . . Jesus was born again.[25]

By teaching that Jesus was "born again" through his resurrection and that his divine nature and spirit were reintroduced into his body, leaders of the Word Faith movement divorce themselves from historic Christianity.

"A Course in Miracles." According to the writer and founder of *A Course in Miracles*, the resurrection should not be understood as a literal physical return from the dead. In fact the body does not exist and death does not exist. Thus Jesus could not have been raised from the dead in any real sense. The resurrection instead is "the symbol of sharing because the reawakening of every Son of God is necessary to enable the Sonship to know its wholeness."[26] It "is a reawakening or rebirth: a change of mind about the meaning of the world."[27] "A slain Christ has no meaning. But a risen Christ becomes the symbol of the Son of God's forgiveness on himself; the sign he looks upon himself as healed and whole."[28]

A Course in Miracles thrives in the West due to our large-scale abandonment of belief in propositional truth and absolute meaning. The *Course's* teachings underscore the priority of personal encounter over verifiable truth. Resurrection, according to the proponents of the Course, is a symbol of our individual reawakened encounter with ourselves as Sons of God. Founder Helen Shucman made herself the "author" of New Testament texts, construing their meaning on the basis of her personal identity and subjective experience. She claimed to receive such revelations from Jesus himself, channeled through her to the world.

Rosicrucianism. In the theological system of Rosicrucianism, everyone has three bodies with which they operate in various realms: (1) the "dense" (physical) body, to operate in the physical world, (2) the "vital" (invisible) body, to operate in the "etheric" (spiritual) plane, and (3) the desire body, to operate in the realm of emotion. "In order to function in the dense Physical World it is necessary to have a dense body. . . . We must have a vital body before we can express life, grow, or externalize the other qualities peculiar to the Etheric Region."[29]

In Jesus, all three of these "bodies" were abrogated by "the Christ":

> After the destruction of the dense body [Christ's crucifixion], Christ appeared among His disciples in the vital body, in which He functioned for some time. The vital body is the vehicle which He will use when He appears again, for He will never take another dense body. . . . Upon the death of the dense body of Christ Jesus, the seedatom was returned to the original owner, Jesus of Nazareth, who for some time afterward, while functioning in a vital body which he had gathered temporarily, taught the nucleus of the new faith which Christ had left behind.[30]

In Rosicrucian writings it is difficult to determine the exact nature of who or what visited the disciples after the first Easter. Was it "the Christ" or Jesus who appeared to the disciples in a vital body?

Responding to the New Religious Movements

Church of Jesus Christ of Latter-day Saints. Contrary to Mormon teachings, the death of Jesus satisfied the holiness and justice of the Father in relation to the sin of humankind and needed punishment for sin. Christ is the propitiation[31] for our sins: "Your sins have been forgiven on account of his name" (1 Jn 2:12). Our sins are forgiven in light of God's having taken away the certificate of our debt and nailing it to the cross, in the imagery of Colossians 2:13-15.

Peace is now possible with God through Jesus Christ because sin and death have been defeated completely on the cross (Rom 5:1-2). Christ's resurrection is a guarantee of the salvation that he purchased for us.

Jehovah's Witnesses. First Peter 3:18 says that Jesus "was put to death in the body but made alive by the Spirit." This does not mean that he was raised a spirit but that he was raised from the dead by the power of the Holy Spirit.

The Jehovah's Witness teaching of a "spiritual" resurrection is in direct contradiction to the plain teaching of Scripture (see, for example, Lk 24:36-42, where the risen Jesus asks the disciples for food and eats it in their presence). Jehovah's Witnesses teach that Jesus gave up his "fleshly body" at death as a sacrifice for humankind and thus lost it forever. But this has nothing to do with offering his life for the sins of human beings. Jesus died in the flesh; there was no requirement that he abandon that body. He took it back again at his resurrection (Acts 2:22-31). "In Christ all the fullness of the Deity *lives* [present tense] in bodily form" (Col 2:9).

Jehovah's Witnesses argue that the reason Jesus appeared to his disciples *bodily* was to demonstrate that he was still "alive." But if his body was indeed dead and buried, what was the point? If Jesus wanted to demonstrate that he was still alive as a "spirit creature," it would have made no sense to make them think he was resurrected as a man of flesh and bone.

When he was in human form, Jesus humbled himself to the point of death (see Phil 2:8); this does not imply that Jesus was in a humiliated state for having taken on a human nature. Certainly God's demonstration of the extent of his love for us through the incarnation is amazing. It is also true that we humans were created "a little lower than the heavenly beings" (Ps 8:5). But when the second Person of the Trinity assumed a human nature along with his divine nature, he elevated humanity rather than diminishing himself. By virtue of the incarnation, we will be above the angels.

Christian Science. When the Scriptures speak of resurrection generally, the common wording is "a resurrection *[anastasis]* of dead ones." There is never—ever—a suggestion of spirits rising or being reborn or living on in other than bodily form. In Romans 1:4 Jesus' resurrection itself is referred to as "a resurrection of dead ones," the very same wording. The same terminology is used in 1 Corinthians 15:21, where the Greek text could be literally translated: "For since through a man death came, so also through a Man came a resurrection of dead persons."

Jesus actually died physically on the cross (Mt 27:50-60; Rom 5:6; 8:34), and this was attested to by a plethora of witnesses, sympathetic as well as hostile (1 Cor 15:5-6; Gal 1:1-11; 2 Pet 1:16). His resurrection, personal and physical, from the dead is also verified by historical facts and eyewitness testimony (Mt 28:9, 16-17; Lk 24:13-15, 28-35, 51) and was confirmed by as many as fifteen postresurrection appearances (Acts 1:3, 9; 1 Cor 15:6-8). Without these corroborative facts of history, Christianity would be the most elaborate hoax ever devised (1 Cor 15:1-4, 14-19; Gal 2:20-21). The bodily resurrection of Jesus is an absolutely necessary belief for salvation (Rom 10:9).

"A Course in Miracles." The physical nature of Jesus' resurrection was part and parcel of the apostolic message. These men who turned the world upside down were convinced that Jesus of Nazareth was risen from the grave just as he had predicted, as a sign of the truth of his claim to be God in human flesh. On the Day of Pentecost, Peter said that the messianic psalms "spoke of the resurrection of the Christ, that he was not abandoned to the grave, nor did his body see decay" (Acts 2:31). The reality that Christ "died for our sins" and "was raised on the third day" is the heart of the gospel (1 Cor 15:3-4).

The account of Jesus' appearance to "doubting Thomas" and the other apostles to show his pierced hands, feet and side (Jn 20:26-29) makes it clear that he was showing his body of flesh and that this was not a visionary experience. The unequivocal language of Luke 24 also shows that Jesus had a fleshly body, a literal death and a literal physical resurrection.

Word Faith movement. A few Scriptures speak clearly to the errors of this movement's teachings regarding Jesus' death and resurrection.

> Jesus, the author and perfecter of our faith, . . . for the joy set before him endured the cross [not torture at the hands of Satan and his demons in hell], scorning its shame, and sat down at the right hand of the throne of God. (Heb 12:2)
>
> In him we have redemption through his blood, the forgiveness of sins, in accordance with the riches of God's grace. (Eph 1:7)

> . . . Him who loves us and has freed us from our sins by his blood. (Rev 1:5)
>
> The reason my Father loves me is that I lay down my life—only to take it up again. No one takes it from me, but I lay it down of my own accord. I have authority to lay it down and authority to take it up again. (Jn 10:17-18)
>
> As the Father has life in himself, so he has granted the Son to have life in himself. (Jn 5:26)

The New Testament is quite clear that Jesus had authority to lay his life down and take it up again. The resurrection of Jesus Christ was not possible because some "technicality" prevented Satan from holding him forever; it was possible because he was not subject to sin and death. As the perfect human representative, in rising Jesus demonstrated to people and demons the power and authority he possesses now and forever as the Son of God. That "life in himself" is his eternal deity and power, setting him apart from every created thing. This power brought his dead body back to life and will also bring our dead bodies back to life on the glorious morning of eternity.

Rosicrucianism. Over and against the Rosicrucian teaching that upon the death of Jesus' body the "seedatom" (whatever this means) was returned to the original owner, Jesus of Nazareth, the New Testament clearly teaches that the resurrected body of Jesus was both spiritual and physical. Christ's resurrection body was fully capable of engaging in all physical earthly pursuits—eating, walking on earth and subject to gravity, touching and holding physical objects—activities that require a physical body at least similar to if not exactly like the bodies we possess at present.

The Jesus of Rosicrucianism emerges from deep within the recesses of ancient Gnostic myth and the occult, not the New Testament.

Conclusion

The theological systems of the six organizations examined here all in one way or another distort or deny the doctrine of Christ's physical resurrection from the dead. The orthodox church has always maintained that to deny the bodily resurrection of Christ—or to distort the New Testament's clear teaching about it—is to deny the very basis of eternal salvation.

What one believes about God, Christ and the gospel is of vital importance, just as it was for the early church (see Gal 1:6-9). The first Christians, like us, competed with numerous other truth claims about the nature of God, human nature and salvation, and so were compelled to guard the gospel message jealously.

6

THE HOLY SPIRIT

What Can We Know About Him?

In the realm of Christian theology, the twentieth century can best be described as the century of the Holy Spirit. Never before in the history of the church had so much attention been given to the third Person of the Trinity. In the latter half of the century the once-belittled Pentecostal movement burgeoned into the charismatic movement, bringing a renewed emphasis on holiness and fervency of worship around the world.

Yet how much do most Christians really know about the Spirit? What do the Scriptures say about him? What did Jesus, the apostles and the early church fathers teach about him? Christian thought regarding the nature and work of the Holy Spirit has been intermittent and irregular since those first centuries. In the West, Augustine ascribed power to internal grace rather than to the Holy Spirit, and medieval thinkers substituted the church and its sacraments for the Spirit and the Word as bringing salvation to humankind. Serious study of the Holy Spirit (or pneumatology) was thus neglected for centuries. "Only Eastern Orthodoxy, with its rigorous Trinitarian formulation, and Evangelicalism out of Reform, Methodist and pietist stables, with its experiential-ethical emphasis, have ever made much of the theme," notes J. I. Packer.[1]

The early church dealt with a wide assortment of views regarding the nature of the Holy Spirit. As late as A.D. 380, Gregory of Nazianzus reported in a sermon that some considered the Holy Spirit to be a force, some a creature, while others considered him to be God; yet others, due to Scripture's vagueness on the topic, refrained from committing themselves altogether. Among those who considered the Holy Spirit to be God, some held the belief privately, others declared it in the open. Others maintained that the three persons of the Trinity possess deity in unequal degrees.[2]

The early church emphasized the Spirit as the guiding and moving force in the production of the Bible.[3] Later, although the Holy Spirit was revered, his exact status and nature remained only vaguely understood. Many theologians thought of the Holy Spirit as "one of the things which have come into existence through the Son," according to Eusebius of Caesarea's exegesis of John 1:3.[4] Eusebius spoke of the Spirit as "in the third rank," "a third power" and "third from the Supreme Cause."[5] The actual working out of a definitive doctrine of the Holy Spirit was a byproduct of the christological work done in the fourth and fifth centuries by Athanasius when he responded to the *Tropici,* persons engaged in figurative interpretations of Scripture, who also maintained that the Spirit is a "creature" brought into existence from "nothingness."[6]

Athanasius maintained that the Spirit is fully divine, consubstantial with the Father and the Son, and that the Spirit "belongs to and is one with the Godhead which is in the Triad." Thus the Holy Spirit should be recognized as possessing the same nature as the Father and the Son and should be given the same honor and worship.[7]

The Orthodox Understanding of the Holy Spirit

A brief look at some of the creeds and confessions of the church can show the development of thought regarding the third Person of the Trinity. The Apostles' Creed (third-fourth centuries), a brief confession used primarily for baptismal affirmations of faith, makes a pronounced emphasis on the second Person of the Trinity, Jesus Christ. God the Father is referred to in the first line as maker of heaven and earth. The second paragraph is devoted exclusively to the ministry of God the Son. The Holy Spirit is given a passing reference in the last line: "I believe in the Holy Spirit; the holy catholic Church; the communion of saints; the forgiveness of sins; the resurrection of the body; and the life everlasting." Beyond belief in him, nothing about the Holy Spirit is affirmed or denied.

The Nicene Creed (325; revised at Constantinople in 381), like the Apostles' Creed, focuses mainly on Jesus Christ. This is understandable, since the theological controversies of the time had to do primarily with the nature of the Son's relationship with the Father. Regarding the Holy Spirit it says, "[I believe] in the Holy Spirit, the Lord and Giver of life; who proceedeth from the Father and the Son;[8] who with the Father and the Son together is worshiped and glorified; who spake by the Prophets." The Nicene was the first creed to explicitly acknowledge the Holy Spirit as participating in the Trinity.

In the Chalcedonian Definition (Chalcedonian Creed of 451), which focuses on the hypostatic union, the Holy Spirit is not even mentioned by name. In the Athanasian Creed (fourth-fifth centuries) the Holy Spirit is referred to directly, though this creed's emphasis, particularly in the opening propositions, is on the unity of the Godhead: "The Godhead of the Father, of the Son, and of the Holy Spirit, is all one: the Glory equal, the Majesty coeternal."

In the Articles of Religion, or the Thirty-nine Articles of the Church of England (1571), the Holy Spirit is mentioned in article 5: "The Holy Spirit, proceeding from the Father and the Son, is of one substance, majesty, and glory, with the Father and the Son, very and eternal God." The Westminster Confession of Faith (England, 1647), in the spirit of Puritan Calvinism, is a sharpening of the Thirty-nine Articles. The Holy Spirit is mentioned in chapter 1, "Of the Holy Scripture," as "speaking in Scripture." He is mentioned many times throughout the rest of the Confession along with the Father. The Son, of course, is afforded the most honor and mention.

Why do all the creeds emphasize the Son? Jesus himself gives us the answer.

> When he, the Spirit of truth, comes, he will guide you into all truth. He will not speak on his own; he will speak only what he hears, and he will tell you what is yet to come. *He will bring glory to me by taking from what is mine and making it known to you.* All that belongs to the Father is mine. That is why I said the Spirit will take from what is mine and make it known to you. (Jn 16:13-15)

The Holy Spirit's ministry is to convict the world of guilt and judgment and to bring glory to Jesus Christ, the only name under heaven by which we can be saved. The Spirit's intent is to deflect attention from himself and lead us back to the Son.

But what of the Spirit's nature? Charles Hodge notes that since *Father* and *Son* are relational terms, it is natural to infer that *Spirit* is to be understood in the same way. "The Son is called the Word, as the revealer or image of God, and the Third Person is called Spirit as his breath or power."[9] In the Old Testament the spirit *(ruach)* of Yahweh is God's power in action. According to J. I. Packer, the distinct personhood of the Spirit can and should (according to the New Testament) be read into the Old Testament but cannot be read out of it.[10] *Ruach* can mean both breath blown out and wind blowing, which is often viewed as God's breath (Is 40:7; Ezek 37:9). In one hundred of its four hundred Old Testament appearances, *ruach* evokes powerful and lucid images of God's power unleashed. God's Spirit shapes creation, animates animals and humankind, directs the course of nature and history, reveals God's word to his messengers, teaches the way of righteousness, elicits faith and obedience, and equips for tasks requiring divine wisdom and effective leadership.[11]

In the New Testament, Spirit is *pneuma,* a Greek word similarly associated with wind or breath. He appears as a person who is distinct from the Father and the Son, with a ministry all his own.[12] We see that his nature is absolutely holy, and the cause of holiness in all creatures.[13] Although all things said against the Father and the Son will be forgiven, blaspheming the Holy Spirit will never be forgiven—though this statement by Jesus appears to refer to rejection of the Spirit's redemptive work in revealing Jesus, not simply speaking against the Spirit.

Some unorthodox groups portray the Holy Spirit as merely the "power" of God, or the Father's influence. The personality of the Holy Spirit, however, had few detractors even during the chaotic early years of theological controversies in the church.[14] The Scriptures clearly teach that the Holy Spirit is a person. He is given to the church as Counselor, taking over the role performed by Jesus on earth. Like the Father and the Son, he acts as only a person can do: he speaks, hears, acts, testifies, glorifies, convinces, guides, teaches, punishes, prompts, commands, forbids, desires, intercedes with groanings too profound for human understanding. Like the Father and the Son, he can be personally insulted, lied to, resisted and grieved by sin.[15]

When Jesus speaks of the ***paraklētos*** (counselor, comforter) he always uses the personal pronoun. In John's Gospel Jesus says the Spirit mediates his presence among his church in knowledge of and communion with the ascended and glorified Savior. "Less explicitly Christocentric statements about the Spirit elsewhere in the NT should be understood as rooted in this understanding, which is the tap-root of apostolic spirituality from first to last."[16] Only after Christ's return to the Father could the Spirit's ministry (not the Spirit age) begin; it was inaugurated at Pentecost not many days afterward. The Spirit assures believers that they are children of God, mediates fellowship with the Father and the Son, prompts missionary action in the world, and elicits pastoral concern for the building up of Christ's body. "This Christocentric focus of the Spirit's paraclete ministry is consistently sustained in NT thought."[17]

The Old Testament contains predictions that the presence of the Holy Spirit would be poured out in unprecedented degree, bringing multiplied blessings on God's people.[18] Isaiah foresaw a time when the Spirit would inaugurate a great spiritual renewal:

> The fortress will be abandoned,
>   the noisy city deserted . . .
> till the Spirit is poured upon us from on high,
>   and the desert becomes a fertile field,
>   and the fertile field seems like a forest.
> Justice will dwell in the desert
>   and righteousness live in the fertile field.
> The fruit of righteousness will be peace;
>   the effect of righteousness will be quietness and confidence
>   forever.
> My people will live in peaceful dwelling places,

in secure homes,
in undisturbed places of rest. (Is 32:14-18)

For I will pour water on the thirsty land,
and streams on the dry ground;
I will pour out my Spirit on your offspring,
and my blessing on your descendants. (Is 44:3)

In contrast, the withdrawal of the Holy Spirit meant misery and judgment: "Yet they rebelled and grieved his Holy Spirit. So he turned and became their enemy and he himself fought against them" (Is 63:10).

In the New Testament the Holy Spirit blesses by giving new life in regeneration, as Jesus emphasizes to Nicodemus: "Flesh gives birth to flesh, but the Spirit gives birth to spirit. You should not be surprised at my saying, 'You must be born again'" (Jn 3:6-7). Jesus also says, "The Spirit gives life; the flesh counts for nothing" (Jn 6:63). On the day of Christ's return the Holy Spirit will raise our dead bodies to immortality: "He who raised Christ from the dead will also give life to your mortal bodies through his Spirit, who lives in you" (Rom 8:11).

The Holy Spirit also gives power for special service to perform God's will. The Spirit empowered Joshua with special leadership skills and military acumen. He also filled certain Israelites in the wilderness with artistic and metallurgic understanding and abilities so they could construct the tabernacle according to God's plans. The Holy Spirit fell upon Saul to arouse him to anger to battle against Israel's enemies (1 Sam 11:6). When David was anointed king over Israel, the Holy Spirit came upon him with great power from that day forward (1 Sam 16:13). The Spirit also went in the midst of his people to protect them and do battle for them.[19] The Old Testament further predicts a time when the Servant-Messiah will be anointed by the Spirit in awesome power and fullness:

> The Spirit of the LORD will rest on him—
> the Spirit of wisdom and of understanding,
> the Spirit of counsel and of power,
> the Spirit of knowledge and of the fear of the LORD—
> and he will delight in the fear of the LORD. (Is 11:2-3)

In New Testament accounts the Spirit performs this same empowerment for service, most fully in his empowering and anointing of Jesus as Messiah. The Holy Spirit descended on Jesus at his baptism (Mt 3:16; Jn 1:32). The Spirit, pleased to dwell in Jesus, empowered him to perform the mighty miracles he wrought with a word. Jesus possessed an anointing from the Holy Spirit without measure, and this anointing "remained on him" (see Jn 1:32).[20]

The Spirit further empowers Christians to overcome spiritual darkness and opposition to the preaching of the gospel and to God's work in people's lives. Jesus said, "But if I drive out demons *by the Spirit of God,* then the kingdom of God has come upon you" (Mt 12:28). In Cyprus, Paul's rebuke of Elymas the magician, who was subsequently blinded, is said to be a work of the Spirit (Acts 13:9-12).

The Spirit witnesses with our spirits that we are children of God (Rom 8:16). Furthermore, the Spirit teaches certain things to God's people by illuminating them regarding spiritual matters.[21] Speaking to the disciples prior to his crucifixion, Jesus said that "the Holy Spirit, whom the Father will send in my name, will teach you all things and will remind you of everything I have said to you" (Jn 14:26). This statement not only bears witness to the distinct personality of the Holy Spirit but highlights the profound unity and diversity within the Trinity. In 1 Corinthians 2:12 we read, "We have not received the spirit of the world but the Spirit who is from God, that we may understand what God has freely given us." This is a power and function performed by the Holy Spirit, *sent* by the Father, *in the name* of Jesus. Here we see Three in One, in perfect unity, distinct in their personalities and their works.

As for the deity of the Holy Spirit, in the Old Testament "the LORD" and "the Spirit of the LORD" are used interchangeably, and thus, according to Hodge:

> If the latter is not a mere paraphrase for the former, he must of necessity be divine. The deity and personality of the Holy Spirit was affirmed in the subsequent church creeds because it was found clearly taught in the Scriptures. For instance, the New Testament passage in Acts 5:1-4, wherein Peter charges the errant Ananias of not lying to men but to God, is one of the most forceful examples of Scripture where we find the Holy Spirit acknowledged as both God and a distinct Person. The expressions, Jehovah [the Lord] said, and, the Spirit said, are constantly interchanged; and the acts of the Spirit are said to be acts of God.[22]

Hodge points out that Isaiah 6:9 reads, "He [the Lord] said, 'Go and tell this people . . .'" This same passage is quoted by Paul in Acts 28:25-26 thus: "The Holy Spirit spoke the truth to your forefathers when he said through Isaiah the prophet: 'Go to this people and say . . .'"[23] Paul is clearly identifying the Lord who spoke to Isaiah in that passage with the Holy Spirit. This is powerful evidence for the New Testament's teaching of the deity and personhood of the Holy Spirit.

Jesus put his personal stamp of approval on the divine authority and origin of the Old Testament. His apostles, who wrote the New Testament documents under his direction through the illuminating power of the Holy Spirit (as he promised), confirmed the unity between the Old and New Testaments. There can be no doubt or equivocation: the Lord God who spoke through the prophets of the Old Testament is the Holy Spirit we have come to recognize in the New Testament.

Unorthodox Teachings on the Holy Spirit

Church of Jesus Christ of Latter-day Saints. Mormons make distinctions between the nature and function of "the Holy Ghost" and those of "the Holy Spirit." The Holy Ghost is a spirit-man, the third god of the Trinity, like the Father and the Son. The Holy Spirit is an impersonal influence that proceeds from the Father. This distinction is drawn from the King James Version's use of the two terms. "The Holy Ghost is an individual personage, the third member of the Godhead; the Holy Spirit, in a distinctive sense, is the 'divine essence' by means of which the Godhead operates upon man and in nature."[24] The Mormons insist on referring to the Holy Spirit as "a personage of spirit."

> The term Holy Ghost and its common synonyms, Spirit of God, Spirit of the Lord, or simply Spirit, Comforter, and Spirit of Truth occur in the Scriptures with plainly different meanings, referring in some cases to the person of God the Holy Ghost, and in other instances to the power and authority of this great personage, or to the agency through which He ministers. . . . The Holy Ghost undoubtedly possesses personal powers and affections; these attributes exist in Him in perfection. Thus, He teaches and guides, testifies of the Father and the Son, reproves for sin, speaks, commands, and commissions. . . . These are not figurative expressions but plain statements of the attributes and characteristics of the Holy Ghost.[25]

In *The Articles of Faith* James Talmadge writes:

> It has been said, therefore, that God is everywhere present; but this does not mean that the actual person of any one member of the Godhead can be *physically* present in more than one place at one time. . . . Admitting the personality of God, we are compelled to accept the fact of His materiality; indeed, an "immaterial" being, under which meaningless name some have sought to designate the condition of God, cannot exist, for the very expression is a contradiction in terms. If God possesses a form, that form is of necessity of definite proportions and therefore of limited extension in space. It is impossible for Him to occupy at one time more than one space of such limits.[26]

Parley P. Pratt, another Mormon theologian, writes:

> There is a divine substance, fluid or essence, called Spirit, widely diffused among these eternal elements. . . . This divine element, or Spirit, is the immediate, active or controlling agent in all holy miraculous powers. . . . The purest, most refined and subtle of all these substances and the one least understood or even recognized by the less informed among mankind is that substance called the Holy Spirit.[27]

According to Pratt, then, the Holy Spirit is a substance, a fluidlike material, in contrast to Talmadge's statement that the Holy Spirit is a person.

Jehovah's Witnesses. According to Watchtower theology, the Holy Spirit is God's active force, not a personal being. Through this force God accomplishes his purposes. "A comparison of Bible texts that refer to the holy spirit shows that it is spoken of as 'filling' people; they can be 'baptized' with it; and they can be 'anointed' with it. . . . None of these expressions would be appropriate if the holy spirit were a person."[28] Notice the lowercase letters. And again, "From God there goes forth an invisible active force by means of which he gets his will done. . . . He sends it forth to accomplish what is holy. So it is correctly called 'holy spirit.'"[29]

The Holy Spirit, according to the Watchtower, is God's active force—like a radar beam: "The Bible's use of 'holy spirit' indicates that it is a controlled force that Jehovah God uses to accomplish a variety of his purposes. To a certain extent, it can be likened to electricity, a force that can be adapted to perform a great variety of operations."[30] "The holy spirit is not a person and it is not part of a Trinity. . . . It is not equal to God but is always at his disposition and subordinate to him."[31]

Freemasonry. Freemasonary is a distinctive religious movement that began as far back as the Middle Ages (fourteenth century). Its modern equivalent has come a long way from the early attempts to form trade unions (lodges). Its members, including politicians, clergymen and scientists, gradually began to fashion esoteric rituals and doctrines to accompany some of the symbols already in use by working masons (usually tools of the trade). At this time occultism began to make headway in the lodges. Eventually the various "grades" that workers went through in developing and perfecting their craft were paralleled by degrees of advancement in esoteric knowledge.

In Freemasonry the Holy Spirit is

> a Life-Principle of the world, a universal agent, wherein are two natures and a double current, of love and wrath. This ambient fluid penetrates everything. It is a ray detached from the glory of the Sun, and fixed by the weight of the atmosphere and the central attraction. It is the body of the Holy Spirit, the universal Agent, the Serpent devouring his own tail.[32]

Freemasonry's concept of the Holy Spirit, as well as of the Father and the Son, is actually a modification of mystical Jewish philosophy:

> In the KABALAH, or Hebrew traditional philosophy, the infinite Deity, beyond the reach of the Human Intellect, and without Name, Form, or limitation, was represented as developing Himself . . . in ten emanations or out-flowings, called SEPHIROTH. . . . Here is the origin of the Trinity of the Father, the Mother or Holy Spirit, and the Son or Word.[33]

"A Course in Miracles." For the *Course,* the Holy Spirit is the voice of God inside every person—a conscience, one might say. The Holy Spirit was created by "God" at the time human beings gained the *illusion* of separation from God. The Holy Spirit tells us that we have made "mistakes" or errors but, according to the *Course,* never says we have "sinned."

> Jesus is the manifestation of the *Holy Spirit,* Whom he called down upon the earth after he ascended into Heaven. . . . The Holy Spirit, being a creation of the One Creator, . . . is eternal and has never changed. . . . The Holy Spirit abides in the part of your mind that is part of the Christ Mind. He represents your Self and your Creator, Who are one.[34]

> The Holy Spirit is part of you. Created by God, He left neither God nor His creation. He is both God and you, as you are God and Him together.[35]

> The Holy Spirit is the Christ Mind which is aware of the knowledge that lies beyond perception. He came into being with the separation as a protection, inspiring the Atonement principle at the same time.[36]

> The Holy Spirit dispels [guilt] simply through the calm recognition that it has never been.[37]

> The Holy Spirit cannot punish sin. Mistakes he recognizes, and would correct them all as God entrusted Him to do. But sin He knows not, nor can He recognize mistakes that cannot be corrected.[38]

Mind Science groups. For the Mind Science groups the Holy Spirit is not an actual person but a "characterization" of God, a feminine quality or spiritual truth. In Religious Science, for example, "the Holy Ghost signifies the feminine aspect of the Divine Trinity. It represents the divine activity of the higher mental plane."[39] Unity School of Christianity teaches that "the very Spirit of truth is lying latent within us each and every one."[40]

The glossary of *Science and Health, with Key to the Scriptures* provides the Christian Science understanding of the Holy Spirit: "HOLY GHOST. Divine Science; the development of eternal Life, Truth, and Love."[41] In the writings of Mary Baker Eddy the term *God* is relative, abstract and impersonal; she readily interchanges *God* with the terms *Life, Truth, Love, Principle, Mind, Substance, Intelligence, Spirit* and *Mother.*[42]

Christian Science, like other Mind Science groups, denies that the Holy Spirit is personal. Eddy denied both the personality and the office of the Holy Spirit and for his exalted role in salvation substituted "Divine Science."[43]

Responding to the New Religious Movements

Church of Jesus Christ of Latter-day Saints. In the Bible, including the King James Version, there is no distinction between the Holy Spirit and the Holy Ghost. In English-language New Testaments "Holy Ghost" and "Holy Spirit" are both translated from the same Greek word, *pneuma.* The Holy Spirit, as we have affirmed above, is the third Person of the Trinity, fully God. He possesses the very same nature as the other members of the Godhead yet is distinguished from them (Mt 28:19; Mk 3:28-29; Jn 14:26; 16:7-14; Acts 5:3-4; 1 Cor 2:10-13; 12:11; Eph 4:30).

Mormon apologist James Talmadge propounds that the Holy Spirit is a personage of spirit, "an immaterial being," and also God (Doctrine and Covenants 20:28). However, since as Talmadge acknowledges the Holy Spirit does not possess a form of material nature, he is not limited to extension and space and can occupy more than one space at one time.

There is another major problem in the Mormon view of God the Holy Spirit and his alleged corporeal body of spirit. In Mormon cosmology the universe is eternal.[44] It has always existed. The gods allegedly caused the universe to come into being. However, these entities have always existed within this "eternal" universe and are subject to the very laws they supposedly brought into being.

If matter exists without being caused by God, then God must be subject to certain laws that determine his relationship to matter despite what he may will to do. Where did these laws come from if the universe is eternal? How could God transcend matter he did not create? By situating God within the space-time continuum, Mormonism has concocted a god who cannot be the cause of the laws that govern his being.

Jehovah's Witnesses. The Bible, in contrast to the Watchtower Society, clearly describes the Holy Spirit as a person. Personal pronouns are always used in reference to the Holy Spirit, never neuter (see Jn 14:17; 15:26; 16:13-14). The Holy Spirit is *never* referred to as a thing or as a force of God. The Holy Spirit is called a "witness" (Acts 5:32), and speech is attributed to him (Acts 8:29; 10:19-20; 11:12; 13:2).

Attributes that can be possessed only by a personal being are ascribed to the Holy Spirit. He feels love and grief (Is 63:10; Rom

15:30; Eph 4:30), has a mind with which to intercede (Rom 8:27), possesses knowledge (1 Cor 2:11), can be lied to (Acts 5:3), can be insulted (Heb 10:29), can teach (Jn 14:26), can bear witness (Jn 15:26), can hear (Jn 16:13) and can make value judgments (Acts 15:28). The Bible also ascribes personal descriptive titles to the Holy Spirit, such as Helper, Comforter and Counselor (Jn 14:26). When Witnesses insist that these verses merely describe the acts of God the Father through the agency of "the holy spirit," they are presupposing that the Spirit is an impersonal force that emanates the attributes of God. Instead of conducting exegesis (reading the meaning out of the text), they conduct eisegesis (reading into the text).

Consider this quote from a Watchtower publication affirming the personality of Satan: "Can an unintelligent force carry on a conversation with a person? Also, the Bible calls Satan a manslayer, a liar, a father . . . and a ruler. Only an intelligent person could fit all those descriptions."[45] I agree! That is why the early church was compelled to attribute personality and deity to the Holy Spirit. If the Watchtower view were true, at least *one* biblical passage should refer to a "holy active force." But the concept "holy active force" does not appear in Scripture.

Freemasonry. The Scriptures unequivocally teach the deity of the Holy Spirit. Freemason notions of the Spirit are based on pagan traditions and gnostic worldviews rather than on the Bible.

"A Course in Miracles." Contrary to *Course* teachings, the Holy Spirit is God, the third Person of the triune Godhead. The Holy Spirit is called "God" (Acts 5:3-4) and is identified in the New Testament as Yahweh (see Acts 28:25-27, quoting Is 6:9-10; also Heb 10:15-17, quoting Jer 31:33-34). These references to the Spirit as Deity, and to "the eternal Spirit" (Heb 9:14), demonstrate that the Holy Spirit always existed. The members of the Godhead are not eternal merely from now on but have existed from eternity past. The Holy Spirit was not created at a point in time.

Neither is the Holy Spirit both "God and you"; he is only God. There is an impassable gulf between the essence of deity and that of humanity. Holy Writ says, "The Spirit of God lives in you"—in Christians (Rom 8:9; 1 Cor 3:16). It never says, "The Spirit of God *is* you."

Finally, the Holy Spirit was sent into the world by God to "convict the world of guilt in regard to sin and righteousness and judgment" (Jn 16:8). The Holy Spirit is sent to convince us that sin and judgment are real and divinely established. The *Course* denies this, yet the Holy Spirit as the author of Scripture (Eph 3:2-5; 2 Pet 1:21) affirms the reality of sin and judgment to come. Part of the work of the Holy Spirit is to "contend" with humans (Gen 6:3) in order to lead people to repentance (Rom 2:4).

Mind Science groups. The God of the Bible does what only a personal Being can do, and his personal attributes forever separate him from the pantheistic god of Christian Science and the other Mind Science groups. We need only reiterate what the biblical writers and the Lord Jesus himself said about the Holy Spirit. In John 16, for instance, Jesus instructs his disciples about their new ministry and duties and promises them the presence of the "Comforter" who will guide them into all truth and strengthen them after Jesus' ascension. Jesus reassures them that it is essential that he first depart before the Comforter will come to them: "I tell you the truth: It is for your good that I am going away. Unless I go away, the Counselor will not come to you; but if I go, I will send him to you" (Jn 16:7-8).

CONCLUSION

The Holy Spirit, like any other person, can display personality passively.[46] He can be lied to, as in the case of Ananias and Sapphira (Acts

5:3-4). Paul warns us about the sin of grieving the Holy Spirit (Eph 4:30) and quenching the Holy Spirit (1 Thess 5:19). Stephen accuses his Jewish audience of always resisting the Holy Spirit (Acts 7:51). While it is possible, of course, to resist a "force," one cannot lie to or grieve an impersonal force. One can lie to and grieve only a person. Neither can one blaspheme a force. No radar beam has ever received—or is ever likely to receive—insults. Only a very holy and sensitive person can be blasphemed: the Holy Spirit can be blasphemed and grieved to such a degree that Scripture declared the sin unforgivable (Mt 12:31; Mk 3:29). Those are chilling prospects.

Further, the Holy Spirit performs ministries and moral actions that can be performed only by a person: teaching, regenerating, speaking, searching, interceding, commanding, revealing, illuminating, testifying, guiding. Certainly Paul has a person in view when he writes of how the Spirit assists us in our weakness: "We do not know what we ought to pray for, but the Spirit himself intercedes for us with groans that words cannot express" (Rom 8:26).

The Holy Spirit is not a force but a person with a will, intellect and emotions. And this person shares the essence of deity with the Father and the Son. He is truly God Almighty.

7

HUMANITY AND SIN

Who Are We, and What Have We Done?

Throughout the past two thousand years of Western history, heavily influenced by the Christian worldview, people have understood themselves to be creatures created in the image of God. Damaged by the entrance of sin, people require redemption from a perfect source outside themselves. That perfect source is God. Outside of occasional challenges, this was the prevailing view of human nature until the advent of the Enlightenment era of the eighteenth century, which challenged the Christian worldview from an a priori rationalistic position. The middle of the nineteenth century witnessed the advent of Charles Darwin's theory of evolution, which directly challenged the Genesis account of the unique creation of a man and a woman and their fall into sin. As the nineteenth century closed, the twentieth century dawned as an age of progress buoyed by unprecedented confidence—propelled by Darwin's hugely successful theory of natural selection—in mankind's eventual taming of nature and itself.

This essentially atheistic and anthropocentric approach to human nature inevitably led to a denigration of objectivity and any genuine knowledge of God. Humans are no longer regarded as fallen creatures in need of salvation from God. We are quite alone in the universe. Human sin has come to be regarded merely as a life lived "inauthentically."

The Orthodox View of Humanity and Sin

The doctrine of human nature. The great Princeton theologian Charles Hodge provides a helpful statement of human nature in comparison to the Creator's:

> God is a Spirit, the human soul is a spirit. The essential attributes of spirit are reason, conscience, and will. A spirit is a rational, moral, and therefore also, a free agent. In making man after his own image, therefore, God endowed him with those attributes which belonged to his own nature as a spirit. . . . He belongs to the same order of being as God Himself, and is therefore capable of communion with his Maker.[1]

Humans, then, are a composite unity of flesh and spirit (soul).[2] The body is material and the spirit is immaterial. Scripture is very clear that each of us possesses a spirit that is distinct from our physical body, and it appears to be able to function somewhat independently of our normal thought processes (Rom 8:16; 1 Cor 14:14) and can function consciously and relate to God even after we die.[3] Jesus said to the dying thief crucified next to him, "Today you will be with me in paradise" (Lk 23:43), even though their physical bodies were soon to die. His statement clearly teaches that the spirit survives death in a conscious state.

Scripture also teaches that in our physical universe body and spirit act together in unison as one person. Our humanity is an integrated whole, and we should not devalue any aspect of our nature—our intellect, emotions, will or body.

> We will not think of our bodies as inherently evil or unimportant. Such a view of dichotomy within unity will also help us to remember that, in this life, there is a continual interaction between our body and our spirit, and that they affect each other: "A cheerful heart is good medicine, but a downcast spirit dries up the bones" (Prov 17:22).[4]

The moral fall of the human race is an essential element of the revelation of salvation mediated through Christ. To understand humans as anything less than beings created by God in perfection, who fell into moral degradation, is to make meaningless the work of Christ and the regenerating office of the Holy Spirit.[5] Unless humans had a real beginning in time and space as Adam and Eve, the entire edifice of redemption given to us through biblical revelation must fall.

An important biblical expression employed to describe the original form of humanity is that God created us in his "image and likeness."[6] This is what distinguishes us from the entire created order, though we too are creatures of the universe and made from "the dust of stars." God's image in us is what makes us human.[7]

A useful definition is provided by Wayne Grudem: "The fact that man is in the image of God means that man is like God and represents God."[8] Humans are beings similar to God. The Hebrew words for "image" *(tselem)* and "likeness" *(demuth)* both refer to something that is similar but not identical to the thing it represents. *Tselem* means an object similar to something else and representative of it, such as a statue or idol representing a deity (2 Kings 11:18; Ezek 7:20) or a painting of ancient soldiers on a wall (Ezek 23:14).[9]

Theologians throughout history have struggled to identify a particular characteristic that would best encapsulate what it means for us to be made in the image and likeness of God. Yet when the original hearers heard "Let us make man in our image, in our likeness" (Gen 1:26), they would have naturally understood this to mean simply "Let us make man to be *like* us, to *represent* us."[10] The rest of the passage underscores the reason for this: men and women are to rule over all creation as God's representative. It is not necessary, therefore, to provide elaborate explanations of what the words *image* and *likeness* convey, such as intellectual ability, moral sense, spiritual nature, rational and abstract thinking, language, creativity, dominion over the earth, relationships, masculinity and femininity.

> No such list could do justice to the subject: the text only needs to affirm that man is *like God*, and the rest of Scripture fills in more details to explain this. In fact, as we read the rest of Scripture, we realize that a full understanding of man's likeness to God would require a full understanding of *who God is* in his being and in his actions and a full understanding of *who man is* and what he does. The more we know about God and man the more similarities we will recognize, and the more fully we will understand what Scripture means when it says that man is in the image of God. The expression refers to every way in which man is like God.[11]

Unlike any other creature in God's creation, human beings have a unique and privileged capacity for rational, moral and spiritual fellowship with the Creator. In a limited, finite sense, humans reflect the image of their infinite Creator through various godlike means. In *dominion*, they rule over God's creation as his representatives: "God blessed them and said to them, 'Be fruitful and increase in number; fill the earth and subdue it. Rule over the fish of the sea and the birds of the air and over every living creature that moves on the ground'" (Gen 1:28). In *communication*, humans reflect God's ability to communicate and apprehend abstract ideas and concepts: "The LORD God commanded . . . The LORD God said," (Gen 2:16, 18). Through *rational and moral decision making,* humans reflect their Creator's nature.

The doctrine of sin. The great Reformer John Calvin (1509-1564) perhaps articulated the best definition of sin: "This is the inherited corruption, which the church fathers termed, 'original sin,' meaning by the word 'sin' the depravation of a nature previously good and pure."[12] Sin comes from human beings' failure to uphold their moral obligations to their Creator. The apostle John refers to sin as "lawlessness" (1 Jn 3:4). Other definitions of sin have been offered.[13] The most popular is that sin is essentially self-interest. Yet Scripture does not support this interpretation. Some self-interest is good and commended by Scripture (Mt 6:20), such as when we desire to grow in maturity and sanctification (1 Thess 4:3). God appeals to our self-interest to seek his solution for sin (John 1:12).

When Paul seeks to demonstrate the universality of sin, he appeals to the law of God, whether it be the Mosaic law (Rom 2:17-29) or an unwritten law in the heart of the Gentile (Rom 2:15). In each case, sin is defined as a lack of moral conformity to the law of God.[14]

God neither sinned nor is responsible for the entrance of sin into the universe. He cannot be blamed for sin in any way. James quite tersely dismisses God as the source of sin or of human temptation: "When tempted, no one should say, 'God is tempting me.' For God cannot be tempted by evil, nor does he tempt anyone" (Jas 1:13). To suggest otherwise is blasphemy against God's nature. The responsibility—in every way—for sin lies squarely at the feet of humanity. "Each one is tempted when, by his own evil desire, he is dragged away and enticed. Then, after desire has conceived, it gives birth to sin; and sin, when it is full-grown, gives birth to death" (Jas 1:14-15).

Grudem rightly cautions us against skidding into the opposite extreme by supposing that a corresponding evil influence exists in the universe similar to, or equal to, God in power. "To say this would be to affirm what is called an ultimate 'dualism' in the universe, the existence of two equally ultimate powers, one good and the other evil." Nor must we entertain the notion that sin somehow surprised God or overcame his omniscience or omnipotence.[15]

The narrative of the fall of Adam and Eve in Eden needs to be understood as historically accurate. If it were mere myth, the rest of biblical revelation that unfolds the story of human redemption would have no foundation at all. Grudem argues for the fall's historicity from New Testament theology: "The New Testament authors look back on this account and affirm that 'sin came into the world through one man' (Rom 5:12) and insist that 'the judgment following one trespass brought condemnation' (Rom 5:16) and that 'the serpent deceived Eve by his cunning' (2 Cor 11:3; cf. 1 Tim 2:14)."[16]

Sin entered the universe through the willful disobedience of Adam and Eve, which was the "first sin." All of Adam and Eve's children were born thereafter with "original sin."

God had clearly commanded the man not to eat the fruit of a particular tree situated in the middle of the Garden. He included a dire warning regarding the consequences that would follow disobedience. So Adam and Eve were without excuse and culpable.

The consequence of sin is death, which is described in Scripture in various ways. The first is the physical decay of all creation, including the ultimate death of every human being born into this world:

> To Adam [God] said, "Because you listened to your wife and ate from the tree about which I commanded you, 'You must not eat of it,'

Cursed is the ground because of you;
 through painful toil you will eat of it
 all the days of your life . . .
for dust you are
 and to dust you will return." (Gen 3:17, 19)

As a result of the entrance of sin, God instituted death and decay to reign throughout the universe. Otherwise sin would exist forever: "For the creation was subjected to frustration [futility], not by its own choice [not as a normal course of nature], but by the will of the one who subjected it [God]" (Rom 8:20).

Another consequence of sin is the spiritual death of all humanity. This death is the utter demise of the intimate relationship with God for which we were originally created. "All have sinned and fall short of the glory of God" (Rom 3:23). The Greek verb "to sin" in this passage is in the aorist tense, which implies that this incident took place at a specific time, or at least as a particular event. Further, "sin entered the world through one man, and death through sin, and in this way death came to all men, because all sinned" (Rom 5:12). This text, and others related to it, would be mere religious nonsense if not rooted in the historical reality of Adam and Eve who disobeyed God in the Garden. Paul continues this theme in 1 Corinthians: "For as in Adam all die, so in Christ all will be made alive" (1 Cor 15:22).

Since the fall of humanity, all men and women have inherited the guilt of Adam. It is the same as if we were all in the Garden with Adam, egging him on as he took the fruit from Eve's hand, looked at it, considered it and finally brought it to his mouth. We all share in the guilt. This means we all share in the consequences for Eve and Adam's relationship with God, as elucidated by Millard Erickson: "In the case of Adam and Eve, trust, love, confidence, and closeness were replaced by fear, dread, and avoidance of God. Whereas they had previously looked forward with positive anticipation to their meetings with God, after the fall they did not want to see him. They hid themselves in an attempt to avoid him."[17]

God's anger toward us is another consequence of our sin. In the Old Testament, God's anger regarding human disobedience is imaged as "snorting" (Hebrew *anaph;* Deut 1:37; Is 12:1), suggesting a strong physical expression of anger.[18] Sometimes it is described as fire or fierce heat: "My wrath will break out and burn like fire because of the evil you have done—burn with no one to quench it" (Jer 4:4). God is clearly angered by sin.

The final consequence for our sin is God's punishment. The only solution that frees us is Christ's atoning death on the cross, allowing God's forgiveness, and eventually death's release from the temporal effects of sin in our life.[19] If there is no forgiveness for our sins, then the final solution is eternal death. At the last judgment, if one's name is not found written in the Lamb's Book of Life, the only destiny for that person is eternal death in the lake of fire, making permanent what the sinner chose in life.

Unorthodox Teachings on Human Nature and Sin

Church of Jesus Christ of Latter-day Saints. The doctrine of human nature in the Mormon system involves an "eternal being" who sprang from eternal "spiritual" matter. After a period of steady progression, God the Father reached the status of "Godhood," and he and his celestial wife procreated spirit children just as we humans procreate.

Man was also in the beginning with God. Intelligence, or the

> light of truth, was not created or made, neither indeed can be. (Doctrine and Covenants 93:29)
>
> Life, intelligence, mind, the "light of truth," or whatever name one gives to the center of the personality of man, is an uncreated, eternally existent, indestructible entity. . . . In the first stage, man was an eternally existent being termed an intelligence. . . .
>
> The next realm where man dwelt was the spirit world . . . . Eternally-existing intelligences were clothed with spirit bodies. . . . Numerous sons and daughters were begotten and born of heavenly parents into that eternal family in the spirit world.[20]

Jesus came into existence in the spirit world in the same manner all people do. Everyone lived in heaven with Jesus before coming to earth.

> These spirit children were organized, possessing divine, eternal, and godlike attributes, inherited from their Heavenly Father and Mother. There in the spirit world they were reared to maturity, becoming grown spirit men and women prior to coming upon this earth.[21]
>
> Jesus is man's spiritual brother. We dwelt with Him in the spirit world as members of that large society of eternal intelligences, which included our Heavenly Parents and all the personages who have become mortal beings upon this earth or who ever shall come here to dwell. . . . Jesus was the "firstborn," and so He is our eldest brother.[22]

The spirits come to earth in "tabernacles of flesh" (human bodies).

> Following his stay in the spirit world, man comes on earth in a probationary state preparatory to the eternal existence beyond

> the mortal confines of this world [in preparation for life after one dies on earth]. . . . It is true that when we are born into mortality a veil is drawn over our minds, so that we have forgotten our pre-mortal life.[23]

Eventually each person dies and awaits the resurrection and judgment, when they will be given either rewards or punishments: "Mortal death comes upon all. The eternal spirit goes to the spirit world to await resurrection and judgment."[24] But the Mormon spirit world is not the same heaven that Christians look forward to, nor are the rewards and punishments in any way the same.

For Mormonism, death and sin came into the world through the fall of Adam and Eve. Their deed, however, is not regarded as a sin in the Mormon scheme; it is rather a *blessing,* since it enabled humankind to continue progressing on toward eternal life: "They [the Christian world] have been long taught that Adam and Eve were great transgressors. . . . We, the children of Adam, . . . should rejoice with them, that through their fall and the atonement of Jesus Christ, the way of eternal life has been opened up to us."[25]

Jehovah's Witnesses. Jehovah's Witnesses seem to understand the significance of Adam's sin. When Adam sinned, his punishment was death. Everyone is a condemned sinner because of Adam: "By the disobedience of Adam sin became active and he was sentenced to death, and condemnation resulted to all his offspring. Hence all were born sinners."[26]

According to the Watchtower Society, when a person dies he or she completely ceases to exist. "The dead are shown to be 'conscious of nothing at all' and the death state to be one of complete inactivity. . . . In both the Hebrew and the Greek Scriptures, death is likened to sleep."[27] "When a person is dead he is completely out of existence. He is not conscious of anything."[28] Two Scriptures are cited as evidence:

> For the living know that they will die,
> but the dead know nothing;
> they have no further reward,
> and even the memory of them is forgotten. . . .
>
> Whatever your hand finds to do, do it with all your might, for in the grave, where you are going, there is neither working nor planning nor knowledge nor wisdom. (Eccles 9:5, 10)
>
> When their spirit departs, they return to the ground;
> on that very day their plans come to nothing. (Ps 146:4)

For the Jehovah's Witness, people do not have souls; they *are* souls. A soul is a combination of a body and the "life force" that only Jehovah God can impart.[29] "How, then, did this belief about an immortal soul find its way into the teachings of Christendom's churches? Today it is frankly acknowledged that this has come about through the influence of pagan Grecian philosophy."[30]

Mind Science groups. Mind Science teaches that human beings have the power to remove the idea of sin and hence have authority to forgive themselves. More precisely, we have no sin for which to be forgiven. We can simply deny it out of existence! Mary Baker Eddy uses that very verb: "To get rid of sin through Science, is to divest sin of any supposed mind or reality, and never to admit that sin can have intelligence or power, pain or pleasure. You conquer error by denying its veracity."[31] Religious Science says, "As we correct our mistakes, we forgive our own sins."[32] According to the Unity School of Christianity, since "Jesus was able to say, 'All authority is given to me in Heaven and on earth,' we too can say truthfully that this authority has been given to us."[33]

Death and disease—the consequences of sin—are denied as well. "The cardinal point in Christian Science [is] that matter and evil (including all inharmony [sic], sin, disease, death) are unreal."[34] A Gnostic influence is quite evident here. Religious Science seeks "to show that there is no sin but a mistake, and no punishment but a consequence. The Law of cause and effect. Sin is merely missing the mark."[35] The verdict? "THERE IS NO SIN, SICKNESS, OR DEATH."[36]

Because in the Mind Science groups human beings are regarded as part of the divine essence, they are spiritual beings and therefore perfect and sinless. "Man is not matter—made up of brains, blood, bones, and other material elements. . . . Man is spiritual and perfect; and because of this, he must be so understood in Christian Science. . . . Man is incapable of sin, sickness, and death, inasmuch as he derives his essence from God."[37] Eddy also says:

> There is that within every individual which partakes of the nature of the Universal Wholeness and—in so far as it operates is God. That is the meaning of the word Immanuel, the meaning of the word Christ. There is that within us which partakes of the nature of the Divine Being, and since it partakes of the nature of the Divine Being, we are divine.[38]

As a part of our inheritance in the divine essence, human beings can presume to claim all knowledge and understanding in the universe: "Never say, I don't know; I can't understand. Claim your Christ understanding at all times and declare: I am not under any spell of human ignorance. I am one with Infinite Understanding."[39]

Rosicrucianism. This complex integration of doctrines lifted from ancient mystical traditions of China, India and Persia teaches that everyone preexisted prior to being born on earth. "Every one of us is an individual spirit, which existed before the bodies we call races and will exist after they have ceased to be."[40]

Like the Mind Sciences, the Rosicrucians teach that everything in reality is "spirit." What we see is spirit substance crystallized. God and humankind share the same nature:

> Rosicrucians teach that MATTER is the external manifestation of an internal or invisible "PRINCIPLE." That "Principle" is SPIRIT. . . . MATTER may be termed the external manifestation of SPIRIT substance, in other words, CRYSTALLIZED SPIRIT. . . . The ABSOLUTE and Man, both being spirit, are therefore of the same substance. . . . Man is thus Divinity incarnated in Humanity.[41]

Humankind, according to Rosicrucianism, is divine by nature, but this truth has been forgotten. Rosicrucianism is designed to help us rediscover this truth: "The Rosicrucian Order is in existence today and has been for centuries, offering people a way to realize their own infinitely powerful and divine nature."[42]

New Age movement. For members of this fast growing movement, there is no sin or evil in the world:

> But where is the place of evil in this scheme then? It doesn't exist. That's the point. Everything in life is the result of illumination or ignorance. Those are the two polarities, not good and evil. And when you are totally illuminated such as Jesus Christ or Buddha, or some of those people, there is no struggle any longer.[43]

If evil and sin do not exist, why resist them? "You must not resist what you call evil."[44] Good and evil actually arise from the same source, so what we mistakenly regard as evil is in reality good as well.[45]

New Age thought has adopted into its hodgepodge belief system a Westernized version of reincarnation as a solution to the problem of sin and evil in the universe. Although some New Agers do not believe in reincarnation, the vast majority do.[46] It plays a prominent role in the thinking of such celebrities as Shirley MacLaine, Tina Turner and Sally Kirkland. Reincarnation is the belief that all human souls are involved in a cyclic pattern of death and rebirth in which the soul is eventually purged of all evil through suffering myriad tragedies, administered through the law of karma.[47]

Karma is the fixed and immutable law which states that "a person pays for the evil [or good] he does in this life by suffering [or being rewarded] for it in the next life." If an individual is reborn as a fly or a crippled child, it is because of his or her bad karma. That person is merely being rewarded for engaging in evil in a previous incarnation. Because everything is ultimately God, and individuality and personality are illusions, "a person's soul . . . is eternal and is part of the 'world soul' or 'ultimate being.'" The Westernized version of reincarnation tells us that human souls return only as human beings whereas the original Eastern version, also known as transmigration, tells us that human souls can return as another creature, such as a fly or cow.[48]

Karma solves the sin problem by teaching that the human soul is actually just a part of the "ultimate impersonal God."[49] The basic human problem is the illusion of self-awareness (I am) and the subject-object distinction (I-Thou). Through cyclic rebirth, the person who thinks he is a "something" will be purged of this illusion and return to "nothing" in absorption into a nonconscious union with the Absolute (God).[50]

The Way International. According to The Way, humans originally had a threefold nature: body, soul and spirit. These aspects are reflected in the Bible's use of the words *formed*, *made* and *created* in the account of humankind's creation.[51] "God formed man of the dust of the ground. . . . The body of man was formed *(yatsar)* of the dust of the ground."[52] The soul is the life-force God breathed into the first man. God *made* man a living soul by giving him that which brought life to his body. It was made only once:

> Leviticus 17:11: For the life of the flesh is in the blood. . . . The soul life is in the blood and is passed on when the sperm impregnates the egg. . . . The soul is passed on from one person to his progeny. If a person has no offspring, his soul is gone when he dies; it is no more.[53]

> How many times did God create soul? The Bible says that (except for the birth of Jesus) God created it just once and that was when animals first came into being. God simply took the previously created soul life and gave it to man. . . . The soul life which was in Adam was carried on in his children. . . . To this day the same soul life continues in humanity which God originally put in Adam.[54]

The spirit was that aspect that God created so that he and human beings could spiritually communicate. The spirit placed in humans was actually part of God himself. "God created within man his Spirit *(ruach)*, His image. . . . It is that part of man which made it possible for God to talk to man and for man to communicate with God."[55]

When the first humans fell, according to The Way, they lost their spirit. The image of God in human beings has been erased, and they are no more than highly intelligent animals: "The spirit which God originally created in man was given on a condition. . . . In not fulfilling the conditions which God had prescribed, man became a twofold being of just body and soul."[56]

When people are born again, they once again receive "spirit":

> On the day of Pentecost, every believer for the first time could have the spirit from God born within, so man could again become a tripartite being of body, soul, and spirit. This anointing with spirit from God places the believer again in the position where God can communicate directly with tripartite man. . . . The spirit from God is created in the believer and at the end of natural life this created spirit must return to God of whom it is a part.[57]

Responding to the New Religious Movements

Church of Jesus Christ of Latter-day Saints. In contradistinction to the Mormon idea of the eternal existence of human spirit-beings, the Scriptures teach clearly that each human is a finite being whose existence has a definite beginning. The first man, Adam, was created at a specific point in time and space. This is one difference between an eternal being like God and a finite creature. God has existed for all eternity and is the *only* being who has so existed. Humankind could not have existed when God was first creating the universe, for if we had, God's question to Job would have made no sense: "Where were you when I laid the earth's foundation?" (Job 38:4). Humans were created lower than the angels, who were created prior to us, so that even David wondered why God would have any regard for him (Ps 8:3-5; 144:3).

Not *one* verse in the entire biblical corpus even remotely suggests that God has a wife. Isaiah says that the Lord made all things by himself. Moreover, several passages in Isaiah teach that there is only one God and none beside him (Is 44:8; 45:6) or like him (Is 46:8).

Jesus is Almighty God from everlasting to everlasting. He is the Creator of all that exists and is the "firstborn" over all creation, that is, the preeminent One, the originator of life and the universe

(Ps 90:2; Mic 5:2; Jn 1:1-3; Acts 3:14-15; Col 1:16-17; Heb 1:2).[58] He is not simply another, better human being.

Contrary to Mormon teaching, human beings have no existence before birth; the body and soul of each person is formed in his or her mother's womb (Job 10:8-12; 31:15; Ps 119:73; 139:13-16; Zec 12:1). The Scriptures speak of God's having known Jeremiah before he formed him in the womb (Jer 1:5), but this does not hint at pre-existence but rather God's foreknowledge and omniscience. God "calls those things which do not exist as though they did" (Rom 4:17 NKJV).

To the Mormon, the fall of Adam and Eve was a blessing that enabled humankind to continue progressing toward eternal life. Rejoicing, however, is hardly the appropriate response to Adam's sin and its consequence. The misery human beings have suffered over the millennia is agonizing testimony to the heinous effects of sin in God's once perfect universe. The entire creation "groans" under the weight of it (Rom 8:22)! Human beings have been destined to be born dead in sins, children of God's wrath by nature.[59] The appropriate response to sin is mourning.

Jehovah's Witnesses. Most Christian conservatives maintain, contrary to the Witnesses, that the soul survives death in a temporary disembodied state while awaiting the resurrection.[60] It is not a matter of choosing either for the immortality of the soul versus the resurrection, it is rather that both play a part in the future of mankind.[61] To survive as a soul in a disembodied state is a temporary state; to be resurrected to eternal life is the joyous culmination of our ultimate salvation.

Jehovah's Witnesses believe that a person completely ceases to exist upon death and does not retain consciousness. Yet the oft-cited Ecclesiastes 9:5, 10 and Psalm 146:4 say nothing about consciousness after death but of a person's earthly knowledge and participation in earthly events. Jesus himself suggests that there is consciousness after death (Lk 16:19-31). And during his transfiguration Jesus conversed with a conscious Moses who had died physically centuries earlier.

The Hebrews believed in an immortal soul existing separate from the body long before Greek philosophy could influence Christian thought. Genesis 35:18 speaks of a woman's "soul" departing; 1 Kings 17:21 recounts how Elijah asked God to let the soul of a child return to him. Such descriptions also appear in the New Testament (Mt 10:28; Acts 20:10; Rev 6:9-11).

Mind Science groups. Contrary to Mind Science denial and do-it-yourself forgiveness, the apostle John writes, "If we claim to be without sin, we deceive ourselves and the truth is not in us. If we confess our sins, he is faithful and just and will forgive us our sins and purify us from all unrighteousness. If we claim we have not sinned, we make him out to be a liar and his word has no place in our lives" (1 Jn 1:8-10). God's remedy for sin is for us to confess our sin to him (Ps 32:5; 38:18) and accept his payment for it that we can never make for ourselves (Rom 3; Jas 2:10; Heb 9:11-22).

The biblical teaching on sin and forgiveness is very plain. Since all people sin, it is universal and quite real (Rom 3:23). Human beings are sinners in action and nature (Jer 17:9; Mk 7:21-23; Rom 5:12-21). Whatever does not proceed from faith is sin (Jas 2:11), all lawlessness is sin (1 Jn 3:4), and any wrongdoing is sin (1 Jn 5:17). Sin separates us from God (Rom 6:23). Jesus came into the world to save us sinners (1 Tim 1:15). Only God can forgive sin (Mt 9:6).

Sin, evil, disease and death are very real in history and in our experience. To attempt to redefine them or deny them does not help us deal with them but rather compounds their negative effects. The monistic worldview of Mind Science denies clear sensory data and leaves adherents bereft of any means of dealing with real life struggles.

Rosicrucianism. The Bible nowhere suggests the preexistence of the soul. We are composite beings of matter and spirit (or soul). Though there has been debate throughout church history as to where the soul originates—do we receive our soul in the womb (creationism) or is it passed down through procreation (traducianism)?—the church has never taught or endorsed the notion of the soul's preexistence.

"The spiritual did not come first, but the natural, and after that the spiritual. The first man was of the dust of the earth" (1 Cor 15:46-47). Zechariah 12:1 sheds more light on the subject: "This is the word of the LORD concerning Israel. The LORD, who stretches out the heavens, who lays the foundation of the earth, and who forms the spirit of man within him . . ." This informs us that God forms the spirit of a person only after the physical shell is formed to house it. We are not arguing for either a creationist or traducianist understanding of the soul's formation, only that Scripture affirms the formation of the "spirit" (or soul) of a human being "within him" by God.

Further, the God of the Bible makes it plain that he is transcendent and separate from his creation.

As the heavens are higher than the earth,
so are my ways higher than your ways
and my thoughts than your thoughts. (Is 55:9)

I am the LORD,
who has made all things,
who alone stretched out the heavens. (Is 44:24)

God, being a noncontingent being, created all things and existed before all things, including time and space. He is eternal, infinite, unmade, uncreated; humans will forever be made of created and finite substance.

To say that "all is god" is equivalent to saying that all things are equal or on the same level; then it would be just as true to say that "nothing is god" or that "nothing is important." The God of the Bible is a unique being, separate and distinct from his creation. Isaiah 46:9 says, "I am God, and there is no other; I am God, and there is none like me" (compare Ex 9:14). Clearly, if God is just part of the substance of all reality, then any such distinctions between him and his creation would be meaningless.

New Age movement. In contrast to the New Age denial of evil, the God of the Bible has both defined and drawn sharp distinctions between good and evil. After Adam disobeyed God in Eden and acquired a guilty conscience, God said, "The man has now become like one of us, knowing good and evil" (Gen 3:22). Very soon after, human wickedness increased and grieved the Creator: "The LORD saw how great man's wickedness on the earth had become, and that every inclination of the thoughts of his heart was only evil all the time" (Gen 6:5). God abhors evil:

> You are not a God who takes pleasure in evil;
> with you the wicked cannot dwell. (Ps 5:4)

> The face of the LORD is against those who do evil,
> to cut off the memory of them from the earth. (Ps 34:16)

Human beings' ability to discern good and evil is linked to maturity: "But solid [spiritual] food is for the mature, who by constant use have trained themselves to distinguish good from evil" (Heb 5:14).

While God does not want his people taking personal revenge for wrongdoing (see Mt 5:39), he does expect us to oppose evil in ourselves and in society:

> Put on the full armor of God, so that when the day of evil comes, you may be able to stand your ground, and after you have done everything, to stand. (Eph 6:13)
>
> Submit yourselves, then, to God. Resist the devil, and he will flee from you. (Jas 4:7)
>
> Be self-controlled and alert. Your enemy the devil prowls around like a roaring lion looking for someone to devour. Resist him, standing firm in the faith, because you know that your brothers throughout the world are undergoing the same kind of sufferings. (1 Pet 5:8-9)
>
> Learn to do right!
> Seek justice,
>   encourage the oppressed.
> Defend the cause of the fatherless,
>   plead the case of the widow. (Is 1:17)
>
> This is what the LORD says: Do what is just and right. Rescue from the hand of the oppressor the one who has been robbed. (Jer 22:3)

New Age belief understands good and evil as emerging from the same source, so that what we regard as evil is in reality good as well. This is patently false. Good and evil are not one and the same; they are diametrical opposites. To say that good and evil originate from the same source violates a key principle of logic: something cannot be both *A* and non-*A* at the same time and in the same sense. There can be no legitimate attempts to contradict logic in this case, or to deny its efficacy in any metaphysical language, for to attempt to deny logic, one must first employ it. The very fabric of the universe is woven with logic. When good and evil are equated, logic is violated and meaningful communication is vitiated.

The problem of sin, suffering and evil cannot be addressed through karma, reincarnation and the teaching that the human soul is a part of the "ultimate impersonal God." This sort of thinking is laden with logical inconsistencies and absurdities.[62] If one claims that there was a first life, then one cannot appeal to any previous lives to account for the evil and suffering in that life. If one says that there is an infinite regress of previous lives, then in principle one can never arrive at a previous life or lives that could account for all of the tragedy in one's present life. In this case reincarnation betrays the fallacy of infinite regress.

The Way International. The three Hebrew verbs Genesis uses in reference to human origins—*bara, yatsar* and *asah,* or *created, formed* and *made*—are simply different words used to describe a single event. Nothing in the language or the context would suggest that each word is used to differentiate an aspect of the first human being. The Way's definition of those Hebrew words to support its understanding of human nature is imposed on the text, not derived from it—eisegesis rather than exegesis.[63]

The Way's teaching on the soul contrasts to the biblical teaching that a new soul is formed in the womb at the conception of each human child. The Bible does not say that one's soul is passed on through the blood. It only states that life, survival or existence is inseparable from blood. A person would die without the regenerative process of blood's circulation in the body. Nowhere does Scripture require that there is a kind of soul-life essence that circulates among humans and is passed from parent to child.

The human spirit, according to The Way, was created so that God could communicate with the first man, and this spirit was actually part of God himself. This goes well beyond the teaching of Scripture. Humankind is flesh as well as spirit, created in the image of God.

There is nothing innately wrong with physical flesh. God created flesh, walked with human flesh and at a pivotal point in history took on human flesh. The Way's strict dualistic distinction of the human being is fabricated and unbiblical.

Contrary to The Way's teaching that human beings lost their spirit when they fell, Scripture is replete with references to human beings in an unregenerate state possessing a "spirit" (Ps 51:10; 77:6; 142:3-4; 143:7; Prov 15:13). Zechariah 12:1 says that God forms the spirit of each person within him, and Hebrews 4:12 speaks of God's Word as so powerful that it can divide the soul from the spirit. How could God's Word do this if human beings have no spirit? Our spirit is an intrinsic part of who we are—and the stamp of our identity with God's very image, however marred.

When people are born again, says The Way, they receive "spirit" loaned by God so that he and they can communicate. But God's ability to communicate with human beings is not dependent on whether they are indwelt by the Spirit of God. For example, God spoke to Abimelech, the Philistine King of Gerar (Gen 20:3), an unregenerate man. God spoke in a miraculous way while Saul, an unregenerate man at the time, was on the road to Damascus (Acts 9:3-6).

CONCLUSION

Some critics of the Christian doctrines of human nature and sin have argued forcefully that God himself set up our first parents to fall. Why did God find it necessary to place temptation before Adam and Eve? Why didn't he simply create them morally perfect?

The first systematic theologian in church history, Irenaeus, wrestled with this question.

"Could not God have made humanity perfect from the begin-

> ning?" Yet one must know that all things are possible for God, who is always the same and uncreated. But created beings, and all who have their beginning of being in the course of time, are necessarily inferior to the one who created them. Things which have recently come into being cannot be eternal; and, not being eternal, they fall short of perfection for that very reason. And being newly created they are therefore childish and immature, and not yet fully prepared for an adult way of life. And so, just as a mother is able to offer food to an infant, but the infant is not yet able to receive food unsuited to its age, in the same way, God, for his part, could have offered perfection to humanity at the beginning, but humanity was not capable of receiving it. It was nothing [sic] than an infant.[64]

Our first parents were not morally perfect, they were morally *innocent.* Thus, for Irenaeus, the moral responsibility for sin lies at the feet of Adam, who, because of his moral and spiritual frailty, committed the first act of disobedience.[65] The fault does not lie with God.

The teachings of some groups exemplify the extent to which people will go to deny culpability for our sinful nature. But the Scriptures provide us with a vivid portrayal of the first sin. Spiritual death is demonstrated by human beings' inherent bondage to a "sin nature." "When we were controlled by the sinful nature, the sinful passions aroused by the law were at work in our bodies, so that we bore fruit for death" (Rom 7:5). "All of us also lived among them at one time, gratifying the cravings of our sinful nature and following its desires and thoughts. Like the rest, we were by nature objects of wrath" (Eph 2:3).

Our redemption comes from Jesus Christ, who paid the penalty for our sins by dying on the cross on our behalf (Col 2:13-14). Once redeemed, we still struggle with our old sin nature, but we are no longer in bondage to it.

> There is now no condemnation for those who are in Christ Jesus, because through Christ Jesus the law of the Spirit of life set me free from the law of sin and death. (Rom 8:1-2)

> My dear children, I write this to you so that you will not sin. But if anybody does sin, we have one who speaks to the Father in our defense—Jesus Christ, the Righteous One. (1 Jn 2:1)

8

THE ATONEMENT

How Can We Be Saved by the Death of Christ?

The atonement of Christ, his death on the cross, provides forgiveness for sin. But what is the atonement, and why is it necessary?

What Jesus Christ did on the cross is the very heart of the gospel. The atonement is the central doctrine of Christianity. After our first parents fell, the atonement of humankind was prefigured by God. Amidst the curses came the promise of redemption. We were promised a champion, one who would come and defeat the serpent who brought evil into the world: "I will put enmity between you and the woman, and between your offspring and hers; he will crush your head, and you will strike his heel" (Gen 3:15). This is the first prophecy of the promised deliverer of humans, the Redeemer who would save his people from their sins.

The Orthodox View of the Atonement of Christ

The Old Testament prefigures and anticipates Christ's atonement for humankind. Jesus' atoning death must be viewed against the backdrop of the Old Testament sacrificial system. These elaborate sacrifices were instituted for the express purpose of atoning for sin—not to reform the sinner or to deter others from sinning. Sins that had been committed against God had to be set right.

The most commonly used Hebrew word in the Old Testament for the various sorts of atonement is *kaphar,* which literally means "to cover." Something had to be interposed between the offender's sin and God in order for punishment to be averted. The atoning sacrifice acted as a covering. This meant that the just penalty against the perpetrator no longer had to be exacted.

The sacrifice had to be spotless and without blemish of any kind, as close to actual perfection as possible. The one for whom the sacrifice was intended brought the animal before the priests and laid hands on it. The sacrificial animal then symbolically bore the offender's guilt. This bringing of the sacrificial animal and laying hands on it constituted an admission of guilt by the sinner.

The Bible is clear regarding the necessity for the shedding of blood to atone for sin. "For the life of a creature is in the blood, and I have given it to you to make atonement for yourselves on the altar; it is the blood that makes atonement for one's life" (Lev 17:11). The writer of Hebrews corroborates this ancient principle: "The law requires that nearly everything be cleansed with blood, and without the shedding of blood there is no forgiveness" (Heb 9:22). This author goes on to demonstrate at great lengths how the Old Testament sacrificial system was a "type" of the ultimate sacrifice that was to come in fullness in the person of Christ. We have been given peace through the *blood* of his cross.

"While the legal portions of the Old Testament typify with considerable clarity the sacrificial and substitutionary character of Christ's death, the prophetic passages go even further. They establish the connection between the Old Testament sacrifices and Christ's death."[1] The clearest example of this prophetic link between the sacrifices of the Old Testament and Christ is Isaiah 53.

> Surely he took up our infirmities
>   and carried our sorrows,
> yet we considered him stricken by God,
>   smitten by him, and afflicted.
> But he was pierced for our transgressions,
>   he was crushed for our iniquities;
> the punishment that brought us peace was upon him,
>   and by his wounds we are healed. (Is 53:4-5)

Having described the Messiah and the extent of the sins of humanity, Isaiah makes reference to Christ's sacrifice: "We all, like sheep, have gone astray, each of us has turned to his own way; and the LORD has laid on him the iniquity of us all" (Is 53:6). The iniquity of sinners, then, is to be transferred from them to the perfect sacrifice that was to come.

The cause of the atonement. As anticipated in the Old Testament and fulfilled in the accounts of the Gospels, Jesus Christ's death on the cross provided atonement for sin. "God demonstrates his own love for us in this: While we were still sinners, Christ died for us" (Rom 5:8). *Atonement* is "the . . . work Christ did in his life and death to earn our salvation."[2] Ultimately, why did Christ have to come to earth and die for our sins? This question is answered by the character of God, specifically the *love* and *justice* of God.

God's love for us as a cause of the atonement is expressed in the classic and most popular text of the Bible: "For God so loved the world that he gave his one and only Son, that whoever believes in him shall not perish but have eternal life" (Jn 3:16). Paul explains that God sent Christ into the world to be a *propitiation* (Rom 3:25), that is, a sacrifice that bears God's wrath in order for him to be *propitious*, favorably disposed, toward us. This was in order that the righteousness of God might be made evident.

Prior to the cross, God passed over former sins. Paul explains that God had been forgiving sins in the past before the penalty for those sins had been paid. But God's justice required that a way be found for that penalty to be paid so that God might have fellowship with human beings. Could a perfect God forgive sins without a penalty? No! Surely no God who is holy and just could gloss over the horror of sin. Thus when God sent Jesus to die and pay the penalty for our sins, "he did it to demonstrate his justice at the present time, so as to be just and the one who justifies those who have faith in Jesus" (Rom 3:26).

> Therefore, both the love and the justice of God were the ultimate cause of the atonement. It is not helpful for us to ask which is more important, however, because without the love of God, he would never have taken any steps to redeem us, yet without the justice of God, the specific requirement that Christ should earn our salvation by dying for our sins would not have been met. Both the love and the justice of God were equally important.[3]

The necessity of the atonement. Was there any other way? Could anyone have been saved from the penalty of sin without God's having to send his Son to die in our place? No![4] First of all, God was under no moral obligation to save anyone. This is important to remember. The God who did not spare the angels, but consigned them to the nether gloom until the judgment, could very well have determined the same fate for us with perfect justification. Justice did not oblige God to remove our sin and guilt from us—that is true for the *entire* human race, not only for Adam. Hence the atonement was not necessary at all.

However, when God decided, in his love, to redeem human beings, there was absolutely no way to accomplish this other than through the voluntary sacrificial death of his Son. Therefore justice did not require the atonement, but as a "consequence" of his decision to redeem humankind, the atonement *was* absolutely necessary. This concept is sometimes referred to as the "consequent absolute necessity" theory of the atonement.

Consider the drama that unfolded in the Garden of Gethsemane: "*If it is possible,* may this cup be taken from me. Yet not as I will, but as you will" (Mt 26:39). The "cup" Jesus would have to drink—death on a cross—was absolutely necessary if God was to redeem the creation. Matthew gives us a glimpse into a very private moment between the Father and the Son in order to demonstrate the necessity of Christ's sacrifice. We know that Jesus fulfilled God's will in every way. The writer shows us that it was not possible for Jesus to avoid death on a cross if he was going to accomplish the work his Father set for him. There *was* no other way.

After his resurrection, Jesus reiterates this necessity when he spoke with the two disciples on the road to Emmaus. Very sad that Jesus had died, the two listened in rapt attention as this "stranger" demonstrated from the Scriptures the *necessity* that the Messiah should suffer these things and enter into his glory (Lk 24:25-26).

The writer to the Hebrews explains masterfully that if God were to be righteous and still save human beings, he had to send Jesus to pay the penalty for sins: "For this reason [Christ] had to be made like his brothers in every way, in order that he might become a merciful and faithful high priest in service to God, and that he might make atonement for the sins of the people" (Heb 2:17). And since "it is impossible for the blood of bulls and goats to take away sins" (Heb 10:4), a far better sacrifice is required (Heb 9:23). Only Christ's sacrificial death can take away sins (Heb 9:25-26). There was simply no other way for God to save us.

The nature of the atonement. What exactly did the atonement accomplish?[5] In order for us to be established in righteousness forever before God, as opposed to being simply forgiven and back in the original "innocent" state of Adam and Eve, Christ had to earn our righteousness by living in perfect obedience. This is sometimes referred to as his "active obedience." Christ "became" our righteousness by living a life perfectly pleasing to the Father from start to finish. To John the Baptist Jesus said, "It is proper for us to do this to fulfill all righteousness" (Mt 3:15). Christ for all eternity had shared an existence of perfect fellowship and love. His fulfillment of "all righteousness" was for *our* sake. He could have easily been sacrificed as a young child to pay the penalty for our sins, if only his sinlessness had been necessary and not also a life of perfect obedience.

In addition Christ took upon himself the sufferings necessary to pay the penalty for our sins. His sufferings for us are sometimes referred to as his "passive obedience." Overall, not only his passion but the suffering he endured throughout his entire earthly life took on redemptive worth. Who can possibly fathom the tremendous suffering he endured during his wilderness sojourn, for instance? In predicting the coming Messiah, Isaiah describes him as "a man of sorrows, and familiar with suffering" (Is 53:3).

During the Passion Week, Jesus' sufferings began to increase. He gave his disciples just a glimpse of the wrenching emotion he was enduring as the cross loomed before him. This is not to say that Jesus was about to suffer more physical pain than anyone else. The Bible never makes such a claim. However, death on a cross was one of the most horrible forms of execution ever devised. Jesus' death was excruciatingly painful, agonizing. Death usually took days to occur, and that not by loss of blood but by asphyxiation, for the victim had to flex every muscle in his body to draw and exhale every breath. This sapped the victim of strength until it was impossible to breathe. The searing pain in his flayed back scraping against rough wood and the cramping of his legs and arms with the constant grinding of bones and nerves against the iron nails took its toll on Jesus. Yet more terrible than the physical pain was the psychological horror of enduring the guilt of the sin of the entire human race. Who can fathom this?

> Now Jesus was perfectly holy. He hated sin with his entire being. The thought of evil, of sin, contradicted everything in his character. Far more than we do, Jesus instinctively rebelled against evil. Yet in obedience to the Father, and out of love for us, Jesus took on himself all the sins of those who would someday be saved. Taking on himself all the evil against which his soul rebelled created deep revulsion in the center of his being. All that he hated most deeply was poured out fully upon him.[6]

Scripture repeatedly refers to our sins' being put on Christ: "The LORD has laid on him the iniquity of us all," and he "bore the sin of many" (Is 53:6, 12). Paul goes so far as to write that God made Christ "to be sin for us" (2 Cor 5:21) and to become "a curse for us" (Gal 3:13). And Peter says, "He himself bore our sins in his body on the tree" (1 Pet 2:24). The verses from 2 Corinthians and Isaiah indicate that it was God the Father who put our sins on Christ. This is a great mystery and often misunderstood. In the very same way that Adam's sins were imputed to us, so God imputed our sins to Jesus. Since God is the great Judge and ultimately defines what is in the universe, when God regarded our sins as having belonged to Christ, they actually did belong to him.[7]

Furthermore, Jesus had to endure all this agony utterly alone.

Though not separated from the Father in any ontological or experiential manner, judicially Jesus was declared sinful and thus came under the judgment of God. The eyes of God, pure beyond description, cannot bear the sight of sin in practice or the guilt of sin. Now his Son bore the guilt of the sins of millions. Having been judicially declared guilty by his Father, with whom he had known deep love and fellowship from eternity past, Jesus hung suspended above the earth, naked, near death, wracked by intense physical pain and mental anguish. He faced God's wrath for the guilt of millions all alone.

Many outside of evangelical Christianity have objected to the idea that Christ had to bear the wrath of God. They believe this is inconsistent with the loving character of God, who would not display such anger toward his creation, regardless of their sinful condition. A loving Father, it is argued, would not harbor such ill-will toward his children.[8] However, the Old Testament is replete with illustrations of God's white-hot anger toward sinners. And the whole argument of Paul's letter to the Romans is built on the premise that God's wrath is being revealed against the Jews and the Gentiles without distinction.

Three passages refer to Jesus' death on the cross as a "propitiation": Hebrews 2:17 and 1 John 2:2 and 4:10. The Greek verb *hilaskomai*, "to make propitiation," and the noun *hilasmos*, "a sacrifice of propitiation," used in these passages, carry the idea of "a sacrifice that turns away the wrath of God," thereby making us favorable in his sight.[9] These verses simply mean that Jesus bore God's wrath against our sin. We learn of God's wrath against sin in passages like Romans 1:18; 2:5, 8; 4:15; 5:9; 9:22; 12:19; 13:4-5; Ephesians 2:3; 5:6; Colossians 3:6; and 1 Thessalonians 1:10; 2:16; 5:9. Thus *hilaskomai* means much more in Paul's writings than "to expiate," to cleanse from sin; it means rather "to propitiate," to turn away the wrath of God from the one who commits sin, as if the sinner had never sinned at all.

The Atonement and the New Religious Movements

Church of Jesus Christ of Latter-day Saints. In the Mormon scheme of things, the atonement (Christ's death on the cross) canceled the penalty of death imposed through Adam's sin and thus ensured that all people will be redeemed—resurrected and given immortality, spirit reunited with body—as a gift. "If there had been no atonement, temporal death would have remained forever, and there never would have been a resurrection. The body would have remained forever in the grave." "Redemption from death, through the sufferings of Christ, is for all men, both the righteous and the wicked." "Immortality is a free gift which comes by grace alone without works on man's part."[10]

In Mormon thinking the atoning death of Jesus, then, does not remove personal sins. It can only provide an opportunity to achieve resurrection, or eternal life:

> The Individual Effect of the Atonement makes it possible for any and every soul to obtain absolution from the effect of personal sins, through the mediation of Christ; but such saving intercession is to be invoked by individual effort as manifested through faith, repentance, and continued works of righteousness. . . . The blessing of redemption from individual sins, while open for all to attain, is nevertheless conditioned on individual effort.[11]

The believer must remove the effects of her sin and guilt by personal effort. The promised absolution occurs only as the recipient continues in Mormon redemption, which is to be invoked by individual effort manifested in faith, repentance and continued works of righteousness. This Mormon absolution, then, is conditional on works righteousness—not the atonement as understood within orthodox Christianity: "Redemption from personal sins can only be obtained through obedience to the requirements of the gospel, and a life of good works."[12]

The removal of personal sins according to Mormon theology is not by the perfect sacrificial death of Jesus on the cross. Consequently the Jesus of Mormon theology is not the Jesus of the Apostles', Nicene and Athanasian creeds; nor is this the Jesus of the apostles who launched the most explosive religious movement in human history.

Brigham Young, the second president of the Mormon Church, explained how he viewed Christ's atonement:

> Suppose you found your brother in bed with your wife, and you put a javelin through both of them, you would be justified, and they would atone for their sins, and be received into the kingdom of God. I would at once do so in such a case; and under such circumstances. I have no wife whom I love so well that I would not put a javelin through her heart, and I would do it with clean hands. . . . There is not a man or woman, who violates the covenants made with their God, that will not be required to pay the debt. The blood of Christ will never wipe that out, your own blood must atone for it; and the judgments of the Almighty will come, sooner or later, and every man and woman will have to atone for breaking covenants. . . . All mankind love themselves, and let these principles be known by an individual, and he would be glad to have his blood shed. . . . I could refer you to plenty of instances where men have been righteously slain, in order to atone for their sins. . . . This is loving your neighbor as ourselves; if he needs help, help him; and if he wants salvation and it is necessary to spill his blood on the earth in order that he may be saved, spill it.[13]

So plain was Young's denial of the all-sufficiency of the atoning sacrifice of Jesus that Mormons since have struggled to explain away his words.[14] Generally they argue that his reference was to the death sentence imposed on a criminal for a capital offense. Yet clearly Young was not discussing this subject at all, but what Christ's sacrifice for sins cannot do and what the shedding of a person's own blood can do.[15]

Jehovah's Witnesses. For the Jehovah's Witness, Jesus' death paid only for Adam's sin, not for the sins of all humanity: "[God] could not set aside the judgment that he had entered against Adam. He could, however, be consistent . . . by permitting another to pay the debt of Adam and thereby to open the way for Adam and his offspring to be released from sin and death."[16] "To redeem or ransom man from the grave means that God will provide a means of satisfaction of the judgment against Adam."[17]

Jehovah's Witnesses maintain that the Atonement is not entirely of God, but instead half of God and half of man.[18] Jesus removed the effects of Adam's sin by his sacrifice on the cross, but the culmination of Christ's work will not be realized until the survivors of Armageddon return to God through free will and accept Jehovah's theocratic rule. The atonement will only be realized once people have become reconciled with God, completed in the realization of the millennial kingdom. The blood of Christ possesses only partial cleansing power. Note the words of the Watchtower:

> Jesus, no more and no less than a perfect human, became a ransom that compensated exactly for what Adam lost—the right to perfect human life on earth. . . . The perfect human life of Jesus was the "corresponding ransom" required by divine justice—no more, no less. A basic principle even of human justice is that the price paid should fit the wrong committed. . . . So the ransom,

> to be truly in line with God's justice, had to be strictly an equivalent—a perfect human, "the last Adam." Thus, when God sent Jesus to earth as the ransom, he made Jesus to be what would satisfy justice, not an incarnation, not a god-man, but a perfect man, "lower than angels."[19]

By implication we are responsible for eradicating our own sin through following the only organization on earth instituted by God, the Watchtower Bible and Tract Society, and performing good works.

"A Course in Miracles." According to Helen Shucman, to partake in the atonement we must simply recognize our original state of being; then all that we were will be restored to us. Shucman attributes the following statement to Jesus:

> I am in charge of the process of Atonement, which I undertook to begin. When you offer a miracle to any of my brothers, you do it to yourself and me. The reason you come before me is that I do not need miracles for my own Atonement, but I stand at the end in case you fail temporarily. My part in the Atonement is the canceling out of all errors that you could not other-wise correct. When you have been restored to the recognition of your original state, you naturally become part of the Atonement yourself.[20]

Notice that there is no mention of the word *sin*. We commit some "errors" that are canceled out by Christ. Shucman's language glosses over human depravity and guilt. Hitler's determined program to exterminate all the Jews of Europe was an "error." Stalin's political purges of the late 1930s to do away with any potential intrigue or challenge to his authority were "errors." It was an "error" when Mao Zedong obliterated millions of his own compatriots during the Cultural Revolution.

For the *Course*, "the purpose of the Atonement is to restore everything to you; or rather, to restore it to your awareness."[21] The *Course* denies that the suffering of Christ ever took place. God did not allow his Son to die on the cross for our salvation. Instead:

> If the crucifixion is seen from an upside-down point of view, it does appear as if God permitted and even encouraged one of His Sons to suffer because he was good. . . . Yet the real Christian should pause and ask, "How could this be? Is it likely that God Himself would be capable of the kind of thinking which His Own words have clearly stated is unworthy of His Son? . . .
>
> Persecution frequently results in an attempt to "justify" the terrible misperception that God Himself persecuted His Own Son on behalf of salvation. The very words are meaningless. . . . In milder forms a parent says, "This hurts me more than it hurts you," and feels exonerated in beating a child. Can you believe our Father really thinks this way? It is so essential that all such thinking be dispelled that we must be sure that nothing of this kind remains in your mind. I was not "punished" because you were bad. The wholly benign lesson the Atonement teaches is lost if it is tainted with this kind of distortion in any form.[22]

According to the Jesus of the *Course*, "Sacrifice is a notion totally unknown to God."[23]

The atonement is a recognition of one's former state of being. The implication is that humankind's original state is perfection. Participating in "the Atonement" means undoing the misbelief that we are separated from God and are sinful, imperfect beings limited within a body. The *Course* envisions "the process of Atonement" as something that occurs within our own experience, whereby we gradually evolve to a certain state of self-awareness.

Urantia Foundation. This group is very unusual: since its foundation in Chicago in 1950 there has been no membership published, though those who advocate Urantia meet regularly in small groups to study its teachings. The primary purpose of the Urantia Foundation is to publish and disseminate the teachings of *The Urantia Book,* a 2,097-page collection of assorted revelations allegedly received from angelic beings between 1929 to 1942 by an anonymous person.

Urantia-oriented groups meet as a "society," typically on Sundays. During these gatherings a creedal statement is read. There are no other rites or rituals and no clergy. Each meeting is designed simply to discuss the various "truths" being learned from *The Urantia Book.* Since the mid-1970s several thousand *Urantia Book* readers believe they have been contacted by "supermortal intelligences" with additional revelations concerning humanity, divine truth and the future.

The Urantia Book supposedly answers many of life's most perplexing questions: Why do evil and suffering exist? Is there intelligent life on other planets? Who is Jesus? What did he teach? Where is he now? What is God's purpose for your life?[24] It repudiates the doctrines of the Trinity, the deity of Christ, his virgin birth, his atonement for our sins, his physical resurrection from the dead and other Christian teachings. "Modern culture must become spiritually baptized with a new revelation of Jesus' life and illuminated with new understanding of his gospel of eternal salvation."[25]

According to *The Urantia Book,* Christ's death was not in God's original plan. Something went terribly wrong: "It was man and not God who planned and executed the death of Jesus on the cross. . . . The Father in Paradise did not decree, demand, or require the death of his Son."[26] The concepts of sacrifice and atonement are actually repugnant to God:

> The barbarous idea of appeasing an angry God, of propitiating an offended Lord, of winning the favor of Deity through sacrifices and penance and even by the shedding of blood, represents a religion wholly puerile and primitive, a philosophy unworthy of an enlightened age of science and truth. Such beliefs are utterly repulsive to the celestial beings and the divine rulers who serve and reign in the universe. It is an affront to God to believe, hold, or teach to win his favor or to divert the fictitious divine wrath.[27]

Christadelphianism. According to the Christadelphians, Christ's death on the cross did not atone for sins. He died in need of personal redemption as well as for all as a representative of humanity:

> The common doctrine of the Atonement, which sets forth Jesus as a substitute sacrifice, does not reveal God as just. This doctrine suggests that Jesus died instead of others; that he paid a debt of death that they had incurred but to which he was not associated. . . . Jesus did not die instead of others; he died as a representative of humanity . . . in need of redemption from that death-doomed state as much as anybody else.[28]

Christ's death, for Christadelphians, revealed the effects of sin to the world while demonstrating the holiness of God through Christ's perfect life. Through this demonstration of good and evil, people now can see how they should live.

> Jesus Christ, son of Adam, . . . was of the same flesh and blood nature . . . and, as such, under the same sentence . . . and the righteousness he manifested came from denying the flesh, not obeying it. But, God also raised him from the dead, because His justness made it impossible that one manifesting complete

> righteousness "should be holden of death." . . . It is comforting to recognize this, for it shows that virtue will never go unrewarded. . . . He [God] realizes that flesh is weak and prone to sin, and that unless one is Divinely strengthened, he must inevitably succumb to it.[29]

The atonement, then, in the Christadelphian system is merely an example for us to follow. It does not blot out sin or guilt from God's sight.

RESPONDING TO THE NEW RELIGIOUS MOVEMENTS

Church of Jesus Christ of Latter-day Saints. In contrast to the Mormon perspective that all will be redeemed, that is, resurrected, through the atonement of Christ, the Bible teaches that only those who accept Jesus' sacrifice, as God's gift (Rom 10:9), will receive forgiveness of sins (Acts 10:43) and salvation (Rom 3:24). Eternal life "in Christ"—not simply eternal existence through resurrection—is the gift offered by God to humanity (Rom 6:23). This gift is attainable only by grace through faith (Eph 2:8-10). Moreover, Jesus' death serves to reconcile all believers to God (Rom 5:10). In his death he demolished the wall of separation between God and us that had been erected as a result of human disobedience (Eph 2:11-22).

In Jesus Christ we have redemption. His blood is all-sufficient for cleansing the conscience (Heb 9:14) and for the permanent removal of sin (Rev 1:5). It is the very bedrock of our justification.

Jehovah's Witnesses. The atonement in the Watchtower system is very limited, since Jehovah's Witnesses believe that only the penalty of Adam's sin was paid. This Bible, on the contrary, teaches that Jesus' death paid not only for Adam's sin but also for our sins (1 Cor 15:3; Gal 1:4; Heb 9:28; 1 Pet 2:24).

The blood of Jesus has more than partial cleansing power.[30] It must not be turned into a mere preliminary offering for a works-righteousness religious system. Without the all-sufficiency of Christ's blood, we would be hopelessly lost.

"A Course in Miracles." We will never know the depth of suffering that engulfed the second Person of the Godhead as he endured the weight of the sins of the whole world during his passion. Human sin was not swept under the rug or canceled out by a wave of God's hand; it was dealt with in all its totality and horror. Nothing was left out. The pain was not muffled. The humiliation was not veiled. Sin had its awful way with Christ on a level that we mortals (even in our eventual immortality) will never fathom totally.

The Christian concept of atonement stems from the Old Testament. The *Course* errs in failing to take seriously the meaning of the word *atonement* within its Old Testament context. "Atonement" translates the Hebrew noun *kippur*, related to the verb *kaphar,* which means "to cover or conceal." Human sin was lawfully "covered" by the Jewish priest's offering of blood: "In this way the priest will make atonement for them, and they will be forgiven" (Lev 4:20). This verse is also translated with the word *reconcile,* since the act of covering sin reconciles humans to God. Though sin offerings were made daily, the Jews were commanded to participate in the Day of Atonement (Yom Kippur) once a year, "because on this day atonement will be made for you, to cleanse you" (Lev 16:30).

Atonement does not open our eyes to our own perfection; it covers our sins before the eyes of God. The New Testament testifies to Christ's death on the cross for the sins of the world: "Christ died for sins once for all, the righteous for the unrighteous, to bring you to God" (1 Pet 3:18).

At Pentecost Peter told the Jews that it *was* God's will to offer up Jesus for us: "This man was handed over to you by God's set purpose and foreknowledge; and you, with the help of wicked men, put him to death by nailing him to the cross. But God raised him from the dead, freeing him from the agony of death, because it was impossible for death to keep its hold on him" (Acts 2:23-24).

Urantia Foundation. Not once does *The Urantia Book* show the New Testament teaching of the atonement to be false, logically flawed or just plain wrong. Saying that the atonement is a doctrine unworthy to be held by an enlightened member of this modern scientific age is mere rhetoric. Science cannot speak to or disprove the theological questions of the atonement. One does not do away with the doctrine of the atonement by dismissing it; it is either true or false, and that can be determined only through careful study of the Scriptures using a grammatical and historical method.

Far from being a mistake, the sacrificial death of Jesus Christ not only was foretold in Old Testament prophecies but was the intentional plan and will of the triune God (Is 53:10). Jesus rebuked Peter for suggesting that he did not have to die (Mt 16:23). After his resurrection, Jesus reminded the disciples that his death was ordained in the Scriptures (Lk 24:25-26). Peter's perspective was altered by the time he proclaimed on the Day of Pentecost that Jesus was crucified "by God's set purpose and foreknowledge" (Acts 2:23).

As for the assertion that the very idea of sacrifice and atonement is repugnant to God, the practice of sacrifice is rooted in the Old Testament, and God said he gave it to the people of Israel (Lev 17:11). It is not "an affront to God" to believe that blood sacrifice was necessary for our forgiveness. On the contrary, it is an affront to God to refuse to believe what he has said about the atonement required by his holiness and provided through his great mercy: "He loved us and sent his Son as an atoning sacrifice for our sins" (1 Jn 4:10). This mercy is extended to all who would hear the message of forgiveness in Jesus' name and believe.

Christadelphianism. Scripture teaches that Jesus died in the place of others (1 Pet 2:24; 3:18). Jesus himself did not need redemption, for he was without sin (1 Pet 1:19) and it is sin that brings death (Rom 6:23). "It is by grace you have been saved, through faith—and this not from yourselves, it is the gift of God—not by works, so that no one can boast" (Eph 2:8-9). Salvation comes through trusting in Christ and his all-sufficient atoning sacrifice on the cross (Rom 6:8-9; 2 Tim 2:12).

To add anything else as a requirement after the atoning sacrifice of Jesus Christ, even a "lifelong attempt to emulate Christ," is to insult the Spirit of grace and invite God's condemnation (Rom 4:14-15). God will have none of our pride. He requires nothing but simple childlike trust in his Son for us to enter the kingdom of God (Mk 10:15).

Conclusion

The atonement is not a solution devised by a God struggling with an internal conflict of mind or between the members of the Trinity,[31] as if a loving Son persuaded the Father to abandon his wrath and adopt a loving, forgiving attitude toward humankind. There is no conflict within the mind of God regarding propitiation. It was a loving Father who sent his Son to die in our place. Thus it is not true that the sacrifice of Jesus changed a wrathful God into a loving God. It is true, however, that the God who hates sin is loving toward the humanity he created.[32]

> The love that prompted God to send his Son was always there. While the Father's holiness and righteousness and justice required that there be a payment for sin, his love provided it. The propitiation is a fruit of the Father's divine love. This is indicated quite clearly in 1 John 4:10: "Herein is love; not that we

> loved God, but that he loved us, and sent his Son to be the propitiation for our sins."[33]

The atonement demonstrates how great God's love is for us. God could not possibly disregard sin and still be God. He was willing to take the extraordinary route of sending the second Person of the Godhead to be the sacrifice and satisfaction for our sins. Such selflessness is beyond human comprehension. God's heavy payment for our salvation demonstrated his justice and holiness; his personal provision of that payment demonstrated his love. This is why there can be no hope for any who reject "so great a salvation." Outside of this provision, what else is there?

Here, then, in Jesus' death, we see the intersection of God's love and justice: "The holiness requires payment of the penalty, and the love provides that payment."[34]

9

SALVATION

Is It by Faith or by Works?

In Islam, salvation is achieved by belief in the five pillars of Islam (reciting the confession, prayer, fasting, almsgiving, pilgrimage to Mecca) and good works, and even then there is no assurance of salvation.[1] In Zen Buddhism, salvation is the achievement of nirvana, the annihilation of dualistic thinking (I-thou distinctions), the elimination of logic, and transcending all physical reality in order to achieve ultimate happiness.[2] In Hinduism, salvation or union with Brahman can be achieved only through adherence to one of the following paths: meditation and mind control, work, knowledge, or love and devotion. And it must be accompanied with a detachment or indifference to any action, whether good or evil.[3]

In every human religious system, the motivation for acts of works righteousness is an abundant supply of moral guilt. Guilt is the catalyst and the perennial justification for a constant stream of works of righteousness performed in hopes of soothing, if not eradicating, a guilt-ridden conscience. This is due not only to the universal moral guilt we all share with Adam but also to human pride. Somehow we believe we can draw ourselves up from the muck of our depravity by our bootstraps and ascend to the stars of heaven—if only we try hard and long enough. God would "owe" us for all our effort and sincere devotion to the project.

But nothing could be further from the truth. Salvation is achieved in a very exclusive way.[4] Just as God was the author and progenitor of the atonement for human sin, so he is the supreme Author of our salvation. Only God can pay the penalty of our sins; only God can provide for our ultimate justification.

THE ORTHODOX DOCTRINE OF SALVATION

As we learned in the chapter on the atonement, sin has caused complete separation of humanity from God. Salvation is the complete restoration of human beings through the totality of God's work on their behalf, delivering them from a lost, sinful condition to a position of glorious righteousness. It is in salvation that we humans experience God's grace and peace. His justice demands a penalty that we are completely unable to pay, yet his justice also provides eternal life through the means of grace. We humans are left in awe of the contrast between our sinfulness and God's love.

Regeneration. Salvation involves *regeneration,* the instantaneous spiritual re-creation of a person when he or she comes to faith in Christ. Again, regeneration—"the new birth"—is accomplished by God alone. The apostle John specifies that the true children of God are those who are born of God; our human will ("human decision") has nothing to do with it (Jn 1:13). Scripture refers to it as being "born from above" (Jn 3:3-8 NRSV; Jas 1:18; 1 Pet 1:3).[5] Our will had nothing to do with our conception and birth. This analogy strongly suggests that we are entirely passive in our regeneration.

Conversion is the human being's response to God's offer of salvation.[6] Regeneration is entirely God's work; it is God's transformation of the believer into something new. We are given a new spiritual life, a vitality that was not there before we accepted Christ.

Underlying this doctrine of salvation is an inherent assumption regarding human nature. Human beings before regeneration are spiritually dead, unresponsive to spiritual stimuli, completely unable to alter their spiritual blindness and natural proclivity toward sin. Romans 3:9-20 shows that some transformation of human nature is required to bring about conversion. This is no mere readjustment or modification of the person—it is a far more radical change. Paul describes the converted person as "a new creation" or "a new creature" (2 Cor 5:17).

This transformation of humanity into a new creation was prophesied in the Old Testament.

> I will give them an undivided [new] heart and put a new spirit in them; I will remove from them their heart of stone and give them a heart of flesh. Then they will follow my decrees and be careful to keep my laws. They will be my people, and I will be their God. (Ezek 11:19-20)

> I will give you a new heart and put a new spirit in you; I will remove from you your heart of stone and give you a heart of flesh. And I will put my Spirit in you and move you to follow my decrees and be careful to keep my laws. (Ezek 36:26-27)

This is heart surgery that only God can perform. It is a transformation of the human will—not to be forced beyond its will, but to "be moved," to be inclined to follow God's will. And God accomplishes all of this for us. The moral legacy of Israel at the time of this prophetic writing was utter failure. The contrast between Israel's miserable moral state and God's promise to restore them by re-creating them is profound. Spiritual re-creation is as miraculous as bringing a dead person back to life.

The Greek word that most vividly conveys the idea of regeneration is *palingenesia,*[7] found only twice in the New Testament. In Matthew 19:28 the term is employed for the "renewal" of God's creation. In Titus 3:4-5 it refers to salvation: "When the kindness and love of God our Savior appeared, he saved us, not because of righteous things we had done, but because of his mercy. He saved us through the washing of rebirth and renewal by the Holy Spirit."

The best-known depiction of the new birth is in John 3. Jesus is giving Nicodemus, an expert on the Hebrew Scriptures, a lesson in basic theology: "I tell you the truth, no one can see the kingdom of God unless he is born again" (Jn 3:3). Later in the conversation Jesus states, "You must be born again" (Jn 3:7). The Greek word translated "again" is ***anōthen,*** which is better rendered "from above," since the context speaks of heavenly versus earthly, or spiritual versus physical, reality.

During the same conversation Jesus speaks of being "born of the Spirit" (Jn 3:5-8).[8] This supernatural birth cannot be accomplished by human work or planning. It can be accomplished only "from above." This new birth is indispensable if one is to enter the kingdom of God. It is also spoken of as being "born of God" (Jn 1:12-13; Jas 1:18; 1 Pet 1:3, 23; 1 Jn 2:29; 5:1, 4).

Nicodemus had great difficulty grasping the idea, despite the theological training that was supposed to equip him to understand such concepts, as Jesus gently reminded him (Jn 3:10). Jesus compares it to trying to understand wind: we hear its sound and feel it, but no one understands where it comes from or where it goes. So it is with the work of the Spirit in the new birth.

The new birth involves God's doing something new to a human

being. It involves the reversal of a person's natural tendencies, not just an amplification or intensification of one's natural abilities. Indeed the new birth includes the putting to death, or crucifixion, of present qualities. Paul says, "Those who belong to Christ Jesus have crucified the sinful nature with its passions and desires. Since we live by the Spirit, let us keep in step with the Spirit" (Gal 5:24-25). Millard Erickson elaborates: "The idea of one's being made dead to the flesh (the natural way of acting and living) and alive in the Spirit is evidence that regeneration is the production of a totally new creation (as Paul correctly labeled it), and not merely a heightening of what is already the basic direction of one's life."[9]

Being made alive in regeneration, although totally new to us, is not "unnatural;" it is, rather, a restoration of a human condition that was ours from the beginning of our physical creation in Adam before the Fall. "It is simultaneously the beginning of a new life and a return of the old life and activity."[10] This new birth happens not only instantaneously, it occurs only *once*.[11] At one moment we are spiritually dead; the next, we are born "out of God" or "from above." There may not be a crisis event to clearly mark the passage from "sinner to saint." But the change generally will be evident over time in the thought and behavior patterns of the new believer, though specific changes may not all be evident to others.[12]

Conversion involves both repentance and faith, turning from sin to trusting faith in the work of Christ, in response to the enabling work of God in the heart. Repentance is a change of mind (*metanoia*). We see ourselves and the world around us in a new light. The Greek word does not suggest emotion, but deep sorrow, which may precede repentance. One sees one's former state for the detestable thing it is, renounces that condition and turns to walk with Jesus in newness of life. Jesus says, "Take my yoke upon you and learn from me, for I am gentle and humble in heart, and you will find rest for your souls" (Mt 11:29). The sinner is relieved of the awful weight of sin and guilt and given a new outlook on life, a joy so complete that Jesus' "yoke" feels like no yoke at all!

Not by works. Salvation is achieved *solely* by God's grace. *Sola gratia* was the great Reformation proclamation that revolutionized the lives of millions. This theme turned Christian Europe on its head, in much the same way as the early church turned the classical world on its head. Salvation is achieved by God's grace alone. It is *not* achieved by observing the Mosaic law in order to earn God's favor. There is absolutely nothing a sinner can do to please God apart from trusting in his mercy. Works serve, rather, as demonstrable evidence of God's new birth in the heart of the believer.

We have been acquitted before God, judged to stand in right relationship to God, that is, to have fulfilled every requirement of that relationship. We did not achieve this "foreign" righteousness. God's own nature is understood to be the very standard and requirement for a right relationship (righteousness) with God.[13]

> "What must we do to do the works God requires?"
>
> Jesus answered, "The work of God is this: to believe in the one he has sent." (Jn 6:28-29)

Paul continues with this theme: "Now when a man works, his wages are not credited to him as a gift, but as an obligation. However, to the man who does not work but trusts God who justifies the wicked, his faith is credited as righteousness" (Rom 4:4-5).

"It is by grace you have been saved, through faith—and this not from yourselves, it is the gift of God—not by works, so that no one can boast" (Eph 2:8-9). Then how do works figure into the equation at all? Paul continues, "For we are God's workmanship, created in

Christ Jesus *to do good works,* which God prepared in advance for us to do" (Eph 2:10). We are not saved *by* good works; we are saved by God's grace, through our faith, *for* good works. Now at last our good works will be pleasing to God, for we have been made pleasing to him by being clothed in the righteousness of his Son.

All the good works done in creation will not earn salvation. Yet good works are to come from the believer who has been justified by God. Indeed "faith by itself, if it is not accompanied by action [works], is dead" (Jas 2:17). If we have been united to Christ in faith, then our lives are to reflect his character. We should not live according to the base dictates of the flesh but according to the divine imperatives of the Spirit (Rom 8:1-17).

Justified by grace through faith, we are actually adopted as sons and daughters of the Most High God. "Yet to all who received him, to those who believed in his name, he gave the right to become children of God—children born not of natural descent, nor of human decision or a husband's will, but born of God" (Jn 1:12-13). Paul states that this adoption is a fulfillment of the plan of God: "He predestined us to be adopted as his sons through Jesus Christ, in accordance with his pleasure and will" (Eph 1:5).

As children of God, we have the unmerited favor of our Father in heaven. Thus we can know the same love that Christ experienced from the Father when he was on earth. "May they be brought to complete unity to let the world know that you sent me and have loved them even as you have loved me" (Jn 17:23).

Salvation According to the New Religious Movements

Church of Jesus Christ of Latter-day Saints. According to Mormon theology, the atonement of Christ does not remove personal sins.

Christ's death on the cross merely gave everyone the opportunity to be resurrected. Salvation, then, is eternal life that must be earned. It is *not* a gift of God: "Eternal life is the reward for 'obedience to the laws and ordinances of the Gospel.'"[14]

It is not uncommon to find in Mormon publications the statement that "all men are saved by grace alone." This sounds orthodox—but we need to look further. One official Mormon publication, written by the eminent Mormon apologist Bruce R. McConkie, defines salvation by grace thus:

> Grace is simply the mercy, the love and the condescension God has for his children, as a result of which he has ordained the plan of salvation so that they may have power to progress and become like him. . . . All men are saved by grace alone without any act on their part, meaning that they are resurrected and become immortal because of the atoning sacrifice of Christ. . . . In addition to this redemption from death, all men, by the grace of God, have the power to gain eternal life. This is called salvation by grace coupled with obedience to the laws and ordinances of the gospel. Hence Nephi was led to write: "We labor diligently to write, to persuade our children, and also our brethren, to believe in Christ, and to be reconciled to God; for we know that it is by grace that we are saved *after all we can do*" [2 Nephi 25:23, Book of Mormon].
>
> Christians speak often of the blood of Christ and its cleansing power. Much that is believed and taught on this subject, however, is such utter nonsense and so palpably false that to believe it is to lose one's salvation. Many go so far, for instance, as to pretend and, at least, to believe that if we confess Christ with our lips and avow that we accept Him as our personal Savior,

> we are thereby saved. His blood, without other act than mere belief, they say, makes us clean. . . . Finally in our day, he has said plainly: "My blood shall not cleanse them if they hear me not." Salvation in the kingdom of God is available because of the atoning blood of Christ. But it is received only on condition of faith, repentance, baptism, and *enduring to the end in keeping the commandments of God.*[15]

Mormons thus must strive incessantly for perfection, sanctification and godhood. Grace is merely incidental.[16]

Brigham Young, second president of the Mormon Church, taught: "But as many as received Him, to them gave he power to *continue* to be the sons of God."[17] The Mormon doctrine of the preexistence of spirits holds that we are *already* sons of God and that God's acceptance merely enables us to "continue to be the sons of God."

Mormon apostle and spokesman R. H. Evans teaches universal salvation: "Mormons believe in universal salvation, that all men will be saved, but each one in his own order."[18] Yet eternal life in the Mormon scheme of things is the reward for "obedience to the laws and ordinances of the Gospel." One receives the privilege of earning one's ultimate salvation, which in Mormonism is exaltation to godhood.

Jehovah's Witnesses. The Watchtower points to an opportunity to work for one's salvation after Christ cleared away the penalty of Adam's sin: "It is for the reward of eternal life that every last person on earth should now be working. Are you?"[19] The obstacle that Christ removed was that which blocks the path to a course of works righteousness. "To get one's name written in that book of life will depend upon one's works, whether they are in fulfillment of God's will and approved by his Judge and King."[20] One's personal efforts, then, will determine one's eternal destiny.

The Watchtower is not vague regarding its requirements for salvation:

> Jesus Christ identified a first requirement when he said in prayer . . . 'This means everlasting life, their taking in knowledge of you.' . . . Many have found the second requirement more difficult. It is to obey God's laws. . . . A third requirement is that we be associated with God's channel, his organization. . . . To receive everlasting life in the earthly Paradise we must identify that organization and serve God as part of it. The fourth requirement . . . requires that prospective subjects of his Kingdom support his government by loyally advocating his Kingdom rule to others.[21]

Note that a vital requirement for salvation is loyalty to the earthly "channel" of God's will on earth. "Make haste to identify the visible theocratic organization of God that represents his king, Jesus Christ. It is essential for life. Doing so, be complete in accepting its every aspect."[22] That theocratic organization, of course, is the Watchtower Bible and Tract Society of Brooklyn, New York.

According to Jehovah's Witnesses, even during the millennial reign of Christ true believers will not be known until after a final test is completed: "Jehovah God will justify, declare righteous, on the basis of their own merit all perfected humans who have withstood that final, decisive test of mankind (the release of Satan from bondage after the 1000-year reign of Christ)."[23]

"A Course in Miracles." As observed in chapter seven, this group considers sin illusory. If your brother sins against you, it is a sin only if you believe it is a sin. Thus forgiveness is also illusory: "Forgiveness recognizes what you thought your brother did to you has not occurred. It does not pardon sins and make them real. It sees there was no sin. And in that vow are all your sins forgiven."[24] Thus if someone breaks into my home, ties up my family and me, rapes and tortures my wife, and then kills her and the children in front of me, I only have to realize that what just happened did not in fact happen! To try to forgive the criminal would only make the crime real. There is no sinful act to forgive.

The reason for Christ's crucifixion, according to the *Course*, was to induce people to love one another. "The message of the crucifixion is perfectly clear: 'Teach only love, for that is what you are.' If you interpret the crucifixion in any other way, you are using it as a weapon for assault rather than as the call for peace for which it was intended."[25] These are ostensibly words of Jesus Christ himself, channeled through a Jewish psychologist (now deceased).

Freemasonry. Like leaders of numerous other alternative groups, the Freemasons regard salvation as works righteousness that can be achieved apart from Christ: "[If your life is] without soil or blemish, you will be received at the pearly gates of heaven and there be presented with the pure white robe of righteousness."[26] Salvation by works in the Masonic system is illustrated graphically in the ritual of the Entered Apprentice Degree: "The Lamb has in all ages been deemed an emblem of innocence. By the lambskin, therefore, the Mason is reminded of that purity of life and conduct which is so essential to his gaining admission to the Celestial Lodge above, where the Supreme Architect of the Universe presides."[27] And how is entrance gained? "Perform the duties of your respective stations . . . and you will receive from your Almighty Father an inheritance incorruptible and undefiled, that fadeth not away."[28]

The Masonic plan of salvation includes the ultimate realization that we are not only basically good but divine: "The great secret of Masonry [is] that it makes a man aware of that divinity within him."[29]

When one joins the Masons, one should understand what is really being offered and why the association is formed: "[Masonry's purpose is] to reach the spiritual and divine within himself."[30]

Mind Science groups. Like the Mormons, the Mind Science groups believe in universal salvation. All people will gain salvation and in fact are already saved. We do not even need to ask God for salvation: "Man as God's idea is already saved with an everlasting salvation."[31] Need we fear God as Judge of our souls? No, say the Mind Sciences: "We need fear nothing in the Universe. We need not be afraid of God. We may be certain that all will arrive at the final goal, that not one will be missing. Every man is an incarnation of God. The soul can no more be lost than God could be lost."[32]

According to the Mind Sciences, "being 'born-again,' or 'born from above,' is not a miraculous change that takes place in man; it is the establishment of that which has always existed as the perfect man idea of divine Mind."[33] In order to achieve enlightenment (the divine state), we need to purify our minds and work out our own salvation: "Final deliverance from error [sin], whereby we rejoice in immortality, boundless freedom, and sinless sense, is not reached through paths of flowers nor by pinning one's faith without works to another's vicarious effort."[34] "What more can life demand of us that we do the best that we can and try to improve? If we have done this, we have done well, and all will be right with our souls both here and hereafter. This leaves us free to work out our own salvation—not with fear, or even with trembling—but with peace and in quiet confidence."[35]

Responding to the New Religious Movements

Church of Jesus Christ of Latter-day Saints. To claim to be saved by grace as a saving principle and then to deny it by declaring that it is coupled with obedience to the laws and the ordinances of the gospel violates a law of logic and exemplifies the equivocation fallacy, or the simple ambiguity fallacy, where a word or phrase is imbued with two or more meanings.[36] *Grace* means unwarranted favor. It cannot mean unwarranted and warranted at the same time and in the same sense. When the Mormons speak of grace, they have something altogether different in mind from what orthodox Christianity has taught for two thousand years.

Jehovah's Witnesses. "Jesus Christ identified a first requirement when he said in prayer . . . 'This means everlasting life, their taking in knowledge of you.'" Here the Watchtower misquotes what Jesus says in John 17:3. Jesus states that eternal life is knowing God—in other words, coming to a knowledge or realization of who God is. Nowhere does Jesus equate salvation with an ongoing process of gaining knowledge.

As for having to obey God's laws, Jehovah's Witness statements are only half-true. Scripture instructs us to keep Christ's commandments (Jn 14:15, 21; 15:10; 1 Jn 2:3; 3:22-24; 2 Jn 6). Yet because of sin and the weakness of our flesh, no one can keep the law in whole or in part (Jas 2:10). Consequently, although the law is in and of itself holy (Rom 7:12; 1 Tim 1:8), it has become a curse to us, highlighting our sin like a finger pointed accusingly at us (Gal 3:13). Christ, however, kept the law perfectly (Mt 5:17), and his perfection is imputed to us through faith apart from the law (Rom 3:28). In this way the law is fulfilled in us (Rom 8:3-4).

No one, not even the most earnest Jehovah's Witness, is justified by the law (Rom 3:20; Gal 2:16; 3:11), and those who seek to justify themselves through the law will actually be severed from Christ (Gal 5:3-4). Jesus, according to the Bible, is actually the end of the law (Rom 10:4). We who believe are not under the law but under grace (Rom 6:14).

"A Course in Miracles." In response to the *Course*'s teaching that sin is not real and cannot be forgiven, we need to remember Jesus' parable of the slave who owes ten thousand talents to a king. The king suspends the debt mercifully, but when the slave refuses to forgive a much smaller debt, the king withdraws his suspension and penalizes that slave in full (Mt 18:23-35). Jesus' warning "This is how my heavenly Father will treat each of you" establishes the reality of sin and the necessity of forgiveness.

> The message of the cross is foolishness to those who are perishing, but to us who are being saved it is the power of God. . . . For what I received I passed on to you as of first importance: that Christ died for our sins according to the Scriptures, that he was buried, that he was raised on the third day according to the Scriptures. (1 Cor 1:18; 15:3-4)

It was not the exclusive purpose of the cross to induce people to love one another, nor even the primary purpose. The cross is no less than the physical demonstration of the justice and mercy of God. God is just, and only he can justify. The cross is the solution to the sin problem and the means by which we are saved through faith in the One who paid the price of our redemption.

Freemasonry. Paul disagrees with all teaching of works-righteousness:

> Therefore no one will be declared righteous in his sight by observing the law; rather, through the law we become conscious of sin. (Rom 3:20)

> Know that a man is not justified by observing the law, but by faith in Jesus Christ. So we, too, have put our faith in Christ Jesus that we may be justified by faith in Christ and not by ob-

> serving the law, because by observing the law no one will be justified. (Gal 2:16)

> It is by grace you have been saved, through faith—and this not from yourselves, it is the gift of God—not by works, so that no one can boast. (Eph 2:8-9)

Salvation is not in the performance of certain duties, as the Masons want us to believe.

As in many other alternative religious movements, an appeal to "divinity" in us is the Freemasons' lure. It is the same lure that the deceiver used to snare Adam and Eve. But humankind is not divine. God is Creator; human beings are creatures. It was Satan's temptation to Eve in the Garden to "be like God" that led to sin in the first place (Gen 3:5).

Mind Science groups. The Bible does not teach universal salvation, but rather that some people will finally reject God's love and forgiveness and be lost by their own choice (Mt 7:15-23; 24:45-46; Jn 5:28-29). Universal salvation is wish-fulfillment, flying in the face of unequivocal scriptural evidence. The God of the Bible will in no way allow the guilty to go unpunished (Ex 34:7). All those who reject Jesus Christ and his gospel will be punished by God for eternity (2 Thess 1:8-9; Rev 19:20; 20:15). Salvation is a wonderful gift from God that must be received by grace through faith in the person and work of Jesus Christ (Jn 3:36; Eph 2:8-9).

Only Jesus Christ can save a person; no human person could ever do enough to earn or deserve eternal life. God's remedy for sin is for us to trust in his means to remove it. Philippians 2:12 says, "Continue to work out your salvation with fear and trembling," which means (Phil 2:13) that God makes it possible for us to act in his will. Paul is here urging believers to show evidence of the salvation they already have. Salvation is totally a gift from God appropriated by trusting in Jesus Christ's work of atonement (Rom 5). We must receive Christ and his gift (Jn 1:12; Rev 3:20) and become adopted as children of God through faith in Him (Gal 4:5; Eph 1:5).

CONCLUSION

Works do not play a part in personal salvation. They are, rather, a testimony of the work of salvation accomplished in us, an outward expression of our changed hearts and minds. Anyone who attempts to work for their salvation by following the law—whether the Mosaic law or the law of their own conscience—will reap only guilt and condemnation, for no one in all of history, except for Jesus Christ, has ever kept the *whole* law. Many people believe that God will weigh the totality of good and bad deeds done in their life at the end of time and, hopefully, with a little mercy thrown in, find that the balance tips in their favor. Yet our shared intuitive moral sense is that evil must be punished with a severity matching the offense. There is nothing a sinner can do in and of him- or herself to appease God apart from trusting in his mercy, realized in Christ's death on the cross.

There are a number of benefits that result from our salvation. First, union with Christ: Christ' life becomes the life of the Christian (Rom 8:1; Gal 2:20). Second, justification: God is able to declare believers righteous because Christ took on their deserved punishment (Rom 3:24-26; 5:9, 18; Col 2:13-14). Third, reconciliation: God adopts those who come to him through faith in Christ as his children (Rom 5:10; 2 Cor 5:18-19). Fourth, sanctification: God launches a process in us to make us holy (1 Cor 1:30; 6:11; 1 Thess 4:3-4, 7). Fifth, glorification: all believers will rise from the grave to eternal life in glorified bodies, just like Christ's. This event of glorification will purge all vestiges of sin from the believer forever. All corruption will be eliminated (Rom 8:18-19; 1 Cor 15:42-44; 1 Pet 5:1, 4, 10).

The Holy Spirit is the member of the Trinity who convicts the world of all sin and transforms believers through spiritual birth.

> I tell you the truth, no one can enter the kingdom of God unless he is born of water and the Spirit. Flesh gives birth to flesh, but the Spirit gives birth to spirit. (Jn 3:5-6)

> When [the Spirit] comes, he will convict the world of guilt in regard to sin and righteousness and judgment: in regard to sin, because men do not believe in me; in regard to righteousness, because I am going to the Father, where you can see me no longer; and in regard to judgment, because the prince of this world now stands condemned. (Jn 16:8-11)

Members of unorthodox groups have no conception of the peace of God that reigns in the heart of a believer. Those who strive to work for their salvation are engaged in an exercise in futility. Coming to recognize and receive God's salvation gift is an experience of liberation. Let us always invite them to receive it.

10

CHRIST'S SECOND COMING
Is It Physical or Spiritual?

The early church's belief and interest in Christ's imminent return was intense. By the time of Augustine of Hippo, however, the idea of an imminent return of Christ was not as stressed. In his exegesis of Mark 13:26 Augustine wrote:

> Will not the Lord come again in later times, when all the peoples of the earth shall lament? He came first in preaching, and filled the whole wide world. Let us not resist his first coming, that we may not tremble at his second.[1]

Later the idea that Christ's kingdom was "immanent" began to gain ground: the kingdom is already present within the world and will continue to grow and increase in a gradual fashion.[2] Once the Roman Empire had adopted Christianity as its official state religion (A.D. 380), many thought, what need was there for a visible, physical return of Christ to earth to perfect his glory when his kingdom was advancing across the earth?

Some today argue that the conviction that Jesus believed in and taught an impending return (as the early church taught) was obviously wrong.[3] For the evangelical Christian, such a conclusion about the teaching of Jesus is not only unacceptable but impertinent. One could adopt such an opinion only if one first presupposed that Jesus was not speaking authoritatively. Paul's assertion "For the Lord himself will come down from heaven" (1 Thess 4:16) should leave little doubt regarding the nature of Christ's return; and that is but one of many verses within the New Testament that attest to a physical, visible return of Christ to the earth. As the disciples watched Jesus ascending into heaven, two "men dressed in white" suddenly appeared beside them, saying, "Why do you stand here looking into the sky? This same Jesus, who has been taken from you into heaven, will come back in the same way you have seen him go into heaven" (Acts 1:10-11).

Many sincere Christians take differing positions regarding the events leading up to Christ's physical return to the earth. Some argue that Christ must come before a period of millennial bliss to reign on the throne of David (premillennialism), while others believe Jesus will come after the church has essentially conquered the world for him and established a reign of Christ (postmillennialism), and still others consider "millennium" only a figurative expression (amillennialism). Regarding the tribulation, some believe that Jesus will return to gather the faithful before the beginning of the tribulation (pretribulationism), at the middle of the tribulation (midtribulationism), toward the very end of the tribulation (prewrath) or after the tribulation, immediately before the millennium (posttribulationism).[4] All of the tribulation views are premillennial, involving the belief that Jesus will return to the earth for judgment and reign at the end of the tribulation. In this book we do not take a particular position on any of these issues, but we do stress that a physical, visible return of Christ is the only worthy rendering of the biblical witness.

THE ORTHODOX VIEW OF CHRIST'S SECOND ADVENT

The writers of the New Testament, without question, believed in the literal, physical coming of Jesus Christ for his people.

> Christ was sacrificed once to take away the sins of many people; and he will appear a second time, not to bear sin, but to bring salvation to those who are waiting for him. (Heb 9:28)
>
> You too, be patient and stand firm, because the Lord's coming is near. (Jas 5:8)
>
> But we know that when he appears, we shall be like him, for we shall see him as he is. (1 Jn 3:2)
>
> Amen. Come, Lord Jesus. (Rev 22:20)

This theme, found throughout the New Testament, was the dominant hope of the New Testament church. A sudden, dramatic return of Christ in full view of all creation is depicted: "Look, he is coming with the clouds, and every eye will see him, even those who pierced him; and all the peoples of the earth will mourn because of him" (Rev 1:7). Scripture teaches us to expect a dramatic entrance into human history by the resurrected Jesus Christ in all his glorious splendor.

These passages are far too graphic and explicit to allow for the old liberal notion of a "spiritual" return of Jesus through a growing acceptance of his teaching and imitation of his lifestyle that will gradually win the world over to the kingdom of God. It is not Christ's "spirit" but he himself who will return to this earth: "The Lord himself will come down from heaven, with a loud command, with the voice of the archangel and with the trumpet call of God" (1 Thess 4:16). One could render Christ's coming metaphorically only if one were first predisposed to such a position, for the biblical text does not support such an interpretation anywhere.

There are those who propose that Christ's Spirit has been with us since Pentecost, that his promise of returning was fulfilled in a spiritual coming. After all, he did say, "Surely I am with you always, to the very end of the age" (Mt 28:20). Pointing to the fact that the word *parousia* basically means "presence," those who hold to the "spiritual presence" notion of Christ's second coming insist that Christ has indeed been with each and every believer throughout the church age. It must be noted, however, that while *parousia* can mean "presence," it also means "coming." This is the meaning that is most prominent in the New Testament, its primary meaning. Further, there are other New Testament terms employed plainly to mean "coming": *apokalypsis* and *epiphaneia*. Most important, however, is the fact that most of the promises of Christ's second coming were made *after* the Day of Pentecost. John's Revelation came some sixty years after this event,[5] and he still placed Jesus' return in the future.

In sharp contrast to the humble circumstances surrounding Christ's birth, his second coming will be glorious and awe-inspiring. All humanity will witness the God-man descending to earth clothed in clouds of majesty.

> In my vision at night I looked, and there before me was one like a son of man, coming with the clouds of heaven[6]. He approached the Ancient of Days and was led into his presence. He was given authority, glory and sovereign power; all peoples, nations and men of every language worshiped him. His dominion is an everlasting dominion that will not pass away, and his kingdom is one that will never be destroyed. (Dan 7:13-14)

When asked if he was the Christ, the Son of the Blessed One, by the high priest who was examining him (Mk 14:60-62), Jesus quoted the book of Daniel, affirming that he was the very one described: the

Son of Man at the right hand of the Mighty One, coming on the clouds.

Christ's return will be a literal occurrence within history. The spiritualizing of God's acts in history common among some modern groups would have been inconceivable to first-century Jews. Although Jesus did speak of spiritual, eternal things that transcend physical realities, he did not deny the reality of the physical realm. It is a Greek way of thinking, denigrating or even denying the physical world, that has been used to obfuscate the meaning of the biblical passages regarding Christ's second coming.

But why has the parousia been so long delayed? Where is the promise of his coming? Twentieth-century scholarship was much concerned over the problem of the delay of Christ's advent.[7] Wasn't the early church's expectation that Jesus would return in their generation discredited, and thereby the entire idea of a parousia debunked?

We are convinced that the problem of the delay of the parousia is exaggerated. As noted above, Jesus did not say specifically when he would return, only that it was imminent—it could happen at any time. He did not discuss the "signs of the times" (as in Mk 13:1-25) in order to enable the calculation of a timetable but to warn of certain conflicts that were to be expected throughout history until his return. Next to passages that support the idea of imminence (such as Mk 9:1; 13:30; Rom 13:11-12) are others declaring that the date of the end is unknown. The passages that suggest imminence, then, are declaring the *certainty* of Christ's coming, not necessarily a chronological order between present and future. Events preceding the second coming are foretold—the desolating sacrilege (Mt 24:15), great tribulation (Mt 24:21), darkening of the sun (Mt 24:29)—but they do not point to the exact time of Jesus' return.

The New Religious Movements and the Second Coming

Unity School of Christianity. This Mind Science group denies the visible, bodily, audible, personal return to earth of Jesus. Instead the second coming should be understood as the transformation of the consciousness of all humankind. The *person* Jesus Christ is not coming back. "We believe the second coming of Jesus Christ is now being fulfilled, that His spirit is quickening the whole world"[8] through a gradual process of transforming humanity's earth-bound consciousness into a heavenly one, universally. "The first coming of Christ is the receiving of truth in the conscious mind, and the second coming is the awakening and regeneration of the subconscious through the superconsciousness of Christ-Mind."[9]

Christian Science. Mary Baker Eddy denied the physical death of Jesus on the cross and posited that he actually entered a higher existence of spirituality. Therefore his ascension and return are not physical.

> Until he himself ascended—or, in other words, rose even higher in the understanding of Spirit, God . . . Jesus' unchanged physical condition after what seemed to be death was followed by exaltation above all material conditions; and this exaltation explained his ascension. . . . In his final demonstration, called the ascension, which closed the earthly record of Jesus, he rose above the physical knowledge of his disciples, and the material senses saw him no more.[10]

Since Christ never really died, he is not expected to return physically to the earth.

It was simply on her own authority that Eddy reinterpreted the physical dimensions of Christ's death, burial, resurrection and return in spiritual terms. He now exists in a higher existence of spirituality somewhere, without a human body. Christian Science's basic premise is that matter and spirit cannot possibly coexist; thus any idea of Christ's returning in a physical body is impossible a priori.[11]

Jehovah's Witnesses. The Jehovah's Witnesses maintain that Christ returned *invisibly* in 1914. Initially founder Charles Taze Russell announced that Jesus was scheduled to return to earth and set up his kingdom toward the end of 1874. When that event failed to materialize, he changed it to 1914, and that year was marked by the beginning of World War I. "The 'battle of the great day of God Almighty' (Rev 16:14), which will end in A.D. 1914 with the complete overthrow of earth's present rulership, is already commenced."[12] When the 1914 prediction failed, the invisible return of Christ was taught: "Christ Jesus returns, not again as a human, but as a glorious spirit person."[13] World War I was then regarded as the beginning of the overthrow of the present world rulerships, a "sign" of Christ's "second presence."[14]

> Christ's return does not mean that he literally comes back to this earth. Rather, it means that he takes Kingdom power toward this earth and turns his attention to it. . . . Bible evidence shows that in the year 1914 C.E. God's time arrived for Christ to return and begin ruling. . . . Christ's return is invisible. . . . Christ himself gave a visible "sign" by which we know that he is invisibly present. . . . "NATION WILL RISE AGAINST NATION" . . . Surely you have seen this part of the "sign" being fulfilled since 1914! In that year World War I began.[15]

From the year 1914 on, then, the Witnesses teach that "Christ has turned his attention toward earth's affairs and is dividing the peoples and educating the true Christians in preparation for their survival during the great storms of Armageddon, when all unfaithful mankind will be destroyed from the face of the earth."[16] Christ, then, is already here, invisibly carrying out his purposes through his theocratic organization in Brooklyn, New York.[17] Yet more recently the Jehovah's Witnesses have been altering their prophetic charts to lessen the impact of their earlier teaching on the significance of 1914. As the end of the last millennium approached, the Watchtower Society had to account for the fact that the battle of Armageddon had not yet occurred, even though they taught earlier that it would come at least within the lifetimes of those born by 1914.

For many years the masthead of the Witness magazine *Awake!* carried the following statement: "Most important, this magazine builds confidence in the Creator's promise of a peaceful and secure new world *before the generation that saw the events of 1914 passes away.*" However, the November 8, 1995, issue of *Awake!* and all subsequent issues bore an altered statement: "Most important, this magazine builds confidence in the Creator's promise of a peaceful and secure new world *that is about to replace the present wicked lawless system of things.*"[18]

Following is a sampling of some of the revisions the Watchtower has made regarding the prophecy of the battle of Armageddon and Christ's establishment of his theocratic kingdom on earth:

- *The battle of Armageddon will end shortly after 1914:*
  In the year 1918, when God destroys the churches wholesale and the church members by millions, it shall be that any that escape shall come to the works of Pastor Russell to learn the meaning of the downfall of "Christianity."[19]

- *The battle of Armageddon will come around 1925:*
  The date 1925 is even more distinctly indicated by the Scriptures because it is fixed by the law God gave to Israel. Viewing the present situation in Europe, one wonders how it will be possible to hold back the explosion much longer; and that even before

1925 the great crisis will be reached and probably passed.[20]

- *People who were present and understood the events of 1914 will live to see the battle of Armageddon:*
  Jesus said, "This generation will by no means pass away until all these things occur." Which generation is this, and how long is it? . . . The "generation" logically would not apply to babies born during World War I. It applies to Christ's followers and others who were able to observe that war and the other things that have occurred in fulfillment of Jesus' composite "sign." Some of such persons "will by no means pass away until" all of what Christ prophesied occurs, including the end of the present wicked system.[21]

- *Anyone born by 1914 will live to see Armageddon:*
  If Jesus used "generation" in that sense and we apply it to 1914, then the babies of that generation are now seventy years old or older. And others alive in 1914 are in their eighties or nineties, a few even having reached one hundred. There are still many millions of that generation alive. Some of them "will by no means pass away until all things occur."[22]

- *Anyone who sees the events signaling the end, regardless of any relationship to 1914, will see the battle of Armageddon:*
  Eager to see the end of this evil system, Jehovah's People have at times speculated about the time when the "great tribulation" would break out, even tying this to calculations of what is the lifetime of a generation since 1914. However we "bring a heart of wisdom in" not by speculating about how many years or days make up a generation. . . . "This generation" apparently refers to the peoples of earth who see the sign of Christ's presence but fail to mend their ways.[23]

The Jehovah's Witnesses' teaching that Christ's return is invisible makes reference to two statements by Jesus:

> A little longer and the world will behold me no more. (Jn 14:29 New World Translation)

> For I say to you, You will by no means see me henceforth until you say, "Blessed is he that comes in Jehovah's name!" (Mt 23:39 New World Translation)[24]

They also teach that the early Christians expected Christ's return to be invisible. Paul argued, they contend, that there was insufficient evidence in his day:

> However, brothers, respecting the presence of our Lord Jesus Christ and our being gathered together to him, we request of you not to be quickly shaken from your reason nor to be excited either through an inspired expression or through a verbal message or through a letter as though from us, to the effect that the day of Jehovah is here. Let no one seduce you in any manner, because it will not come unless the apostasy comes first and the man of lawlessness gets revealed, the son of destruction. (2 Thessalonians 2:1-3 New World Translation)[25]

After he died on the cross and was buried in the tomb, Jesus' body is said to have turned into a gaseous cloud as his spirit returned to be the archangel Michael. Naturally, then, no physical return of Jesus can be expected.

Seventh-day Adventists. The Seventh-day Adventists are orthodox, but examining the history of their teachings regarding Christ's second coming is instructive. A look at their doctrinal statements establishes their orthodoxy:

> As our denominational name indicates, the second coming of Christ is one of the cardinal doctrines of the Adventist faith. We give it such prominence in our beliefs because it occupies a pivotal place in Holy Scripture, not only in the New Testament, but also in the Old.[26]

> Jesus will assuredly come the second time. . . . [His] second advent will be visible, audible, and personal. . . . Seventh-day Adventists believe on the evidence of Scripture that there will be one visible, personal, glorious second coming of Christ.[27]

It is clear, then, that Seventh-day Adventists believe in a literal second coming of Jesus Christ to the earth. Yet the group's doctrines of the "sanctuary" and the "investigative judgment" need to be examined in light of Seventh-day Adventist history.

Seventh-day Adventism got its start in the "Great Second Advent Awakening," which jolted the Western religious community just prior to the middle of the nineteenth century.[28] It was a time of strong reemphasis on the second advent of Jesus Christ. The awakening swept through Great Britain, Europe and then America. Talk of "seventy weeks," "twenty-three hundred days" and "the abomination of desolation" from Daniel and Revelation was common in the streets and in theological journals and newspapers. Following the biblical chronological system of Bishop James Ussher, Bible students from a variety of denominations interpreted the twenty-three hundred days of Daniel as twenty-three hundred years and thus predicted that Jesus Christ would return on or about the year 1843. William Miller, a Baptist minister who lived in Lower Hampton, New York, predicted in 1818 that in about twenty-five years Jesus Christ would come again.[29]

Miller's views were not the ravings of a lunatic; they were held in common with some of the leading theological lights of the period.

Even though Miller himself lacked formal theological training, dozens of prophetic scholars had espoused his views before he made them public. Miller's was merely one of many voices announcing the impending fulfillment of Daniel 8:14, or the twenty-three-hundred-day period allegedly starting in 457 B.C. and ending in 1843-1844.

Miller and his followers' hopes were dashed when March 21, 1844, came and went without the Lord's return. They had used a prophecy chart developed by Charles Fitch to fix Jesus' return between March 21, 1843, and March 21, 1844. It is difficult for us to grasp how desperate was the hope of these zealous, sincere Christians. Miller reluctantly endorsed the "Seventh-Month Movement," proposing that Christ would return seven months later on October 22, 1844. Hopes were renewed, but as that date too came and went, shock and disillusionment set in. Christ had not come after all to cleanse the "sanctuary" (the earth), usher in judgment and bring the earth into submission to "the everlasting gospel."

On October 25 Hiram Edson, a devout follower of Miller, and his friend O. R. L. Crosier were walking home from their place of waiting for the Lord's return. In order to avoid the mocking of neighbors, they cut across a cornfield. Deep in meditation, Edson suddenly stopped. He turned his face toward heaven as though receiving a great spiritual revelation.

> Suddenly there burst upon his mind the thought that there were two phases to Christ's ministry in the Heaven of Heavens, just as in the earthly sanctuary of old. In his own words, an overwhelming conviction came over him "that instead of our high priest coming out of the most holy of the heavenly sanctuary to come to this earth on the tenth day of the seventh month at the end of the twenty-three hundred days, He for the first

> time entered on that day the second apartment of that sanctuary, and that He had a work to perform in the most holy before coming to this earth."[30]

On that day, according to Seventh-day Adventists, Edson understood why the Millerites had been disappointed. They had expected Christ to return and cleanse "the sanctuary," but instead of being the earth the sanctuary was located in the heavens! Instead of coming to earth, then, Jesus had passed from one heavenly "apartment" to another to perform a work referred to as the "investigative judgment."

According to Edson and Crosier's new doctrine, in 1844 Christ entered the "second phase" of his ministry in the heavenly sanctuary. They, like the Millerite movement before them, borrowed heavily from Jewish sacrificial rituals to explain their doctrine of the investigative judgment. Ever since 1844 Jesus has been investigating, or reviewing, the cases of believers to determine their worthiness for eternal life. He will leave the "second apartment," return to the earth and finish the "second phase" to usher in judgment of the world in his second coming.

This doctrine justified faithful Millerite-Adventists in continuing to endorse the ideas of Miller. They even believed and taught that God had allowed Miller to make mistakes for the greater blessing of the "little flock." Ellen G. White, prophet of the burgeoning Seventh-day Adventist movement, wrote, "I have seen that the 1843 chart was directed by the hand of the Lord, and that it should not be altered; that the figures were as He wanted them, that His hand was over and hid a mistake in some of the figures so that none could see it until His hand was removed."[31]

With Edson's vision, Adventists began to argue his theory that Jesus passed from one apartment of the heavenly sanctuary into the other to perform the investigative judgment. This was all done invisibly, with no human eye privy to the scene except Edson's. Crosier spelled out and defended Edson's visionary concept in a lengthy article in *The Day Star*, a Millerite publication in Cincinnati, Ohio.[32] Edson believed that Christ had passed from the "holy place" to the "most holy place" in the heavenly sanctuary.[33]

Adventist teaching regarding the sanctuary is that Christ our high priest transferred the sins of believers ("the record of sins") to the heavenly sanctuary, which will be cleansed finally at the conclusion of the great Day of Atonement and the cessation of the investigative judgment.[34] The cases of the believers having been decided, their sins will be blotted out, and the Lord Jesus will return. According to White, the sins transferred to the sanctuary will remain there until the investigative judgment is concluded:

> The blood of Christ, while it was to release the repentant sinner from the condemnation of the law, was not to cancel the sin; it would stand on record in the sanctuary until the final atonement; so then the type, the blood of the sin offering, removed the sin from the penitent but it rested in the sanctuary until the day of atonement.[35]

To substantiate this doctrine, Adventists quote the King James rendering of Acts 3:19: "Repent ye therefore, and be converted, that your sins may be blotted out, when the times of refreshing shall come from the presence of the Lord."

To his credit, Miller, after "the Great Disappointment," disassociated himself from the movement. He never became a Seventh-day Adventist, and later he remarked that he had "no confidence" in the theories that had emerged out of the rubble of the Millerite movement. Some of his followers, like him, admitted their error and went on in their discipleship, greatly humbled. Others, however, driven by shock and embarrassment, went on to greater errors.

RESPONDING TO THE NEW RELIGIOUS MOVEMENTS

Unity School of Christianity. The New Testament teaches unequivocally that Jesus' second coming is to be personal, visible, audible and physical (1 Cor 15:51-52; 1 Thess 4:13-18; Rev 1:7-8; 19:6-16). Jesus himself taught that it would be an event in literal history (Mt 24:37; Lk 17:28-30). It will come unexpectedly (2 Pet 3:10-12), and no one will be able to anticipate its date (Mt 24:36). The second coming of Jesus will be the cataclysmic center of all eschatology. It will be accompanied by discernible "signs" (Mt 24:3-24). The overarching purpose of the second coming is to complete what was begun at Christ's first coming: the fulfillment of redemption, the glorification of the church and the liberation of the created order from sin's enslavement (Rev 21:1-7).

Christian Science. The origin of Christian Science's aversion to physical matter is Greek, not Hebraic. Such a bias against matter infected certain elements of the church early in its history and became the basis for Gnostic thought, as it is today for Christian Science. Origen believed that the Christian's hope is heavenly, not earthly (physical), and that God's object of concern is the human soul, not the body. Thus he rejected notions of Christ's physical rule over a literal kingdom on earth.[36] Similarly, the Christian Scientists, coming to the biblical text with preconceived ideas of what it *should* say, force alien concepts onto it.

Clearly alien presuppositions can have a debilitating effect on the biblical interpreter. We can never come to the text of Scripture without any presuppositions, attitudes or a particular worldview; yet we can *become aware* of our presuppositions and allow Scripture to in-form us; we can work to eliminate any presuppositions that are not congruent with it.

Jehovah's Witnesses. According to Acts 1:9-11, Jesus ascended in bodily form, having demonstrated his bodily resurrection with "many infallible proofs." His ascension was just as "physical" as his resurrection. Immediately upon his ascension, angels appeared to assure the grieving disciples that Jesus' return would be just as physical and visible. Revelation 1:7 declares that when Jesus returns again to the earth, every eye will see him. The Greek word in this instance, *horao,* means "to see, catch sight of, notice of *sense perception*."[37]

As for the Witnesses' claim that Christ is directing his activities invisibly through his theocratic kingdom organization, it would be well for them to heed his own words recorded in Matthew:

> At that time if anyone says to you, "Look, here is the Christ!" or, "There he is!" do not believe it. For false Christs and false prophets will appear and perform great signs and miracles to deceive even the elect—if that were possible. See, I have told you ahead of time.
>
> So if anyone tells you, "There he is, out in the desert," do not go out; or, "Here he is, in the inner rooms," do not believe it. For as lightning that comes from the east is visible even in the west, so will be the coming of the Son of Man. (Mt 24:23-27)

The Jehovah's Witnesses have been forced over the years to revise their predictions of Armageddon and the end of the present world system. Yet the January 1997 issue of the *Watchtower* once again heralds the imminent coming of Armageddon: "In the early 1920s, a featured public talk presented by Jehovah's Witnesses was entitled, 'Millions Now Living Will Never Die.' This may have reflected overoptimism at that time. But today that statement can be made with full confidence. Both the increasing light on Bible prophecy and the anarchy of this dying world cry out that the end of Satan's system is very, very near!"[38] Under Old Testament standards for the evaluation of a prophet's sayings, "God's Prophet on the earth"—the Watchtower Society—would have been stoned.

Jesus' John 14:19 statement "A little longer and the world will behold me no longer" (New World Translation) is referring to his impending death and resurrection, as the context abundantly testifies. Jesus never said that *no one* "would ever see him again in human form." He does promise the disciples to "come to you": "If I go and prepare a place for you, I will come back and take you to be with me that you also may be where I am. You know the way to the place where I am going" (Jn 14:3-4).

Matthew 23:39 really means nothing more than that Jerusalem will not see the Messiah it rejected until it blesses him in repentance as the Anointed of God. Notice that Jesus qualifies his statement with "until," a certain reference to his *visible* return (Mt 24:30).[39]

As for the Watchtower's teaching that the early church expected Christ's return to be invisible, in Paul's epistle to Titus he urges his hearers to "wait for the blessed hope—the glorious appearing of our great God and Savior, Jesus Christ" (Tit 2:13). Paul never looked forward to an "invisible presence" of Christ. Notice what he says to the Thessalonians:

> According to the Lord's own word, we tell you that we who are still alive, who are left till the coming of the Lord, will certainly not precede those who have fallen asleep. For the Lord himself will come down from heaven, with a loud command, with the voice of the archangel and with the trumpet call of God, and the dead in Christ will rise first. After that, we who are still alive and are left will be caught up together with them in the clouds to

meet the Lord in the air. And so we will be with the Lord forever. (1 Thess 4:15-17)

Perfectly in accord with Matthew 24 and Revelation 1, Christ is here depicted as coming *visibly*, and no reputable Greek scholar would allow for a reading of "be present" as opposed to "come down." Other Greek words used in the New Testament to describe Jesus' return to the earth also indicate a visible manifestation: *elthon* and its equivalent *erchomai* mean "to come," "to appear" and "to arrive."[40]

Seventh-day Adventists. The major problem with the Adventist concept of the investigative judgment is that it throws doubt on biblical statements about the justified state of the believer. Christ's second advent is for the gathering up of his church and the punishment of evil. It is not to begin a protracted investigation into the sins of his followers. The Bible states that we are no longer under God's condemnation when we accept Christ as Lord and Savior (Rom 8:1). God freely accepts the believer on the basis of Christ's once-for-all sacrifice. The believer is ushered immediately from spiritual death to eternal life.

The Adventists have always accepted the orthodox understanding of salvation, which makes their acceptance of the investigative judgment doctrine problematic. We shall all certainly appear before the judgment seat of Christ after his return (2 Cor 5:10), but this will be to receive rewards for deeds done for Christ while on earth, not a determination of whether we are worthy to be saved.[41] Hebrews 1:3 informs us that Christ purged our sins on Calvary and immediately sat down at the right hand of the Majesty in heaven. This implies that his redemptive work was accomplished on our behalf forever.

The Greek of Acts 3:19 does not support the Adventist contention that the blotting out of sins will be a separate event from the forgiveness of sins. Modern translations (the Revised, American Standard, Revised Standard and New International versions) render the Greek thus: "Repent therefore, and turn again, that your sins may be blotted out, that times of refreshing may come from the presence of the Lord" (RSV). Peter was urging his listeners to repent and turn from their sins *in order* to receive the forgiveness that comes from God's presence. Outside of an extrabiblical revelation that cannot be substantiated (Edson's cornfield vision), support for the investigative judgment and the heavenly sanctuary is simply not there.

Since Christ has already paid for our sins, no Christian can ever be convicted for them again. At the judgment seat of Christ we will be judged for the way we lived as Christians, with rewards and chastisement given out (2 Cor 5:10). This judgment does not relate to whether we stand justified before God.

Having fashioned doctrines that seemed to explain Christ's failure to return to the earth in glory, the Adventists, under White, rallied to Miller's defense and in effect set themselves up as the only Christian witness to a special "second phase" of Jesus' high-priestly ministry. By accepting these doctrines, our Adventist friends deny by implication the full validity of the atonement of Christ. Strangely, however, Adventists passionately *affirm* the full validity of Christ's atonement. They cannot have it both ways; the atonement and the investigative judgment are logically incongruent. Both cannot be true.

CONCLUSION

The second coming of Christ is an important part of the Christian faith, providing hope of the final resurrection and inheritance with Christ. Groups that deny Christ's literal and physical coming do so in spite of a large array of biblical evidence, as well as the expressed hope of Christians of the early centuries.

Even the Seventh-day Adventists have erred in this doctrine. The Adventists belong firmly within the tradition of the historic Christian church, despite their aberrant doctrines of the sanctuary and the investigative judgment. There is a strong and vibrant evangelical movement within the Adventist camp, with an emphasis on historic Christianity. Most within this evangelical wing either deemphasize White's prophecies and aberrant teachings or renounce them altogether.

No one can fault the Adventists for fervently anticipating Christ's second coming. We share that blessed hope with them. It was the hallmark of the early church, which continually looked up, anticipating the return of their Lord and Master, Jesus Christ. Maranatha!

11

THE DOCTRINE OF REWARDS AND PUNISHMENTS

How Will God Mete Out Justice?

These days one rarely hears sermons on the subject of hell. Evangelical Christians are rarely confronted by their pastors regarding this neglected doctrine. Though during his ministry Jesus spoke often on the subject of hell, eternal punishment for the wicked is treated as taboo by most Christian leaders. The idea of an eternal lake of fire reserved for the lost is not discussed in polite company.

We hear much on the subject of heaven, of rewards, of banquet tables spread for the saints at the marriage supper of the Lamb. We are treated to detailed accounts (usually speculative) of what life will be like in heaven and in the new earth in resurrected glory. Some leaders create "user-friendly" Christian meetings for nonbelievers. Anything that might offend the guests is excised from the message of the gospel. There is rarely any mention of the dire consequences of rejecting Christ's salvation. Many pastors, ministers and priests tolerate sin among members of their congregations without even a word of warning or rebuke. Where sin is tolerated as a necessary evil in a pluralistic society, believers eventually become demoralized. Whatever happened to the idea of landing in the "hands of an angry God"?

Many historians regard Jonathan Edwards as the greatest Christian thinker and philosopher America ever produced.[1] When he read his tightly reasoned treatise "Sinners in the Hands of an Angry God" in a church meeting in Massachusetts, the congregation reacted with wails of grief over their sins. This sermon is regarded by many church historians as the spark that ignited the First Great Awakening of the 1720s and 1730s.[2] One would be hard pressed these days to find preachers of such caliber delivering sermons designed to shock audiences into repentance. This would be regarded by many as fear-mongering and a crass manipulation of emotions.

The great apologist Tertullian responded to pagans who ridiculed the Christian doctrine of hell in *Apologeticus*, his earliest work, written around A.D. 197.

> We are also ridiculed because we proclaim that God is going to judge the world. Yet even the poets and philosophers place a judgement seat in the underworld. In the same way if we threaten Gehenna, which is a store of hidden underground fire for purposes of punishment, we are received with howls of derision. Yet they likewise have the river Pyriphlegethon in the place of the dead. And if we mention paradise, a place of divine delight appointed to receive the spirits of the saints, cut off from the knowledge of this everyday world by a kind of barrier consisting of that zone of fire, then the Elysian Fields have anticipated the faith in this respect.[3]

Despite what appear to be clear scriptural indications regarding rewards and punishment and the existence of an eternal hell, some within the Christian sphere reject the idea of eternal punishment.

One such was Nels Ferré, son of a conservative Baptist minister in Sweden. Ferré preferred *universalism* over a belief in eternal damnation.[4] Noting that most who speak of future rewards and punishments stress the justice of God, he proposed that God's justice is in complete service to his love.[5] Ferré rested his entire concept of God on this one divine attribute. He believed that those who insist on teaching eternal hell do so out of ignorance of the love of God, for to him the notions of love and punishment, heaven and hell, joy and grief, are mutually exclusive.

> Some have never really seen how completely contradictory are heaven and hell as eternal realities. Their eyes have never been opened to this truth. If eternal hell is real, love is eternally frustrated and heaven is a place of mourning and concern for the lost. Such joy and such grief cannot go together.[6]
>
> There can be no psychiatric split personality for the real lovers of God and surely not for God himself. That is the reason that heaven can be heaven only when it has emptied hell, as surely as love is love and God is God. God cannot be faithless to Himself no matter how faithless we are; and His is the power, the kingdom and the glory.[7]

Many devout Christians, like Ferré, are quite uncomfortable with the concept of eternal punishment for those who have rejected Christ. They may have lost loved ones who died seemingly without a confession of Christ as their Lord and Savior.[8] I hope that through this chapter those who have known the heartbreak of such a loss will not only be reminded of divine revelation on this subject but receive divine comfort as well.

It is important to acknowledge that to hold views that diverge from historic Christian teachings on some of these doctrines is not necessarily a departure from the faith or from relationship with Christ. Some who are fully orthodox in all other areas of doctrine depart from the traditional Christian perspectives on eternal punishment due to this doctrine's seeming incongruity with the character of God or its apparent harshness.

The Orthodox View of Rewards and Punishment

Scripture teaches believers to expect that existence after death will bring sublime peace and overflowing joy in the presence of the Lord. "We are confident, I say, and would prefer to be away from the body and at home with the Lord" (2 Cor 5:8). "I desire to depart and be with Christ, . . . but it is more necessary for you that I remain in the body" (Phil 1:23-24).[9]

For the unrighteous, death brings separation from God for all eternity and, if Scripture be understood literally, it also brings great suffering. Holy Writ nowhere gives us grounds to suppose that people will have a second chance to choose God after death. Jesus' story about Lazarus and the rich man leaves no room for hope that people who die in their sins will ever cross the gulf from hell to heaven. Scripture never speaks of judgment based on deeds we do after death, only on what we have done during life.[10]

Although unbelievers pass into eternal punishment after death, they will not face the ultimate judgment until they have been resurrected from death and stand before God. What a tragedy! Beings created for eternal companionship with God will be destined instead for eternal destruction with Satan and his angels.

Resurrection of the just and the unjust. Several passages of Scripture point to the resurrection of the just and the gathering of believers who are alive at Christ's second coming. "Each in his own turn: Christ, the firstfruits; then, when he comes, those who belong to him" (1 Cor 15:23). "If I go and prepare a place for you, I will come back and take you to be with me" (Jn 14:3). No other religion offers such an assurance of future bliss. But that's not the end of the assurances:

> I declare to you, brothers, that flesh and blood cannot inherit the kingdom of God, nor does the perishable inherit the imperishable. Listen, I tell you a mystery: we will not all sleep, but we will all be changed—in a flash, in the twinkling of an eye, at the last trumpet. For the trumpet will sound, the dead will be raised imperishable, and we will be changed. For the perishable must clothe itself with the imperishable. (1 Cor 15:50-53)

What will our resurrection bodies be like? Our bodies will be *physical,* for the resurrection, at a minimum, is the restoration of the idyllic period in the Garden before the intrusion of sin. We were meant for physical immortality with God from the outset of Adam's creation. Paul likens it to the adoption of *imperishable* flesh, as opposed to the dying and decaying flesh we all possess from birth to death in this life. Our physical resurrection bodies will be corporeal and spiritual in just the same way that Christ's body is physical and spiritual (1 Cor 15).

Around A.D. 300 a Lycian bishop, Methodius of Olympus, challenged Origen's tendency to spiritualize the resurrection.[11] Methodius compared the resurrection of the body to the recasting of a damaged metal statue:

> So it seems that it is as if some skilled artificer had made a noble image, cast in gold or other material, which was beautifully proportioned in all its features.
>
> Then the artificer suddenly notices that the image had been defaced by some envious person, who could not endure its

> beauty, and so decided to ruin it for the sake of the pointless pleasure of satisfying his jealousy. So the craftsman decides to recast this noble image. Now notice, most wise Aglaophon, that if he wants to ensure that this image, on which he has expended so much effort, care and work, will be totally free from any defect, he will be obliged to melt it down, and restore it to its former condition.[12]

Methodius's point is that at the resurrection humanity does not lose its physical nature. It does not become "something else." Becoming something "spiritual," as Origen concluded based on his neo-Platonic bias against the goodness of matter, is not the meaning of resurrection at all. The New Testament understanding of resurrection involves glorified matter, not something incorporeal. The second coming of Christ becomes the occasion of deliverance and glorification of our physical bodies from death and decay to immortality.

> We believe that Jesus died and rose again and so we believe that God will bring with Jesus those who have fallen asleep in him. According to the Lord's own word, we tell you that we who are still alive, who are left till the coming of the Lord, will certainly not precede those who have fallen asleep. For the Lord himself will come down from heaven, with a loud command, with the voice of the archangel and with the trumpet call of God, and the dead in Christ will rise first. After that, we who are still alive and are left will be caught up together with them in the clouds to meet the Lord in the air. And so we will be with the Lord forever. (1 Thess 4:14-17)

These remarkable words describe the mysterious events that will usher us into eternity with Jesus. The dead in Christ will rise first; then those who are alive will be suddenly changed from mortal to immortal beings like Jesus, rising to meet those who preceded us and together joining Jesus, who waits for us.

The resurrection of the unjust is radically different. They too will rise: "Multitudes who sleep in the dust of the earth will awake: some to everlasting life, others to shame and everlasting contempt" (Dan 12:2). The destiny of the unrighteous is suffering and shame. There will not be one atheist in this domain: all, though, may be aware of their error and rebellion against God and his Christ.

All human beings will experience a judgment: "For the Son of Man is going to come in his Father's glory with his angels, and then he will reward each person according to what he has done" (Mt 16:27). However, believers will not be condemned but judged for how they conducted themselves as Christians: "We must all appear before the judgment seat of Christ, that each one may receive what is due him for the things done while in the body, whether good or bad" (2 Cor 5:10).[13] Jesus said, "I tell you the truth, whoever hears my word and believes him who sent me has eternal life and will not be condemned; he has crossed over from death to life" (Jn 5:24).

All human beings will be judged according to the revelation that has been given to them: "I tell you that it will be more bearable for Sodom on the day of judgment than for you" (Mt 11:24). "All who sin apart from the law will also perish apart from the law, and all who sin under the law will be judged by the law" (Rom 2:12). But what about those who never heard about Jesus Christ and his salvation? Are they automatically condemned for not hearing about him? No, they are *already* condemned for being sinners. No one deserves mercy! If they did, it would no longer be mercy. "There is no one righteous, not even one; there is no one who understands, no one who seeks God" (Rom 3:10-11). All will be judged according to the light given to them, which is more than sufficient to declare the existence and nature of God:

> The wrath of God is being revealed from heaven against all the godlessness and wickedness of men who suppress the truth by their wickedness, since what may be known about God is plain to them, because God has made it plain to them. For since the creation of the world God's invisible qualities—his eternal power and divine nature—have been clearly seen, being understood from what has been made, so that men are without excuse. (Rom 1:18-20)

God is a perfect and holy being who is unencumbered by our sins and limitations. He is wholly righteous and full of truth (Ps 96:12-13). Thus we can rest assured that God will judge fairly on the last day (Ps 19:9). One missionary to the Mormons reminds us, "The Lord will make a way for the desiring heart to hear the Gospel regardless of geographical barriers."[14]

Entrance into heaven will depend on the righteousness of Jesus alone: "I am not ashamed of the gospel, because it is the power of God for the salvation of everyone who believes: first for the Jew, then for the Gentile. For in the gospel a righteousness from God is revealed, a righteousness that is by faith from first to last, just as it is written: 'The righteous will live by faith'" (Rom 1:16-17). No one is guiltless, as we all know intuitively. All human efforts to seek salvation from whatever source are *active,* bent on achieving some standard of ethical excellence and internal rest from guilt. God's salvation tells us to be passive, rather: believe the gospel and be saved. God's solution to avoid judgment for sin is to accept the righteousness he has achieved for us already in Christ. To reject this is to reject all hope for salvation and eternal life.

Rewards and punishments. There will be various levels of punishment for the wicked:

> That servant who knows his master's will and does not get ready or does not do what his master wants will be beaten with many blows. But the one who does not know and does things deserving punishment will be beaten with few blows. From everyone who has been given much, much will be demanded; and from the one who has been entrusted with much, much more will be asked. (Lk 12:47-48)

God's punishment of sin will be eminently fair and equitable. But the *state* of one's punishment will not change; its duration is eternal.

- "All who sin apart from the law will also perish apart from the law, and all who sin under the law will be judged by the law" (Rom 2:12).
- "Then they will go away to eternal punishment, but the righteous to eternal life" (Mt 25:46).
- "The smoke of their torment rises for ever and ever. There is no rest day or night for those who worship the beast and his image, or for anyone who receives the mark of his name" (Rev 14:11).
- "Their worm does not die, and the fire is not quenched" (Mk 9:48).

For the believer there will be various levels of rewards. Scripture gives a number of examples of the kinds of works that will bring rewards.

- Evangelism: "Those who are wise will shine like the brightness of the heavens, and those who lead many to righteousness, like the stars for ever and ever" (Dan 12:3).
- Hospitality: "Anyone who receives a prophet because he is a prophet will receive a prophet's reward, and anyone who receives a righteous man because he is a righteous man will receive a right-

eous man's reward. And if anyone gives even a cup of cold water to one of these little ones because he is my disciple, I tell you the truth, he will certainly not lose his reward" (Mt 10:41-42).

- Enduring suffering for the sake of Christ: "Blessed are you when people insult you, persecute you and falsely say all kinds of evil against you because of me. Rejoice and be glad, because great is your reward in heaven, for in the same way they persecuted the prophets who were before you" (Mt 5:11-12). "If we are children, then we are heirs—heirs of God and co-heirs with Christ, if indeed we share in his sufferings in order that we may also share in his glory" (Rom 8:17).
- Stewardship: "Store up for yourselves treasures in heaven, where thieves do not break in and steal. For where your treasure is, there your heart will be also" (Mt 6:20).

The New Religious Movements' Treatment of Rewards and Punishments

Church of Jesus Christ of Latter-day Saints. The first phase of the Mormon afterlife is referred to as "spirit prison." It is the realm of the dead, where deceased persons await the resurrection and judgment. Righteous spirits wait in paradise, while unrighteous spirits wait in hell. Jesus bridged the gulf between the two places so that those in paradise and hell can freely associate with one another. This enables unrighteous spirits to repent and gain salvation through the gospel preached to them by the righteous spirits.

> The whole spirit world (including both paradise and hell) is a *spirit prison*. . . . In a more particular sense, however, the *spirit prison* is hell, that portion of the spirit world where the wicked dwell. . . . Before Christ bridged the gulf between paradise and

> hell—so that the righteous could mingle with the wicked and preach them the gospel—the wicked in hell were confined to locations which precluded them from contact with the righteous in paradise. . . . Now that the righteous spirits in paradise have been commissioned to carry the message of salvation to the wicked spirits in hell . . . repentance opens the prison doors to the spirits in hell; it enables those bound with the chains of hell to free themselves from darkness, unbelief, ignorance, and sin. As rapidly as they can overcome these obstacles—gain light, believe truth, acquire intelligence, cast off sin, and break the chains of hell—they can leave the hell . . . and dwell with the righteous in the peace of paradise.[15]

> The wicked and ungodly will suffer the vengeance of eternal fire in hell until they finally obey Christ, repent of their sins, and gain forgiveness therefrom.[16]

There are three degrees of glory in the Mormon afterlife, corresponding to kingdoms of the same name: the *telestial* glory/kingdom, the *terrestrial* glory/kingdom and the *celestial* glory/kingdom. "General salvation," which involves obtaining a position in one of the first two glories/kingdoms (telestial or terrestrial) is achieved by nearly everyone, including non-Mormons and "lukewarm" Mormons.

> Most of the adult people who have lived from the day of Adam to the present time will go to the *telestial kingdom*. . . . They will be the endless hosts of people . . . who have been carnal, sensual, and devilish; who have chosen the vain philosophies of the world rather than accept the testimony of Jesus; who have been liars, thieves, sorcerers and adulterers, blasphemers and murderers.[17]

Those who do not go to one of the kingdoms of glory are termed "sons of perdition": Satan and all his angels, any who have willingly rejected Mormon teachings, apostates from the Mormon Church and extremely evil people. All these will be assigned to the lake of fire for eternity.

> Those in this life who gain a perfect knowledge of the divinity of the gospel cause . . . and come out in open rebellion, also become sons of perdition. Their destiny . . . is to be cast out with the devil and his angels. . . . Their torment is as a lake of fire and brimstone.[18]

> Those who have committed the unpardonable sin . . . will be cast out as sons of perdition to dwell with the devil and his angels in eternity. . . . To commit this unpardonable crime a man must receive the gospel, gain from the Holy Ghost by revelation the absolute knowledge of the divinity of Christ and then deny "the new and everlasting covenant by which he was sanctified, calling it an unholy thing." . . . This is the case with many apostates of The Church of Jesus Christ of Latter-day Saints.[19]

Only the celestial kingdom is considered heaven. This kingdom itself has three degrees, heavens or glories. The highest degree is exaltation, eternal life in the truest sense. This is the reward for which Mormons are working. Only Mormonism offers such salvation.[20] The entire process of obtaining exaltation is known as "eternal progression." It is the same process God the Father went through to become God. Mormons hope to receive the same reward—godhood.[21]

According to Mormonism, we can become gods because we are the literal offspring of beings once like us who progressed to godhood:

> God the Eternal Father was once a mortal man who passed through a school of earth life similar to that through which we are now passing. He became God—an exalted being—through

> obedience to the same eternal Gospel truths that we are given opportunity today to obey.[22]

> As man is, God once was; as God is, man may become.[23]

> Here, then, is eternal life—to know the only wise and true God; and you have got to learn how to be Gods yourselves . . . the same as all Gods have done before you,—namely, by going from one small degree to another . . . to inherit the same power, the same glory and the same exaltation, until you arrive at the station of a God, and ascend the throne of eternal power.[24]

Jehovah's Witnesses. According to the Witnesses there are two classes of Christians: the "little flock" and the "great crowd." The former are born-again children of God; only they participate in the annual memorial service (Communion) and will go to heaven. The latter ("other sheep") will live in "paradise" on earth after "unbelievers" are destroyed through either the great tribulation or Armageddon. The "little flock" will be taken to heaven before the tribulation.

> The Bible shows that only a limited number of persons, a "little flock," will go to heaven. . . . The rest of faithful humankind will live on earth as the subjects of these rulers.[25]

> These dedicated, baptized "other sheep" of the "great crowd" have not been begotten to be God's spiritual sons, with a heavenly inheritance.[26]

> At the celebration of the memorial of Christ's death, only those who make up "the Israel of God" should partake of the emblems of bread and wine. . . . The vast international company of "other sheep," who do not partake, will enjoy everlasting life on the Paradise earth.[27]

Salvation for the "little flock" will include sharing in Jesus' divine nature and joining with him in heaven to become "the Christ." Note that this sharing of Jesus' divine nature does not mean that Witnesses consider Jesus *divine* as Christians understand the term. It only means that whatever godlike qualities Jesus possesses will be shared by the "little flock." They will be gods.

> What is meant by "Christ in you?" . . . Jesus was anointed with the Holy Spirit (Acts 10:38), and thus we recognize him to be the Christ. . . . The saints of this Gospel age are an anointed company [1 Jn 2:27]. . . . Together with Jesus, their chief and Lord, they constitute Jehovah's Anointed—the Christ. . . . *The Christ* (the Anointed) is "not one member, but many." . . . Jesus is anointed to be the Head or Lord over the Church . . . and unitedly they constitute the *promised "Seed"*—the Great Deliverer.[28]

> We are begotten of a divine nature. . . . Jehovah is thus our father . . . hence all such are Gods. . . . Now we appear like men, and all die naturally as men, but in the resurrection we will rise in our true character as Gods.[29]

> The titles, Mighty God, and Everlasting Father . . . are very appropriate to Our Lord Jesus. . . . The same titles are applicable to the Church as his body.[30]

There is no conscious eternal punishment for the wicked in Jehovah's Witness teaching. All "unbelievers" will be annihilated: "The fiendish concepts associated with a hell of torment slander God and originate with the chief slanderer of God (the Devil)."[31]

Mind Science groups. For the Mind Sciences, heaven and hell exist only in our minds. We can create a heavenly experience for ourselves, or we can subject ourselves to a mental hell. Heaven and hell do not actually exist as ontological realities.

> The sinner makes his own hell by doing evil, and the saint his own heaven by doing right.[32]

> God neither punishes nor rewards. Such a concept of God would create an anthropomorphic dualism, a house divided against itself. . . . In the long run, no one judges us but ourselves. . . . If we make mistakes, we suffer. We are our own reward and our own punishment.[33]

> Both [heaven and hell] are states of mind, and conditions, which people experience as a direct outworking of their thoughts, beliefs, words, and acts.[34]

According to the teaching of the Mind Science groups, "sinners" make their own hell by doing evil and "saints" their own heaven by doing right. Anyone has the potential, then, of becoming either a sinner or a saint simply by adopting a particular frame of mind and doing either the right or wrong things.

New Age. According to adherents of this modern version of ancient paganism, the early church used its power to subvert the truth of reincarnation and keep the Western world ignorant of the reality of multiple lives:

> I read that Christ's teachings about reincarnation were struck from the Bible during the Fifth Ecumenical Council meeting in Constantinople in the year 553.[35]

> Since the espousal of reincarnation and karma by the wisest spiritual and philosophical sages, the people of the East have remained in awe of the relentless revolutions of the wheel of life. Not so their counterparts in the Western Hemisphere where reincarnation was buried 14 centuries ago.
>
> The conspiring undertakers were the Church and the State,

> fearful that their authority could be challenged by a doctrine that made individuals responsible for their own salvation. Since A.D. 553, when the monstrous "restoration" of rebirth was denounced by Emperor Justinian, the faithful have been taught to believe in eternal life while ignoring immortality's spiritual sister, reincarnation.[36]

Freemasonry. Masonry promises its members that if they pursue obedience to the Lodge and good works, they will dwell with the Great Architect of the Universe for eternity.

> Let us imitate the good man in his virtuous and amiable conduct, in his unfeigned piety to God, in his inflexible fidelity to his trust, that we may welcome death as a kind messenger sent from our Supreme Grand Master to translate us from this imperfect to that all perfect and glorious Lodge above, where the Supreme Architect of the Universe presides.[37]

Although Masonic literature often mentions afterlife rewards, it says nothing about an eternal afterlife of punishment for sin. According to evangelical apologists John Weldon and John Ankerberg, "hell is not mentioned in any of the rituals or ceremonies of the three degrees of the Blue Lodge, the ten degrees of the York Rite, or the thirty degrees of the Scottish Rite."[38]

Responding to the New Religious Movements

Church of Jesus Christ of Latter-day Saints. Hebrews 9:27 states that it is appointed for a person to die once, after which will come judgment. There is no indication of an open door left for those who heard the gospel in their earthly life and rejected it. Jesus' story of Lazarus and the rich man shows that the righteous and unrighteous dead cannot have any contact with one another. Once this life is over, one's eternal destiny is set and there is no reversing it.

The Mormon doctrine of degrees of glory in the afterlife—telestial, terrestrial and celestial—is a radical misinterpretation of 1 Corinthians 15:40-41: "There are also heavenly bodies and there are earthly bodies; but the splendor of the heavenly bodies is one kind, and the splendor of the earthly bodies is another. The sun has one kind of splendor, the moon another and the stars another; and the star differs from star in splendor." Scripture presents only two ultimate destinations for human beings: eternal life with God (salvation) and eternal separation from God (damnation).

The teaching regarding "sons of perdition"—the condemnation of Satan and his angels along with all those who have rejected the Mormon gospel, particularly those who oppose the Mormon Church—seems to be an attempt to silence critics of Mormonism. Scripture describes the lake of fire, damnation, as the final destination for all those who reject Jesus Christ (Mt 7:21-23; 25:46; Rev 20:15).

Jehovah's Witnesses. Nowhere in Scripture is there any mention of two classes of Christians. All are one in Christ (Gal 3:28), and all share one future hope (Eph 1:18; 4:4; Col 1:5). The "other sheep" referred to by Jesus in John 10:16 are not a class of second-class Christians who will not inherit heaven. Remember that Jesus referred to fellow Jews as "the lost sheep of Israel" (Mt 10:6; 15:24). Those who followed him were called his sheep (Mt 10:16; 26:31). Consequently, with "other sheep" he was referring to non-Jewish people who would become believers and join Jewish Christ-followers to create one body of Christ (Eph 2:11-22).

The Jehovah's Witnesses define the "little flock" as those who will share in Jesus' divine nature, joining with him in heaven to become "the Christ," in fact gods. The Bible consistently identifies Jesus as the Christ (Mt 1:16; 16:16, 20; Lk 2:11; 4:41; Acts 3:20; 9:22; 17:3). The claim that the "anointed ones" of the Jehovah's Witnesses will actually become part of the Christ is a fulfillment of Jesus' warning that many false teachers will come saying they are the Christ (Mt 24:5, 23).

Over against the teachings about the ability of the anointed class to become gods are Scriptures such as Isaiah 43:10 and 1 Timothy 2:5, which declare that there is only one God. To say that the titles of Christ found in Isaiah 9:6 can be applied to the church is not only unwarranted exegetically but blasphemous. The Watchtower actually defines Jehovah's Witnesses as polytheists, given the belief that humans can be gods in the sense that Christ is God.

As for the belief in the "annihilation" of unbelievers, which Jehovah's Witnesses adopt instead of the "fiendish concepts associated with a hell of torment," there is no such teaching anywhere in the New Testament. The orthodox Christian church's concept of hell comes from Jesus Christ and the New Testament (Mt 25:46; Rev 14:11; 19:20; 20:11).

Mind Science groups. The Bible describes heaven and hell as actual places of conscious existence after death for human beings, not simply states of mind. Its vivid depictions of the conditions of both realms would be quite frivolous if they were not meant to describe real places where a human's destiny might lead. These detailed depictions of heaven and hell are meant to encourage followers of Christ and to shock enemies of God into solemn reflection on their eternal destiny.

Hell is described as a place of separation from the blessings and presence of God, a place of punishment for all who reject God's means of salvation, Jesus Christ and his gospel (Dan 12:2; Mt 8:11-12; 13:42, 50; 1 Thess 4:14), a place of eternal shame and torment where there is no escape from God's eternal justice. Heaven, on the other hand, is described as a place of eternal fellowship with the personal triune God of the Bible, a place without pain, sin, sorrow or death, a place to enjoy divine rewards forever (Mt 25:34; Jn 3:5, 16, 18, 21; Rev 21—22). Sadly, multitudes will choose to go their own way in this life and thus not to dwell there (Rev 14:9-11; 19:20; 22:15).

New Age. The New Testament canon was finalized in the fourth century, not the sixth century as some critics allege.[39] There were no "stricken" biblical texts that dealt with reincarnation. Certain apocryphal texts were rejected early on by both Jewish scribes and Christian authorities as not belonging in the Old and New Testaments. During the development of the early church some books (mostly Gnostic writings) were rejected by the fathers because they were inconsistent with the Scriptures and contained doctrines that Jesus and the apostles never taught. In fact, many of the New Testament letters and the Gospel of John were written in response to an early form of Gnosticism, the spiritual forebear of the New Age movement. Moreover, numerous pieces of ancient Greek manuscripts of the early New Testament (from the first through third centuries) are extant, and they do not even hint at any notion of reincarnation.

The notion that the Fifth Ecumenical Council of Constantinople in 553 excised teachings on reincarnation from the Bible and body of Christian tradition is outright historical revisionism. At the prodding of Emperor Justinian, this council condemned the teachings of Nestorius in general, as well as heretical teachings on Christ's incarnation proposed by Theodore of Mopsuestia, Theodoret of Cyrus and Ibas of Edessa.[40] It was also established to reaffirm the Council of Chalcedon (A.D. 451) and to restore church unity. Despite so much to do, the council proceeded to examine and condemn certain teachings of Origen, many of which had become very problematic. For example, his argument for the soul's preexistence stemmed from his heavy indebtedness to Platonism.[41] He argued that God made other worlds before this one and would form more in the future. Origen believed that to deny the eternality of the soul was to deny God's omnipotence. He reasoned that there would have to be eternal intelligences under the rulership of an eternal, omnipotent God; you could not have one without the other. The council declared in response, "If anyone asserts the fabulous pre-existence of souls, and shall assert the monstrous restoration which follows from it: let him be anathema."[42] Thus this council condemned Origen's belief in the preexistence, or eternality, of the soul, not reincarnation, which Origen had not espoused.

Freemasonry. The Bible does commend us to imitate the good conduct of others (1 Cor 11:1; Heb 6:12), but not in order to attain eternal life, since salvation is only by faith in Christ. Hell and eternal punishment are taught by Jesus (Mt 5:22; 25:41; Mk 9:43) and other biblical passages (Jas 3:6; 2 Pet 2:4). Many Freemasons who attend Christian churches are no doubt dedicated to what they regard as true Christianity. However, had they been well established in the fundamentals of the Christian faith, they would never have been deceived to believe that the "Great Architect" and the God of the Bible are one and the same.

Conclusion

In hell there will be no skeptics, agnostics or atheists. There will be people very acutely aware of their surroundings, fully conscious of their mental and physical state, tortured over their lost opportunity. They are those who rejected Jesus Christ—their only hope. There are no longer clever arguments drawn up against the Lord and his Christ. All are committed "believers" there, but too late.

Some have objected that people's being damned to eternal hell cannot possibly have any redemptive value. Yet hell satisfies God's justice and demonstrates how terrible and great a standard it is. In

Jonathan Edwards's words, "The vindictive justice of God will appear strict, exact, awful, and terrible, and therefore glorious."[43] Awful, terrible judgment fits in with Scripture's vision of God's awe-inspiring nature. Anything less than hell, as horrible and final a state of torment as it is, would be beneath God's glory. Edwards is eloquent on this point:

> It is a most unreasonable thing to suppose that there should be no future punishment, to suppose that God, who had made man a rational creature, able to know his duty, and sensible that he is deserving punishment when he does it not; should let man alone, and let him live as he will, and never punish him for his sins, and never make any difference between the good and the bad. . . . How unreasonable it is to suppose, that he who made the world, should leave things in such confusion, and never take any care of the governing of his creatures, and that he should never judge his reasonable creatures.[44]

In contrast, the righteous will experience a final state of bliss, shining with the righteousness of Christ alone. The final state of the righteous is an eternal now that will never cease or wane; the words *boredom* and *banal* will be lost from the tongues of the sons and daughters of God. Scripture gives us only captivating glimpses into the future reward reserved for us. We are told of a new heaven and a new earth, where the moon will shine seven times brighter than it does now.Out of heaven will descend a brilliantly bejeweled city built of rare stones and jewels. There God Almighty and the Lamb will dwell with the redeemed forever.

12

ONWARD CHRISTIAN SOLDIERS

The preceding chapters demonstrate the extent to which the doctrines of the new religious movements deviate from orthodox Christianity. Apart from entering into debates with those holding false teaching, however, what is the Christian to do? And what can Christians do to protect themselves from the spiritual and doctrinal counterfeits all around us?[1]

How Do We Protect Ourselves from Error?

Error has been with the Christian church from its inception. Wherever truth exists, error will arise, and it is important for biblical believers to protect themselves from false doctrines that dishonor the Lord and deplete their spiritual vitality. "Children, it is the last hour; and as you have heard that the antichrist is coming, even now many antichrists have come. . . . I am writing these things to you about those who are trying to lead you astray" (1 Jn 2:18, 26). We should not be surprised to encounter heresies and false doctrines that are contrary to the teachings of our Lord and the apostles.

Recognizing error. How does one recognize a spiritual counterfeit? Usually erroneous teaching is manifest in (1) rejection of the true deity and true humanity of Jesus Christ and (2) replacement of God's free gift in Christ with requirements of works or merit for justification. Attempts to justify such teachings may involve appeals to portions of Scripture.

Heresies regarding the person of Christ seek to diminish his humanity or deity or to exalt one nature above another. For example, some Jews (Ebionites) accepted Jesus as a human Messiah but were unwilling to consider him as having the very nature of God. Others (Gnostics) considered him divine but could not accept the idea that he had a genuine human nature. Some (Nestorians) tried to maintain Christ's deity and humanity by separating his person from his nature, while others (Eutychians) sought to blend the two natures into a third nature, a God-man. Some (Arians) could consider Jesus to have some divine qualities but not to be one God with the Father and Holy Spirit. Each of these heresies was an attempt to eradicate the tension inherent in Scripture's presentation of Jesus Christ as fully man and fully God.

Similarly, false religions of our day seek to emphasize or deemphasize some aspect of our Lord's nature. The beloved apostle makes it clear that the major area in which false religions fail is in reference to the person of Christ: "Who is the liar but the one who denies that Jesus is the Christ? This is the antichrist [that is, one who is against Christ], the one who denies the Father and the Son. No one who denies the Son has the Father" (1 Jn 2:22-23 NRSV).

John makes it clear that Christians can learn to recognize spiritual counterfeits:

> Dear friends, do not believe every spirit, but test the spirits to see whether they are from God; because many false prophets

> have gone out into the world. This is how you can recognize the Spirit of God: Every spirit that acknowledges that Jesus Christ has come in the flesh is from God, but every spirit that does not acknowledge Jesus Christ is not from God. This is the spirit of the antichrist, which you have heard is coming and even now is already in the world. (1 Jn 4:1-3)

Besides distorting Jesus' nature, false religions typically teach that a person must somehow merit the salvation of God. Some deed or rite is required to make a person part of God's kingdom, declared innocent before a righteous Judge. This false teaching places devotees under the control of the group and elicits labor needed to spread the group's message. Such thinking is foreign to the Bible's teaching of God's grace. There is no doubt that humble obedience is the expected response of a child of God, but it in no way determines a person's standing before God in regard to redemption or justification.

The apostle Paul, like John, articulated a basis to distinguish truth from error. In Galatians, probably his first letter, he writes that denial of salvation by grace alone is an evidence of error. He was concerned about a group of Jews who taught that in order to be saved one had to perform works in addition to believing in Christ. Paul declared that if even an angel from heaven should preach another gospel besides salvation by grace through faith alone, he deserved God's condemnation (Gal 1:6-10).

Today various new religions deny the true humanity of Jesus, dispute his incarnation or make him less than true God, coequal with the Father. These groups also want to add something to our salvation—to be saved requires something other than belief in Jesus. Spiritual counterfeits always involve mistakes on these cornerstones of Christian faith.

EQUIPPED FOR MINISTRY

To recognize erroneous teachings is not enough; we must be able to answer the questions posed when unorthodox groups come to our door or when we seek to evangelize them. Not only must we identify their mistakes in interpreting Scripture, but we must be familiar with the true doctrines of the Bible. Training on recognizing counterfeit dollar bills begins with lessons on how to identify genuine dollars; only afterward are trainees shown counterfeits. This is why throughout this book I have outlined the biblical basis for key Christian doctrines.

Though alternative religious groups are in error on a number of subjects, in our responses we must be careful to focus on major Christian doctrines and not be distracted by peripheral issues. For example, the Jehovah's Witnesses hold unusual perspectives on blood transfusions and the celebration of holidays, but these are not the matters we should take up in debate or discussion with them. Our focus must remain on the person of Christ and the nature of justification.

PROTECTING OURSELVES FROM ERROR

Scripture points to several ways for Christians to guard themselves from false teachings.

The work of the Holy Spirit. 1 John 2:20, 27 says we are protected by the anointing of the Spirit of God. But what does John mean by this? The apostle says that the believers he is writing to had an anointing from the Holy Spirit so that they did not need anyone to teach them. John had taught them about Jesus, and that teaching had been confirmed in their lives by the indwelling of the Holy Spirit.

Christians today likewise have the witness of the Holy Spirit when Jesus enters our life. The Spirit bears witness to the truth Christ has presented in the gospel (1 Jn 5:6), that by believing in him we are children of God. No one should be able to steal that witness from us.

Knowing the core of Christian theology. Another means of protection is careful exploration of what a given group teaches about Christ's nature and about salvation. Though there are other important doctrines that may need to be explored, such as their view of Scripture, the Holy Spirit, the Trinity or the church, these matters will usually surface in light of teachings regarding the person of Christ and the matter of salvation.

Recognizing Scripture's sole authority. A third way to avoid falling into doctrinal error is to place all doctrinal teaching under the scrutiny of the Word of God. The Bereans subjected Paul's teaching to the Hebrew Scriptures to determine whether his teaching was true or not and were commended for doing so (Acts 17:10-12).

Paul urged Timothy to pay special attention to sound doctrine. By doing so he would be able to save himself and those who heard his teaching. For Timothy to be able to deliver himself and the Christians under his care from false teaching, said Paul, he must be established in the apostle's teaching. He must not dabble in new ideas, vacillating between different opinions (1 Tim 4:16—5:2; 2 Tim 3:17; 4:1-4).

The Old Testament says prophets were to be judged true or false based on their fidelity to the revealed Word of God. The same is true in the New Testament (1 Cor 14:26-40).

Only the Scripture is able to lead the Christian into maturity (2 Tim 3:16-17); thus Christians must, above all, know Scripture. This ministry has continued from Paul's day to the church today (2 Tim 2:2).

The church's tradition. "The tradition" of the doctrine of Christ and the faith once for all given to the saints (1 Cor 15:1-11; Jude 3) is a biblically based source of protection. The church universal has held common doctrine for the last two thousand years, articulated in the Apostles' Creed, the Nicene Creed and the Chalcedon Creed. One should not lightly set this doctrine aside for new ideas, for one probably does so to one's peril.

We are too readily impressed with the latest idea; we tend to believe that there is always need for change. But being current does not make an idea correct, nor is change always for the good. For protection from false doctrines there is no substitute for being thoroughly versed in the Word of God, reliant on the Spirit's witness to its truth, and in harmony with the orthodox church through the ages.

Members of various groups have come to my (Wayne's) door on several occasions. In conversation with them I've been unwilling to get embroiled in discussions of peripheral issues. I have talked about who Jesus is and the way to salvation he provides. The truth of Christianity ultimately stands or falls on these two pivotal doctrines.

How Do We Minister to Members of Unorthodox Groups?

The key to effectively ministering to those ensnared by an unorthodox group is to follow the teaching of 2 Timothy 2:23-26:

> Don't have anything to do with foolish and stupid arguments, because you know they produce quarrels. And the Lord's servant must not quarrel; instead, he must be kind to everyone, able to teach, not resentful. To those who oppose him he must gently instruct, in the hope that God will grant them repentance leading them to a knowledge of the truth, and that they will come to their senses and escape from the trap of the devil, who has taken them captive to do his will.

It may be interesting to debate whether we should accept blood transfusions (Jehovah's Witnesses) or participate in Mormon rituals or avoid places of entertainment (United Pentecostals). But it is essential to concentrate on doctrinal points that relate to the person's eternal destiny if we are to point them to Christ's saving work.

Walter Martin is reported to have said that the average Christian of twenty years could be tied in knots in a matter of minutes by a recent convert to the Jehovah's Witnesses. Perhaps many Christians shy away from evangelizing unorthodox groups' members because they feel inadequate. This should not be. Believers need to be able to teach the Word to any they meet (1 Pet 3:15) but may only do so by a commitment to study the Word of God: "Do your best to present yourself to God as one approved, a worker who does not need to be ashamed, and who correctly [handles] the word of truth" (2 Tim 2:15). The best way to overcome hesitancy or embarrassment and to become confident and bold is to be knowledgeable in the Scripture.

Our duty is not to cut notches on our Bibles to mark how often we have devastated "the enemy" or won debates with men and women from various groups. Our responsibility is to bring them to Christ. This requires a servant's attitude.

Hank Hanegraaff, concerned for the leaders of the Worldwide Church of God, sought to show them that he was truly interested in helping them know Christ's truth rather than winning an argument with them. His care paid wonderful spiritual dividends, as the leaders of that group reversed their theological positions and embraced the orthodox teachings of the church.

Members of new religious movements are told that Christians are against them; often they thrive on a martyr complex. We must not fulfill their stereotypes of us. Generally people do not join a religious group because they are attracted to its doctrines; rather, they are in need of someone who shows concern, who offers friendship and fellowship, someone who takes away their loneliness. We need to approach these people as straying sheep who need to find the Shepherd of their soul. We need to convince them that we care about them but also help them see that seeking the truth is more important than the facile friendships formed in their group. Friendship not based on honesty and truth is not true friendship.

If we follow these guidelines as we speak to people, God may indeed grant them repentance and lead them to the truth. We must work and pray to this end.

NOTES

Chapter 1: Introduction

[1]Blaise Pascal, quoted in Thomas V. Morris, *Making Sense of It All: Pascal and the Meaning of Life* (Grand Rapids: Eerdmans, 1992), p. 16.

[2]Bruce L. Shelley, *Church History in Plain Language* (Dallas: Word, 1995), p. 47.

[3]Walter Martin is reported to have made this statement often in public, but it cannot be found in his writings according to Bob and Gretchen Passantino, friends of Walter Martin and editors of Martin's book *Kingdom of the Cults* (phone interview, April 6, 2003).

[4]See James W. Sire, *Scripture Twisting: Twenty Ways the Cults Misread the Bible* (Downers Grove, Ill.: InterVarsity Press, 1980).

Chapter 2: Revelation

[1]Carl F. H. Henry, *God, Revelation and Authority* (Waco, Tex.: Word, 1976), 2:8.

[2]John Calvin *Institutes of the Christian Religion* 1.3.4.

[3]Louis Berkhof, *Systematic Theology* (Grand Rapids: Eerdmans, 1946), p. 34.

[4]For more information see Bruce A. Demarest, "Revelation, General," and Carl F. H. Henry "Revelation, Special," in *Evangelical Dictionary of Theology*, ed. Walter A. Elwell (Grand Rapids: Baker, 1984), pp. 944-48.

[5]The Roman Catholic Church adds fourteen books, known as the Apocrypha, to the Old Testament. The world *apocrypha* means "hidden." The apocryphal writings were certainly known among the Jews of Jesus' day, but they did not consider them authoritative or canonical. Jesus himself quoted only from the Old Testament books generally accepted by the Jews as God's Word.

[6]See parts 2-3 of Norman L. Geisler and William E. Nix, *A General Introduction to the Bible* (Chicago: Moody Press, 1986).

[7]Leonard J. Coppes, "Neum," in *Theological Wordbook of the Old Testament*, ed. R. Laird Harris, Gleason L. Archer Jr. and Bruce K. Waltke (Chicago: Moody Press, 1980), 2:541.

[8]Charles L. Feinberg, "Amar," in *Theological Wordbook of the Old Testament*, ed. R. Laird Harris, Gleason L. Archer Jr. and Bruce K. Waltke (Chicago: Moody Press, 1980), 1:54-55.

[9]Eduard Schweizer, "θεόπνευστος," in *Theological Dictionary of the New Testament*, ed. Gerhard Kittel and Gerhard Friedrich, 10 vols. (Grand Rapids: Eerdmans, 1968-1976), 6:454.

[10]One example can be found in William Mitchell Ramsay, *St. Paul, the Traveller and the Roman Citizen*, 14th ed. (London: Hodder & Stoughton, 1925), pp. 7-8.

[11]For examples see Josh McDowell, *Evidence That Demands a Verdict*, rev. ed. (San Bernardino, Calif.: Here's Life, 1979), pp. 325-59.

[12]Geisler and Nix, *General Introduction to the Bible*, p. 46.

[13]John H. Gerstner, *The Rational Biblical Theology of Jonathan Edwards* (Powhatan, Va.: Berea, 1991), 1:112-13.

[14]David L. Edwards and John Stott, *Evangelical Essentials: A Liberal-Evangelical Dialogue* (Downers Grove, Ill.: InterVarsity Press, 1988), p. 92.

[15]See Norman L. Geisler, "Explaining Hermeneutics: A Commentary on the Chicago Statement on Biblical Hermeneutics," in *Hermeneutics, Inerrancy and the Bible*, ed. Earl D. Radmacher and Robert D. Preus (Grand Rapids: Zondervan, 1984), pp. 901-3.

[16]Karl Barth, *The Word of God and the Word of Man,* trans. Douglas Horton (London: Hodder & Stoughton, 1928), p. 43.

[17]R. Laird Harris, *Inspiration and Canonicity of the Bible,* Contemporary Evangelical Perspectives (Grand Rapids: Zondervan, 1969), pp. 102-3.

[18]See Geisler and Nix, *General Introduction to the Bible,* pp. 387-88.

[19]Ibid., pp. 388-94.

[20]Carsten Peter Thiede, "Papyrus Magdalen Greek 17 (Gregory-Aland P64): A Reappraisal," *Tyndale Bulletin* 46 (May 1995): 29-42.

[21]F. F. Bruce, *The New Testament Documents: Are They Reliable?* (Downers Grove, Ill.: InterVarsity Press, 1960), p. 15.

[22]Edwards and Stott, *Evangelical Essentials,* pp. 102-3.

[23]Geisler and Nix, *General Introduction to the Bible,* p. 388.

[24]Charles C. Ryrie, "Illumination," in *Dictionary of Evangelical Theology,* ed. Walter A. Elwell (Grand Rapids: Baker Academic, 2001), p. 502.

[25]See James W. Sire, *Scripture Twisting: Twenty Ways the Cults Misread the Bible* (Downers Grove, Ill.: InterVarsity Press, 1980).

[26]James Talmage, *A Study of the Articles of Faith,* 26th ed. (Salt Lake City: Church of Jesus Christ of Latter-day Saints, 1948), p. 236.

[27]Bruce McConkie, *Mormon Doctrine* (Salt Lake City: Bookcraft, 1977), p. 764.

[28]Ibid., p. 383.

[29]Orson Pratt, "The Bible and Tradition, Without Further Revelation, an Insufficient Guide," *Divine Authenticity of the Book of Mormon,* no. 3 (December 1, 1850): 47, reprinted in *Orson Pratt's Works* (Orem, Utah: Grandin, 1990), p. 62.

[30]Ibid., pp. 62-63.

[31]Joseph Fielding Smith, *Doctrine and Salvation: Sermons and Writings* (Salt Lake City: Bookcraft, 1956), 3:190-91.

[32]*Apostasy and Restoration* (Salt Lake City: Church of Jesus Christ of Latter-day Saints, n.d.).

[33]William A. Morton, *Why I Believe the Book of Mormon to Be the Word of God* (Salt Lake City: Church of Jesus Christ of Latter-day Saints, n.d.), p. 1.

[34]McConkie, *Mormon Doctrine,* pp. 764-65.

[35]"One of the great heresies of modern Christendom is the unfounded assumption that the Bible contains all of the inspired teaching now extant among men. Foreseeing that Satan would darken the minds of men in this way, and knowing that other scripture would come forth in the last days, Nephi prophesied that unbelieving Christians would reject the new revelation with the cry, 'A Bible! A Bible! We have got a Bible, and there cannot be any more Bible' " (ibid., p. 83).

[36]Ibid., p. 34.

[37]Ibid., pp. 764.

[38]Bruce R. McConkie, address at the Book of Mormon Symposium, Brigham Young University, August 18, 1978, quote by Ezra Taft Benson, *Ensign,* November 1984, p. 7.

[39]McConkie, *Mormon Doctrine,* p. 83.

[40]"Bible," in *Aid to Bible Understanding* (New York: Watchtower Bible and Tract Society, 1971), p. xx. Emphasis is in the original.

[41]*Watchtower,* May 1, 1957, p. 274.
[42]*Watchtower,* December 12, 1981, p. 27.
[43]*Watchtower,* December 1, 1981, p. 27.
[44]"They [orthodox Christians] say that it is sufficient to read the Bible exclusively, either alone or in small groups at home. But, strangely, through such 'Bible reading' they have reverted right back to the apostate doctrines that commentaries by Christendom's clergy were teaching 100 years ago" (*Watchtower,* August 15, 1981, pp. 28-29).
[45]"But proper and timely spiritual food was being dispensed by the group of true Christians who were anointed by God's holy spirit and were a part of what Jesus called the 'little flock.' . . . Using the 'faithful slave' and its present-day Governing Body [the Witnesses' twelve-man ruling board], God directs his organized people to make spiritual food, clothing, and shelter available to all who wish to have these provisions" (*Knowledge That Leads to Everlasting Life* [New York: Watchtower Bible and Tract Society, 1995], p. 161; note: except in rare instances, *Watchtower* authors are not identified).
[46]"Let us face the fact that no matter how much Bible reading we have done, we would never have learned the truth on our own. We would not have discovered the truth regarding Jehovah, his purposes and attributes, the meaning and importance of his name, the Kingdom, Jesus' ransom, the difference between God's organization and Satan's, nor why God has permitted wickedness" (*Watchtower,* December 1, 1990, p. 19).
[47]*Theocratic Aid to Kingdom Publishers* (Brooklyn, N.Y.: Watchtower Bible and Tract Society, 1945), pp. 249-50.
[48]*Qualified to Be Ministers* (Brooklyn, N.Y.: Watchtower Bible and Tract Society, 1967), p. 165.
[49]Bruce Metzger, "Jehovah's Witnesses and Jesus Christ," *Theology Today,* April 1953, p. 74.
[50]Mark L. Prophet and Elizabeth Clare Prophet, *The Lost Teachings of Jesus* (Livingston, Mont.: Summit University Press, 1988).
[51]Ibid., p. 1.
[52]Roy Masters, in *Walter Martin Debates Roy Masters* (San Juan Capistrano, Calif.: Christian Research Institute, n.d.), audiocassette 2.
[53]See Randall Price, *The Stones Cry Out: What Archaeology Reveals About the Truth of the Bible* (Eugene, Ore.: Harvest House, 1997); Gary K. Brantly, *Digging for Answers: Has Archaeology Disproved the Bible?* (Montgomery, Ala.: Apologetics Press, 1995); Kenneth A. Kitchen, *The Bible in Its World: The Bible and Archaeology Today* (Downers Grove, Ill.: InterVarsity Press, 1977); Donald J. Wiseman and Edwin Yamauchi, *Archaeology and the Bible: An Introductory Study* (Grand Rapids: Zondervan, 1979).
[54]Robert H. Countess, *The Jehovah's Witnesses' New Testament* (Phillipsburg, N.J.: Presbyterian & Reformed, 1982), p. 91.
[55]Bruce M. Metzger, *The Jehovah's Witnesses and Jesus Christ* (Princeton, N.J.: Theological Book Agency, 1953), p. 8. An excellent treatment of the more salient problems in Witness theology.
[56]"The Time Is at Hand," in *Studies in the Scriptures,* series 2 (Allegheny, Penn.: Watchtower Bible and Tract Society, 1906), p. 101.
[57]*Watchtower,* May 5, 1985, p. 4.
[58]Ibid.

Chapter 3: Who or What Is God?

[1]Robert L. Saucy, "God, Doctrine of," in *Evangelical Dictionary of Theology,* ed. Walter A. Elwell (Grand Rapids: Baker, 1984), pp. 459-64.

[2]Arthur C. Danto, "Persons," in *The Encyclopedia of Philosophy,* ed. Paul Edwards (New York: Macmillan, 1967), 6:110.

[3]What about those human beings, such as infants, the comatose and severly retarded people, who seem to lack these qualities or attributes? The essence of a human being is not derived from its accidents (e.g., sex, complexion, height, intelligence) but from the natural, substantive qualities of the human soul. A human being who is either an infant, in a comatose state or has brain dysfunction is no less a person than a fully functioning one. The potential is still there. Just as an automobile is still an automobile despite the fact that its motor is damaged or removed, so a person is still a person despite the loss or suppression of one or more of its accidental qualities. For more on this see Thomas Aquinas *Summa Theologica* Q 77, Arts. 6-8.

[4]The emotional nature of God has often been understood to be equivalent to human emotion, which is often fickle and subject to change. While God certainly has feelings, neither he nor his eternal plans for his creation are altered by events or persons within creation. He rather wills and acts in a manner consistent with his knowledge and wisdom. See the chapter on impassibility in Norman L. Geisler and H. Wayne House, *The Battle for God* (Grand Rapids: Kregel, 2001).

[5]Louis Berkhof, *Systematic Theology,* 3rd ed. (Grand Rapids: Eerdmans, 1946), pp. 57-58.

[6]Ibid., p. 59.

[7]Ibid.

[8]See Geisler and House, *Battle for God*, on the immutability of God.

[9]Wayne Grudem, *Systematic Theology: An Introduction to Biblical Doctrine* (Grand Rapids: Zondervan, 1994), p. 173.

[10]Herbert Wolf, "*'eḥad* [one]" in *Theological Wordbook of the Old Testament,* ed. R. Laird Harris, Gleason L. Archer Jr. and Bruce K. Waltke (Chicago: Moody Press, 1980), p. 30.

[11]Geoffrey W. Bromiley, "Trinity," in *Evangelical Dictionary of Theology,* ed. Walter A. Elwell (Grand Rapids: Baker, 1984), pp. 1112-13.

[12]There are many interpretations of the use of the plural pronoun here. John Wenham, *Genesis 1-15*, Word Biblical Commentary (Waco, Tex.: Word, 1987), pp. 27-28, lists six views ranging from a declaration of the Trinity to a statement of polytheism. As H. C. Leupold notes, "Those that hold that a reference to the Trinity is involved do not mean to say that the truth of the Holy Trinity is here fully and plainly revealed. But they do hold that God speaks out of the fullness of His attributes in a fashion which man could never employ. Behind such speaking lies the truth of the Holy Trinity" (*Exposition of Genesis*, 2 vols. [Grand Rapids: Baker, 1979], 1:86; see also Gerhard Hasel, "The Meaning of 'Let Us' in Genesis 1:26," *Andrews University Seminary Studies* 13 [1975]: 58-66).

[13] Wenham, *Genesis,* p. 85.

[14]The purpose of church councils was not to invent new doctrines but to clearly and formally set forth the doctrines that Christians already believed. Although the Trinity was not clearly formulated until the Athanasian Creed, its doctrinal building blocks were already being acknowledged by Christians as early as the first century.

[15]Grudem, *Systematic Theology,* p. 267.

[16]Ibid.

[17]Often this expression of monism tends to be pantheistic, viewing the physical universe surrounding us as God.

[18]Mary Baker Eddy, *Science and Health, with Key to the Scriptures* (Boston: First Church of Christ, Scientist, 1994), p. 468. This section begins with a question: "What is the scientific statement of being?"

[19]John De Witt, *The Christian Science Way of Life* (Boston: Christian Science Publishing, 1962), pp. 43-44.

[20]Eddy, *Science and Health,* pp. 331-32.

[21]Charles Fillmore, *Metaphysical Bible Dictionary* (Unity Village, Mo.: Unity School of Christianity, 1931), p. 629.

[22]Helen Shucman, *A Course in Miracles,* vol. 2, *Workbook for Students* (Tiburon, Calif.: Foundation for Inner Peace, 1975), p. 92.

[23]Helen Shucman, *A Course in Miracles,* vol. 1, *Text* (Tiburon, Calif.: Foundation for Inner Peace, 1975), p. 165.

[24]Shucman, *Course in Miracles,* 2:92.

[25]Shucman, *Course in Miracles,* 1:136.

[26]Mark L. Prophet and Elizabeth Clare Prophet, *The Lost Teachings of Jesus* (Livingston, Mont.: Summit University Press, 1988), 1:56. The immediately preceding paragraph used the illustration of one drop of ocean having all the elements of the entire ocean.

[27]Ibid., 1:27.

[28]Brigham Young, *Journal of Discourses* (Salt Lake City: Church of Jesus Christ of Latter-day Saints, 1901), 7:333.

[29]Joseph Smith, *History of the Church* (Salt Lake City: Church of Jesus Christ of Latter-day Saints, 1901), 6:476.

[30]Ibid., 6:474.

[31]Bruce McConkie, *Mormon Doctrine* (Salt Lake City: Bookcraft, 1977), p. 752.

[32]Milton R. Hunter, *The Gospel Through the Ages* (Salt Lake City: Melchizedic Priesthood Course of Study, 1945-1946), pp. 114-15.

[33]Ibid., p. 387. See also *Doctrines and Covenants* (Salt Lake City: Church of Jesus Christ of Latter-day Saints, 1986), pp. 29, 33; Joseph Smith, *The Book of Abraham* (Salt Lake City: Church of Jesus Christ of Latter-day Saints, 1986), 3:18-23.

[34]W. Cleon Skousen, *The First 2000 Years* (Salt Lake City: Bookcraft, 1979), p. 355.

[35]Joseph Fielding Smith, *Teachings of the Prophet Joseph Smith* (Salt Lake City: Deseret, 1976), p. 372.

[36]McConkie, *Mormon Doctrine,* p. 270.

[37]Orson Pratt, "A Discourse by Elder Orson Pratt, February 18, 1855," *Journal of Discourses* (original ed. 1855; London: F. D. Richards, 1966), 2:345.

[38]McConkie, *Mormon Doctrine,* p. 577.

[39]Ibid., p. 321.

[40]Gregory A. Boyd, *Oneness Pentecostals and the Trinity* (Grand Rapids: Baker, 1992), pp. 27-28.

[41]David K. Bernard, *Essential Doctrines of the Bible* (Hazelwood, Mo.: Word Aflame, 1993), p. 7.

[42]Geerhardus Vos, *Biblical Theology: Old and New Testaments* (Grand Rapids: Eerdmans, 1948), p. 78.

[43]For a detailed examination of the problem of infinite regression and a good solution see William Lane Craig, *The Kalam Cosmological Argument* (New York: Barnes & Noble, 1979).

[44]*Let God Be True* (New York: Watchtower Bible and Tract Society, 1952), p. 111.

[45]Victor Paul Wierwille, *Jesus Is Not God* (New Knoxville, Ohio: American Christian, 1975), p. 12.

[46]Ibid., p. 11. Wierwille adds that Hinduism and Greek and Roman religions accept the idea of a trinity. Some Jehovah's Witness literature echoes this allegation, for example, *Let God Be True*, 2nd ed. (New York: Watchtower Bible and Tract Society, 1952), pp. 100-111.

[47]Robert M. Bowman, *Why You Should Believe in the Trinity* (Grand Rapids: Baker, 1989), p. 45.

Chapter 4: Jesus Christ

[1]Millard J. Erickson, *Christian Theology* (Grand Rapids: Baker, 1992), p. 684.

[2]Wayne Grudem, *Systematic Theology: An Introduction to Biblical Doctrine* (Grand Rapids: Zondervan, 1994), pp. 545-46. For one of the most comprehensive and extensive treatments of the subject of Christ's deity, see also Murray J. Harris, *Jesus as God* (Grand Rapids: Baker, 1992).

[3]See Grudem, *Systematic Theology*, p. 546.

[4]Ibid.

[5]Erickson, *Christian Theology*, pp. 703-4.

[6]See ibid., 705.

[7]Grudem, *Systematic Theology*, p. 535.

[8]See Erickson, *Christian Theology*, p. 706.

[9]Ibid.

[10]See Grudem, *Systematic Theology*, p. 530.

[11]Ibid., p. 558.

[12]Ibid., p. 562.

[13]Ibid., p. 563.

[14]Ibid.

[15]E. M. Yamauchi, "Gnosticism," in *New Dictionary of Theology*, ed. Sinclair B. Ferguson, David F. Wright and J. I. Packer (Downers Grove, Ill.: InterVarsity Press, 1988), p. 272.

[16]Ibid.

[17]Alister E. McGrath, "Tertullian on Patripassionism," in *The Christian Theology Reader*, ed. Alister E. McGrath (Oxford: Blackwell, 1995), p. 137.

[18]Ibid.

[19]Erickson, *Christian Theology*, p. 695.

[20]Arius, "A Letter of Arius to Eusebius," in *The Christian Theology Reader*, ed. Alister E. McGrath (Oxford: Blackwell, 1995), pp. 139-40.

[21]Grudem, *Systematic Theology*, p. 553.

[22]Irenaeus, "Against Heresies," in *The Christian Theology Reader*, ed. Alister E. McGrath (Oxford: Blackwell, 1995), pp. 136-37.

[23]Ibid., p. 137.

[24]Ibid., p. 134.

[25]Ibid.

[26]"Apollinarius of Laodicea," in *The Westminster Dictionary of Church History*, ed. Jerald C. Brauer et al. (Philadelphia: Westminster Press, 1971), p. 47.

[27]Erickson, *Christian Theology*, p. 715.

[28]Apollinarius of Laodicea, "On the Person of Christ," in *The Christian Theology Reader*, ed. Alister E. McGrath (Oxford: Blackwell, 1995), pp. 140-41.

[29]*Jehovah's Witnesses in the Twentieth Century* (New York: Watchtower Bible and Tract Society, 1989), p. 13.

[30]*You Can Live Forever in Paradise on Earth* (New York: Watchtower Bible and Tract Society, 1982), p. 58.

[31]*Should You Believe in the Trinity?* (New York: Watchtower Bible and Tract Society, 1989), p. 15.

[32]*Reasoning from the Scriptures* (New York: Watchtower Bible and Tract Society, 1985), p. 218.

[33]*You Can Live Forever*, p. 58.

[34]Ibid., p. 21.

[35]Ibid., pp. 39-40.

[36]Ibid., p. 40.

[37]Ibid., p. 63.

[38]Ibid., p. 138.

[39]*Insight on the Scriptures* (New York: Watchtower Bible and Tract Society, 1988), 1:1189.

[40]Francis J. Beckwith and Stephen E. Parrish, *See the Gods Fall: Four Rivals to Christianity* (Joplin, Mo.: College Free Press, 1997), p. 97.

[41]For an excellent discussion of this topic, see Jerald and Sandra Tanner's *Mormonism: Shadow or Reality* (Salt Lake City: Lighthouse Ministry, 1987). Although the doctrine of Adam-God, for example, is no longer taught openly among the LDS at large, neither is it—nor has it ever been—repudiated.

[42]Bruce R. McConkie, *Mormon Doctrine* (Salt Lake City: Bookcraft, 1977), p. 392.

[43]Ibid.

[44]Milton R. Hunter, *The Gospel Through the Ages* (Salt Lake City: Melchizedic Priesthood Course of Study, 1945-1946), p. 21.

[45]James E. Talmadge, *A Study of the Articles of Faith* (Salt Lake City: Church of Jesus Christ of Latter-day Saints, 1987), p. 472.

[46]Brigham Young, in *Journal of Discourses* (Salt Lake City: Church of Jesus Christ of Latter-day Saints, 1901), 4:259-60.

[47]Orson Hyde, in *Journal of Discourses* (Salt Lake City: Church of Jesus Christ of Latter-day Saints, 1901), 2:81.

[48]"Why We Proclaim Jesus Did Not Pre-exist!" *Herald of the Coming Age* 21, no. 1 (n.d.): 2.

[49]*The Constitution of the Glendale Christadelphian Ecclesia* (Glendale, Calif.: privately published, 1937), p. 18.

[50]"Why We Proclaim," p. 13.

[51]*God Is One Not Three* (n.p., n.d.), p. 9.

[52]"Why We Proclaim," p. 2.

[53]*Constitution*, p. 11.

[54]"Why We Proclaim," p. 3.

[55]"Christ's Death and Your Salvation," *Herald of the Coming Age* 18, no. 5 (n.d.): 76.

[56]Ibid., pp. 69-70.

[57]Quoted in Walter Martin, "The Theosophical Society," rev. and ed. Gretchen Passantino, in *The Kingdom of the Cults*, rev. ed., gen. ed. Hank Hanegraaff (Minneapolis: Bethany House, 1997), p. 291. See also Annie Besant, *Is Theosophy Anti-Christian?* (London: Theosophical Society, 1901), p. 16.

[58]Quoted in Martin, "Theosophical Society," pp. 291-92 (see also Besant, *Is Theosophy Anti-Christian?*).

[59]Mary Baker Eddy, *Science and Health, with Key to the Scriptures* (Boston: Trustees Under the Will of Mary Baker G. Eddy, 1934), p. 196; in the 1881 edition, p. 473.

[60]Ernest Holmes, *The Science of Mind*, rev. ed. (New York: Dodd, Mead, 1938), p. 603.

[61]Ibid.

[62]*Unity Magazine* 57, no. 5: 464; *Unity Magazine* 72, no. 2: 8.

[63]Mary Baker Eddy, *Science and Health,with Key to the Scriptures* (Boston: First Church of Christ, Scientist, 1906), p. 332.

[64]Holmes, *Science of Mind*, p. 367.

[65]*What Unity Teaches* (Lee's Summit, Mo.: Unity School of Christianity, n.d.), p. 3.

[66]*Meet the United Pentecostal Church International* (Hazelwood, Mo.: Word Aflame, n.d.), p. 59.

[67]David K. Bernard, *The Oneness of God*, Series in Pentecostal Theology (Hazelwood, Mo.: Word Aflame, 1983), 1:66.

[68]*Meet the United Pentecostal Church*, p. 59.

[69]For a full discussion of this issue see Roy B. Zuck's "Open Letter to a Jehovah's Witness" (Chicago: Moody Press, 1978), pp. 8-11, or James W. Sire, *Scripture Twisting: Twenty Ways the Cults Misread the Bible* (Downers Grove, Ill.: InterVarsity Press, 1980), pp. 161-63.

[70]See also John 4:21-26. Others claimed that Jesus was the Christ—for example, in Matthew 16:16-20; John 11:27; 20:31; Acts 2:36; 9:22; 17:3; 18:5.

[71]David K. Bernard, *The Oneness of God*, Series in Pentecostal Theology (Hazelwood, Mo.: Word Aflame, 1983), 1:15.

[72]Ibid., 1:57.

Chapter 5: Jesus' Resurrection

[1]Origen *De principis* II.10, in *The Christian Theology Reader*, ed. Alister E. McGrath (Oxford: Blackwell, 1995), p. 357.

[2]Everett Ferguson, "Origen," in *New Dictionary of Theology*, ed. Sinclair B. Ferguson, David F. Wright and J. I. Packer (Downers Grove, Ill.: InterVarsity Press, 1988), p. 481.

[3]Ibid., p. 482.

[4]Ibid. Note that the issue here is not the allegorical method itself but Origen's way of using it.

[5]Wayne Grudem, *Systematic Theology* (Grand Rapids: Zondervan, 1994), p. 608-10.

[6]Earl D. Radmacher, Ronald B. Allen and H. Wayne House, "Facts About the Resurrection," in *Nelson's New Illustrated Bible Commentary*, ed. Earl D. Radmacher, Ronald B. Allen and H. Wayne House (Nashville: Thomas Nelson, 1999), p. 1485.

[7]Grudem, *Systematic Theology*, p. 615.

[8]Radmacher, Allen and House, "Facts About the Resurrection," p. 1487.

[9]William Lane Craig, *Reasonable Faith: Christian Truth and Apologetics*, rev. ed. (Wheaton, Ill.: Crossway, 1994), p. 264.

[10]Ibid., pp. 264-65.

[11]James E. Talmadge, *A Study of the Articles of Faith* (Salt Lake City: Church of Jesus Christ of Latter-day Saints, 1987), pp. 385-86; see also Bruce R. McConkie, *What the Mormons Think of Christ* (Salt Lake City: Deseret, 1973), p. 2.

[12]McConkie, *What the Mormons Think*, p. 2.

[13]*You Can Live Forever in Paradise on Earth* (New York: Watchtower Bible and Tract Society, 1982), p. 172.

[14]Ibid., p. 143.

[15]*From Paradise Lost to Paradise Regained* (New York: Watchtower Bible and Tract Society, n.d.), p. 144.

[16]*Let God Be True*, rev. ed. (New York: Watchtower Bible and Tract Society, 1952), p. 40.

[17]Ibid., p. 41.

[18]Mary Baker Eddy, *Science and Health, with Key to the Scriptures* (Boston: First Church of Christ, Scientist, 1994), p. 593.

[19]Ibid., p. 44.

[20]Ibid., pp. 45-46.

[21]Eddy, *Science and Health*, p. 34.

[22]D. R. McConnell, *A Different Gospel* (Peabody, Mass.: Hendrickson, 1995), p. 166, quoted in Richard Abanes, "The Word Faith Movement," in Walter Martin, *The Kingdom of the Cults*, rev. ed., gen. ed. Hank Hanegraaff (Minneapolis: Bethany House, 1997), p. 514.

[23]Kenneth Copeland, "Jesus Our Lord of Glory," *Believers Voice of Victory*, April 1982, p. 3, quoted in Abanes, "Word Faith Movement," p. 499.

[24]Ibid.

[25]Copeland, quoted in Abanes, "Word Faith Movement," p. 502; also quoted in McConnell, *Different Gospel*, p. 120.

[26]Helen Shucman, *A Course in Miracles*, vol. 1, *Text* (Tiburon, Calif.: Foundation for Inner Peace, 1975), p. 87.

[27]Ibid., vol. 3, *Manual for Teachers*, p. 65.

[28]Ibid., 1:396.

[29]Max Heindel, *The Rosicrucian Cosmo-conception, or Mystic Christianity* (1929; reprint Oceanside, Calif.: Rosicrucian Fellowship, 1974), p. 57.

[30]Ibid., pp. 381, 408-9.

[31]"This is love: not that we loved God, but that he loved us and sent his Son as an atoning sacrifice for our sins" (1 Jn 4:10). See also Isaiah 53:10; Matthew 27:46; Mark 15:34; John 10:17-18; Romans 1:18, 24, 26, 28.

Chapter 6: The Holy Spirit

[1]J. I. Packer, "Holy Spirit," in *New Dictionary of Theology*, ed. Sinclair B. Ferguson, David F. Wright and J. I. Packer (Downers Grove, Ill.: InterVarsity Press, 1988), p. 318.

[2]Millard J. Erickson, *Christian Theology* (Grand Rapids: Baker, 1992), p. 851.

[3]Ibid., p. 848.

[4]Ibid., pp. 848-50.

[5]Ibid., p. 850.

[6]Ibid.

[7]Ibid., pp. 850-51.

[8]The phrase "and the Son" was added to the Nicene Creed at the Council of Constantinople in 381 and is retained by Roman Catholic and Protestant churches today. It is not found in the version used by Eastern Orthodox churches. One of the most important issues in the Great Schism of 1054 was what was termed the *filioque:* did the Holy Spirit proceed from the Father alone as the East believed, or did he proceed from the Father and the Son as the West maintained? The Eastern Church wanted to ensure that the Father was regarded as having final authority over the activities of the other two members of the Trinity. The Western Church wanted to align the work of the Spirit with the Son.

[9]Charles Hodge, *Systematic Theology,* 3 vols. (Peabody, Mass.: Hendrickson, 1999), 1:522.

[10]Packer, "Holy Spirit," p. 316.

[11]Ibid.

[12]Ibid.

[13]Hodge, *Systematic Theology,* 1:522.

[14]Ibid.

[15]Packer, "Holy Spirit," pp. 316-17. See John 14:16—16:15; Acts 2:4; 8:29; 13:2; 16:6-7; 21:11; Romans 8; 1 Corinthians 12:4-6; 2 Corinthians 13:14; Galatians 4:6; 5:17-18; Ephesians 1:3-14; 2:18; 4:4-6; 2 Thessalonians 2:13-14; Hebrews 3:7; 10:15; 1 Peter 1:2, 11; Revelation 1:4-5; 2:7.

[16]Packer, "Holy Spirit," p. 317.

[17]Ibid.

[18]See Wayne Grudem, *Systematic Theology* (Grand Rapids: Zondervan, 1994), p. 635.

[19]See ibid., pp. 637-38.

[20]Ibid., p. 638.

[21]Ibid., pp. 644-45.

[22]Hodge, *Systematic Theology,* 1:527.

[23]Ibid.

[24]James E. Talmadge, *A Study of the Articles of Faith* (Salt Lake City: Church of Jesus Christ of Latter-day Saints, 1987), p. 488.

[25]James E. Talmadge, *The Articles of Faith* (Salt Lake City: Church of Jesus Christ of Latter-day Saints, 1952), p. 115, quoted in Bill McKeever and Kurt Van Gorden, "Church of Jesus Christ of Latter-day Saints (The Mormons)," ed. Gretchen Passantino, in Walter Martin, *The Kingdom of the Cults,* rev. ed., gen. ed. Hank Hanegraaff (Minneapolis: Bethany House, 1997), p. 226.

[26]Ibid., quoting Talmadge, *Articles of Faith,* pp. 42-43.

[27]Parley P. Pratt, *Key to the Science of Theology* (1855; reprint Liverpool: F. D. Richards, 1978), pp. 24-25, 64.

[28]*Reasoning from the Scriptures* (New York: Watchtower Bible and Tract Society, 1985), p. 380.

[29]*Holy Spirit: The Force Behind the Coming New Order* (New York: Watchtower Bible and Tract Society, 1976), p. 11.

[30]*Should You Believe in the Trinity?* (Brooklyn, N.Y.: Watchtower Bible and Tract Society, 1997), electronic version.

[31]Ibid.

[32]Albert Pike, *Morals and Dogma of the Ancient and Accepted Scottish Rite of Freemasonry* (Charleston, N.C.: Supreme Council of the Thirty-third Degree for the Southern Jurisdiction of the United States, Ancient and Accepted Scottish Rite, 1917), p. 734.

[33]Ibid., p. 552.

[34]Helen Shucman, *A Course in Miracles,* vol. 3, *Manual for Teachers* (Tiburon, Calif.: Foundation for Inner Peace, 1975), p. 312.

[35]Ibid., vol. 1, *Text,* p. 312.

[36]Ibid., p. 68.

[37]Ibid., p. 223.

[38]Ibid., p. 377.

[39]Ernst Holmes and Fenwicke I. Holmes, *What Religious Science Teaches* (Los Angeles: Institute of Religious Science, 1944), p. 65.

[40]H. Emile Cady, *Lessons in Truth* (Kansas City, Mo.: Unity School of Christianity, 1939), p. 8.

[41]Mary Baker Eddy, *Science and Health, with Key to the Scriptures* (Boston: First Church of Christ, Scientist, 1994), p. 588.

[42]Walter Martin, *Kingdom of the Cults,* p. 267; the chapter this information is found in was updated, revised and edited by Gretchen Passantino and Cecil Price.

[43]Ibid., p. 268.

[44]Stephen E. Parrish, "Mormonism," in *See the Gods Fall* (Joplin, Mo.: College Press, 1997), chap. 3.

[45]*Awake!* December 8, 1973, p. 27.

[46]Erickson, *Christian Theology,* pp. 862-63.

Chapter 7: Humanity and Sin

[1]Charles Hodge, *Systematic Theology,* 3 vols. (Peabody, Mass.: Hendrickson, 1999), 2:96-97.

[2]Here we will not take up the argument as to whether human nature is bipartite or tripartite—that is, whether we are body and spirit or body, soul and spirit. It is enough to affirm the scriptural witness that human nature possesses both material and immaterial aspects. For a detailed discussion of this ongoing debate, see Wayne Grudem, *Systematic Theology: An Introduction to Biblical Doctrine* (Grand Rapids: Zondervan, 1994), pp. 472-83; Millard J. Erickson, *Christian Theology* (Grand Rapids: Baker, 1992), pp. 520-24. We will refer to humans as comprising body and spirit (as synonomous with "soul").

[3]Grudem, *Systematic Theology,* p. 483.

[4]Ibid., p. 482.

[5]John Miley, *Systematic Theology* (1892-1894; reprint Peabody, Mass.: Hendrickson, 1989), 1:354.

[6]Erickson, *Christian Theology,* p. 497.

[7]Grudem, *Systematic Theology,* p. 442.

[8]Ibid.

[9]Ibid., p. 443.

[10]Ibid.

[11]Ibid.

[12]John Calvin, *Institutes of the Christian Religion,* ed. John T. McNeill, trans. Ford Lewis Battles, Library of Christian Classics (Philadelphia: Westminster Press, 1960), 1:246.

[13]Grudem, *Systematic Theology,* p. 491.

[14]Ibid.

[15]Ibid., p. 492.

[16]Ibid., p. 493.

[17]Erickson, *Christian Theology,* p. 603.

[18]Ibid., pp. 604-5.

[19]Ibid., p. 611.

[20]Milton R. Hunter, *The Gospel Through the Ages* (Salt Lake City: Melchizedic Priesthood Course of Study, 1945-1946), pp. 126-27.

[21]Ibid., p. 127.

[22]Ibid.

[23]Ibid., p. 128.

[24]Ibid., pp. 128-29.

[25]James E. Talmadge, *A Study of the Articles of Faith* (Salt Lake City: Church of Jesus Christ of Latter-day Saints, 1987), p. 476.

[26]J. F. Rutherford, *Life* (Brookly, N.Y.: Watchtower Bible and Tract Society, 1929), p. 194.

[27]*Insight on the Scriptures* (New York: Watchtower Bible and Tract Society, 1988), 1:597.

[28]*You Can Live Forever in Paradise on Earth* (New York: Watchtower Bible and Tract Society, 1982), p. 88.

[29]*Reasoning from the Scriptures* (New York: Watchtower Bible and Tract Society, 1985), p. 375.

[30]Ibid.

[31]Mary Baker Eddy, *Science and Health, with Key to the Scriptures* (Boston: First Church of Christ, Scientist, 1994), p. 339.

[32]Ernest Holmes, *The Science of Mind,* rev. ed. (New York: Dodd, Mead, 1938), p. 633.

[33]Charles Fillmore, *Christian Healing* (Kansas City, Mo.: Unity School of Christianity, 1909), p. 26.

[34]Mary Baker Eddy, *Miscellaneous Writings 1883-1896* (Boston: Trustees Under the Will of Mary Baker G. Eddy, 1896), p. 27.

[35]Holmes, *Science of Mind,* p. 633.

[36]*Unity Magazine* 47, no. 5 (n.d.): 403.

[37]Eddy, *Science and Health,* p. 475.

[38]Holmes, *Science of Mind,* pp. 33-34.

[39]Fillmore, *Christian Healing,* pp. 106-7.

[40]Max Heindel, *The Rosicrucian Philosophy in Questions and Answers,* 2nd ed. (Oceanside, Calif.: Rosicrucian Fellowship, 1910), p. 195.

[41]Khei (George Winslow Plummer), *Rosicrucian Fundamentals: An Exposition of the Rosicrucian Synthesis of Religion, Science and Philosophy* (1920; reprint Kila, Mont.: Kessenger, 1997), pp. 5-6.

[42]*The Ancient and Mystical Order of the Rosae Crusis (AMORC)* (San Jose, Calif.: Supreme Grand Lodge of AMORC, n.d.), 7.

[43]Trance channeler Kevin Ryerson talking with "Vassy," a Russian mystic, about good and evil—quoted in Shirley MacLaine, *Dancing in the Light* (New York: Bantam Books, 1985), p. 247.

[44]The spirit "John" speaking through Ryerson, in ibid., p. 256.

[45]Anthropologist Wade Davis, author of *The Serpent and the Rainbow,* says that "voodoo is good, [and] Haiti will teach you that good and evil are one" (quoted in *Seattle Times*, January 31, 1988).

[46]Francis J. Beckwith, "The New Age Movement," in *See the Gods Fall* (Joplin, Mo.: College Press, 1997), pp. 216-17.

[47]Ibid., p. 217.

[48]Ibid.

[49]Ibid., chap. 6.

[50]Ibid. Note the inherent contradiction of the New Age position regarding good and evil: if they do not exist, only illumination and ignorance, then why the tortuous, cyclical pattern of death and rebirth in order to purge the soul of all evil through suffering myriad tragedies, administered through the law of karma? Any proposition that is invalid should be rejected for what it is, nonsense.

[51]Victor P. Wierwille, *Power for Abundant Living* (New Knowxville, Ohio: American Christian, 1971), pp. 231-32.

[52]Ibid., p. 233.

[53]Ibid., p. 237.

[54]Ibid., pp. 244-45.

[55]Ibid., 239.

[56]Victor P. Wierwille, *Are the Dead Alive Now?* (Old Greenwich, Conn.: Devin-Adair, 1971), pp. 109-10.

[57]Ibid., pp. 110-11.

[58]See the discussion of *firstborn* in the section "Responding to the Cults: Jehovah's Witnesses" in chapter four.

[59]Many more verses could be cited, but refer to Genesis 3:16-24; Romans 3:23; 5:12-15, 17-19; 8:19-22; Ephesians 2:1-5; 1 John 3:4.

[60]Some orthodox Christians do not believe in an immortal soul, and some espouse the idea of "soul sleep" at death. They believe human beings will achieve immortality in the resurrection. We do not quarrel with these Christians but beg to differ on this question in light of the biblical witness.

[61]Erickson, *Christian Theology,* p. 524

[62]Ibid., pp. 217-20. See also the author's further refutation of reincarnation, pp. 220-28.

[63]We are not taking issue with the tripartite view of the human being (body, soul and spirit). Many within Christian orthodoxy have held to the tripartite view.

[64]Irenaeus *Adversus haereses* 4.38.1, quoted in *The Christian Theology Reader,* ed. Alister E. McGrath (Oxford: Blackwell, 1995), p. 212.

[65]Ibid.

Chapter 8: The Atonement

[1]Millard J. Erickson, *Christian Theology* (Grand Rapids: Baker, 1992), p. 805.

[2]Wayne Grudem, *Systematic Theology: An Introduction to Biblical Doctrine* (Grand Rapids: Zondervan, 1994), p. 568. The following discussion relies heavily on Grudem.

[3]Ibid., p. 569.

[4]See ibid., pp. 569-70.

[5]Ibid., pp. 570-81.

[6]Ibid., p. 573.

[7]Ibid., pp. 573-74.

[8]Refer to Leon Morris's work *The Atonement* (Downers Grove, Ill.: InterVarsity Press, 1983), which represents perhaps the finest example of evangelical scholarship in this area. See also Leon Morris, *The Apostolic Preaching of the Cross*, 3rd ed. (London: Tyndale Press, 1965), pp. 114-213, and Grudem's *Systematic Theology*, chap. 12, esp. pp. 205-7.

[9]Grudem, *Systematic Theology*, p. 575. The bias of certain scholars against the idea of God's wrath in the New Testament is evident in the RSV's translation of *hilasmos* as "expiation," which means "an action that cleanses from sin" but does not include the concept of turning away God's wrath.

[10]Bruce R. McConkie, *Mormon Doctrine* (Salt Lake City: Bookcraft, 1977), pp. 63, 65, 377.

[11]James E. Talmadge, *A Study of the Articles of Faith* (Salt Lake City: Church of Jesus Christ of Latter-day Saints, 1987), p. 89.

[12]Ibid., pp. 478-79.

[13]Brigham Young, in *Journal of Discourses* (Salt Lake City: Church of Jesus Christ of Latter-day Saints, 1901), 3:247; 4:219-20.

[14]Walter Martin, *The Kingdom of the Cults*, rev. ed., gen. ed. Hank Hanegraaff (Minneapolis: Bethany House, 1999), pp. 236-37.

[15]Ibid., p. 237.

[16]J. F. Rutherford, *Life* (Brooklyn, N.Y.: Watchtower Bible and Tract Society, 1929), p. 199.

[17]Ibid., p. 206.

[18]Martin, *Kingdom of the Cults*, p. 152.

[19]*Should You Believe in the Trinity?* (Brooklyn: Watchtower Bible and Tract Society, 1997), electronic version.

[20]Helen Shucman, *A Course in Miracles*, vol. 1, *Text* (Tiburon, Calif.: Foundation for Inner Peace, 1975), p. 6.

[21]Ibid., p. 9.

[22]Ibid., p. 32.

[23]Ibid., p. 33.

[24]*The Urantia Book* (Chicago: Urantia Foundation, 1955), p. 1.

[25]Ibid., p. 2084.

[26]Ibid., p. 2002.

[27]Ibid., p. 60.

[28]"Christ's Death and Your Salvation," *Herald of the Coming Age* 18, no. 5 (n.d.): 70-71.

[29]Ibid., p. 71.

[30]Ibid., p. 152.

[31]See Albert Ritschl, *The Christian Doctrine of Justification and Reconciliation* (Edinburgh: T & T Clark, 1900), 3:473.

[32]Erickson, *Christian Theology,* pp. 817-18.
[33]Ibid., p. 818.
[34]Ibid.

Chapter 9: Salvation

[1]Norman Geisler and Abdul Saleeb, *Answering Islam* (Grand Rapids: Baker, 1993), pp. 123-24.

[2]Norman Geisler, "Zen Buddhism," in *Baker Encyclopedia of Christian Apologetics,* ed. Norman Geisler (Grand Rapids: Baker, 1999), p. 791.

[3]Norman Geisler, "Hinduism, Vendanta," in *Baker Encyclopedia of Christian Apologetics,* ed. Norman Geisler (Grand Rapids: Baker, 1999), p. 317.

[4]*Salvation* is a broad term that sometimes refers to justification (our position before God), sometimes sanctification (our spiritual life) and sometimes glorification (our resurrection and presence with God). Most often we think of the first aspect when using the word. See the illuminating study of the aspects of salvation by Earl D. Radmacher, *Salvation* (Nashville: Word, 2000).

[5]See Wayne Grudem, *Systematic Theology: An Introduction to Biblical Doctrine* (Grand Rapids: Zondervan, 1994), p. 699.

[6]Millard J. Erickson, *Christian Theology* (Grand Rapids: Baker, 1992), p. 942. The following discussion is indebted to this section of Erickson's work.

[7]Ibid., p. 943.

[8]It is most likely better to translate this "born of the wind." Water and wind are symbols of God's new life or regenerative work in the Old Testament and in Jewish thought. The background of this passage, which Nicodemus should have known, is the riddle of Proverbs 30:3-5 (compare Jn 3:12-13) and the prophecies of spiritual birth for Israel in Isaiah 44:3-5 and Ezekiel 37:9-10. Here we see Jesus' complete familiarity with prevailing Jewish thought.

[9]Erickson, *Christian Theology,* p. 944.

[10]Ibid.

[11]Grudem, *Systematic Theology,* p. 701. I follow this section of Grudem's work in the ensuing discussion.

[12]See the excellent study of the difference between justification and sanctification in Gary Derickson and Earl Radmacher, *The Disciplemaker: What Matters Most to Jesus* (Salem, Ore.: Charis, 2001).

[13]Erickson, *Christian Theology,* p. 955.

[14]Bruce R. McConkie, *Mormon Doctrine* (Salt Lake City: Bookcraft, 1977), p. 62.

[15]Bruce R. McConkie, *What the Mormons Think of Christ* (Salt Lake City: Deseret, 1973), pp. 27-39.

[16]See Walter R. Martin, *The Kingdom of the Cults,* rev. ed., gen. ed. Hank Hanegraaff (Minneapolis: Bethany House, 1999), p. 239.

[17]Brigham Young, in *Journal of Discourses* (Salt Lake City: Church of Jesus Christ of Latter-day Saints, 1901), 12:100-101.

[18]Rosten Leo, *A Guide to the Religions of America* (New York: Simon & Schuster, 1963), p. 136.

[19]*Watchtower,* August 15, 1972, p. 492.

[20]*Watchtower,* July 1, 1947, p. 204.

[21]*Watchtower,* February 15, 1983, pp. 12-13.

[22]*Watchtower,* October 1, 1967, p. 591.

[23]*Life Everlasting: In Freedom of the Sons of God* (New York: Watchtower Bible and Tract Society, 1966), p. 400.

[24]Helen Shucman, *A Course in Miracles,* vol. 2, *Workbook for Students* (Tiburon, Calif.: Foundation for Inner Peace, 1975), p. 391.

[25]Shucman, *A Course in Miracles,* vol. 1, *Text,* p. 87.

[26]Raymond Allen et al., *Tennessee Craftsmen: Or, Masonic Textbook,* 14th ed. (Nashville: Tennessee Board of Custodians Members, 1963), p. 61.

[27]G. C. Huckaby, comp. *Louisiana Masonic Monitor of the Degrees of the Entered Apprentice, Fellow Craft and Master Mason,* 1941, pp. 44-45.

[28]Allen et al., *Tennessee Craftsmen,* p. 126.

[29]Joseph Fort Nelson, *The Builders: A Story and Study of Freemasonry* (Richmond, Va.: Macoy, 1951), p. 284.

[30]Henry C. Clausen, *Commentaries on Morals and Dogma* (San Diego: Supreme Council, 33, 1974), p. 157.

[31]Mary Baker Eddy, *Miscellaneous Writings 1883-1896* (Boston: Trustees Under the Will of Mary Baker G. Eddy, 1896), p. 261.

[32]Ernest Holmes, *The Science of Mind,* rev. ed. (New York: Dodd, Mead, 1938), p. 383.

[33]Charles Fillmore, *Christian Healing* (Kansas City, Mo.: Unity School of Christianity, 1909), p. 24.

[34]Mary Baker Eddy, *Science and Health, with Key to the Scriptures* (Boston: First Church of Christ, Scientist, 1994), p. 22.

[35]Holmes, *Science of Mind,* pp. 383-84.

[36]Norman Geisler, *Come Let Us Reason Together: An Introduction to Logical Thinking* (Grand Rapids: Baker, 1990), p. 91.

Chapter 10: Christ's Second Coming

[1]Augustine *On the Psalms* 96.14, in *Mark,* Ancient Christian Commentary on Scripture, ed. Thomas C. Oden and Christopher A. Hall (Downers Grove, Ill.: InterVarsity Press, 1998), p. 188.

[2]See Millard J. Erickson, *Christian Theology* (Grand Rapids: Baker, 1992), p. 1188.

[3]Examples are Albert Schweitzer, *The Quest of the Historical Jesus: A Critical Study of Its Progress from Reimarus to Wrede* (New York: Macmillan, 1964), pp. 368-69; Rudolf Bultmann, *Theology of the New Testament,* trans. Kendrick Grobel (New York: Scribner's, 1951), 1:5-6.

[4]Each of these views is examined in H. Wayne House, *Charts of Christian Theology and Doctrine* (Grand Rapids: Zondervan, 1992), pp. 129-36, and H. Wayne House and Randall Price, *Charts of Bible Prophecy* (Grand Rapids: Zondervan, 2002).

[5]Some in recent years have dated the book of Revelation before the destruction of Jerusalem; we find this view untenable but will not make the argument here.

[6]Clouds were associated with deity in ancient Near Eastern thinking.

[7]See S. H. Travis, "Eschatology," in *New Dictionary of Theology,* ed. Sinclair B. Ferguson, David F. Wright and J. I. Packer (Downers Grove, Ill.: InterVarsity Press, 1988), p. 230.

[8]*Unity Statement of Faith* 24 (Unity Village, Mo.: Unity School of Christianity, n.d.).

[9]Charles Fillmore, *The Twelve Powers of Man* (Unity Village, Mo.: Unity School of Christianity, 1931), p. 1.

[10]Mary Baker Eddy, *Science and Health, with Key to the Scriptures* (Boston: First Church of Christ, Scientist, 1994), p. 46.

[11]See J. Stafford Wright, "Sects," in *New Dictionary of Theology*, ed. Sinclair B. Ferguson, David F. Wright and J. I. Packer (Downers Grove, Ill.: InterVarsity Press, 1988), pp. 633-34.

[12]*Studies in the Scriptures*, series 2 (Allegheny, Penn.: Watchtower Bible and Tract Society, 1906), p. 101.

[13]*Let God Be True*, rev. ed. (New York: Watchtower Bible and Tract Society, 1952), p. 196.

[14]*Make Sure of All Things* (New York: Watchtower Bible and Tract Society, n.d.), p. 319.

[15]*You Can Live Forever in Paradise on Earth* (New York: Watchtower Bible and Tract Society, 1982), pp. 147, 150.

[16]*Make Sure of All Things*, p. 319.

[17]See Walter Martin, *The Kingdom of the Cults*, rev. ed., gen. ed. Hank Hanegraaff (Minneapolis: Bethany House Publishers, 1965), pp. 130-36.

[18]Quoted in ibid., p. 132 (italics added).

[19]Charles Taze Russell, *The Finished Mystery* (New York: Watchtower Bible and Tract Society, 1917), p. 485.

[20]*Watchtower*, July 15, 1924, p. 211.

[21]*Watchtower*, October 1, 1978, p. 31.

[22]*Watchtower*, May 14, 1984, p. 5.

[23]*Watchtower*, November 1, 1995, pp. 17-20.

[24]*Make Sure of All Things*, p. 321.

[25]Ibid.

[26]Seventh-day Adventists Answer Questions on Doctrine (Washington, D.C.: Review and Herald Publishing Association, 1957), p. 449.

[27]Ibid., pp. 451-52, 459.

[28]Martin, *Kingdom of the Cults*, pp. 521-88. The following discussion relies on this work.

[29]See Francis D. Nichol, *The Midnight Cry* (Washington, D.C.: Review and Herald, 1944), p. 35, quoted in Martin, *Kingdom of the Cults*, p. 521.

[30]Leroy E. Froom, *The Prophetic Faith of Our Fathers* (Takoma Park, Md.: Review and Herald, n.d.), 4:881, quoted in Martin, *Kingdom of the Cults*, pp. 525-26.

[31]Ellen G. White, *Early Writings* (Washington, D.C.: Review and Herald, n.d.), p. 74, quoted in Martin, *Kingdom of the Cults*, pp. 526-27.

[32]Later in his life Crosier rejected this concept, though it was adopted and endorsed by White and other Adventist leaders (Martin, *Kingdom of the Cults*, p. 526).

[33]This heavenly place was said to comport with the Jerusalem temple, where in the most holy place sat the ark of the covenant, the holiest shrine of Israel. There between the cherubim wings hovered the presence of the Lord. Once a year the high priest entered the most holy place and sprinkled blood upon the "mercy seat," the gold lid of the ark, to make atonement for the sins of the people. In Christian theology the blood symbolized and foreshadowed the sacrificial death of Christ, the Lamb of God, for the sins of all the world.

[34]See Martin, *Kingdom of the Cults*, p. 584.

[35]Ellen G. White, *Patriarchs and Prophets* (Washington, D.C.: Review and Herald, n.d.), pp. 355-56, quoted in Martin, *Kingdom of the Cults*, p. 584.

[36]See "Christ's Second Advent and Millennial Rule," *Integrative Theology*, vol. 3, ed. Gordon R. Lewis and Bruce A. Demarist (Grand Rapids, Michigan: Zondervan Publishing House, 1994), 3:1996; combined volumes edition, p. 372.

[37]*A Greek-English Lexicon of the New Testament and Other Early Christian Literature*, trans. William Arnot and F. Wilbur Gingrich, rev. F. Wilbur Gingrich and Frederick W. Danker, 2nd ed. (Chicago: University of Chicago Press, 1979), p. 581.

[38]*Watchtower*, January 1, 1997, p. 11.

[39]Martin, *Kingdom of the Cults*, p. 135. The following discussion relies on this work.

[40]*Greek-English Lexicon*; and *A Greek-English Lexicon of the New Testament*, trans. and ed. Joseph Henry Thayer, 4th ed. (Edinburgh: T & T Clark, 1901).

[41]See Martin, *Kingdom of the Cults*, pp. 583-88. The following discussion is adapted from this work.

Chapter 11: The Doctrine of Rewards and Punishments

[1]For more on Jonathan Edwards and the intellectual legacy of the Puritans, see Allen Carden, *Puritan Christianity in America* (Grand Rapids: Baker, 1990).

[2]See Jonathan Edwards, "Sinners in the Hands of an Angry God," in *The Christian Theology Reader*, ed. Alister E. McGrath (Cambridge, Mass.: Blackwell, 1998), p. 361.

[3]Tertullian *Apology* 47.12-14, ed. T. R. Glover, Loeb Classical Library (Cambridge, Mass: Harvard University Press, 1960), p. 210.

[4]Universalism, or the theory of universal restoration, is a belief that all will eventually be saved. This idea has had a long history, Origen being its first major proponent. Some universalists hold that all who initially reject Christ will suffer in hell for a limited time; others believe that no one will taste hell at all.

[5]Nels Ferré, *The Christian Understanding of God* (New York: Harper & Brothers, 1951), p. 228, quoted in Millard Erickson, *Christian Theology* (Grand Rapids: Baker, 1992), pp. 1018-19. The following discussion is developed from Erickson.

[6]Ibid., p. 1019.

[7]Ibid.

[8]We, the authors, have experienced this in our own lives. We have known Christians who suffer under the weight of this awareness of loved ones who have apparently died without Christ.

[9]Such verses make it clear that purgatory is a misguided concept. Some Christians believe that souls go to purgatory to be further purged of sin before they are ready to be admitted into the presence of God. This Roman Catholic doctrine is based on certain passages in the Apocrypha, particularly 2 Maccabees 12:42-45. The most serious problem with this doctrine is the notion that Christ's atonement was not sufficient to blot out our sins and secure our eternal salvation.

These verses also disprove soul sleep, the belief that at death believers and unbelievers alike go immediately into a state of unconsciousness until the resurrection. Some Scriptures speak of death as "sleep" or "falling asleep" (Mt 9:24; 27:52; Jn 11:11; Acts 7:60; 13:36; 1 Cor 15:6, 18, 20, 51; 1 Thess 4:13; 5:10), while others seem to suggest that the dead do not possess conscious existence after death (Ps 6:5; 115:17 [but notice v. 18]; Eccles 9:10). Until we are resurrected, our physical state in death *resembles* sleep.

As for the passages that seem to indicate that the dead do not praise God, or that after people die they lose all consciousness, these are to be understood from the perspective of the living in this world. From our perspective, the dead—just like people who are asleep—do not engage in any of life's activities.

[10]Wayne Grudem, *Systematic Theology* (Grand Rapids: Zondervan, 1994), p. 823.

[11]Henry Chadwick, *The Early Church*, rev. ed. (London: Penguin, 1993), p. 112.

[12]Methodius *De Resurrectione* 1.13, quoted in *Christian Theology Reader*, ed. Alister E. McGrath, pp. 357-58.

[13]For an excellent study on the relationship of salvation to rewards, see Joseph C. Dillow, *The Reign of the Servant Kings* (Miami: Schoettle, 1992).

[14]Bill McKeever, *Answering Mormons' Questions* (Minneapolis: Bethany House, 1991), p. 90

[15]Bruce McConkie, *Mormon Doctrine* (Salt Lake City: Bookcraft, 1977), p. 420.

[16]Ibid., p. 816.

[17]Ibid., p. 778.

[18]Ibid., pp. 746, 759.

[19]Ibid., pp. 816-17.

[20]Ibid., p. 670.

[21]Ibid., p. 237.

[22]Milton R. Hunter, *The Gospel Through the Ages* (Salt Lake City: n.p., 1958), p. 104

[23]Lorenzo Snow, quoted in Hunter, *Gospel Through the Ages*, pp. 105-6.

[24]Joseph Smith Jr., *Journal of Discourses* (Salt Lake City: Church of Jesus Christ of Latter-day Saints, 1901), 6:4.

[25]*Watchtower*, February 15, 1984, p. 9.

[26]*Holy Spirit: The Force Behind the Coming New Order* (New York: Watchtower Bible and Tract Society, 1976), p. 157.

[27]*Watchtower*, March 15, 1983, p. 9.

[28]"The Divine Plan of the Ages," in *Studies in the Scriptures* (New York: Watchtower Bible and Tract Society, 1908), pp. 81-82.

[29]*Watchtower*, December 1881, p. 3 (reprint; 1919, p. 301).

[30]*Watchtower*, November 1881, p. 10 (reprint; 1919, pp. 297-98).

[31]*Reasoning from the Scriptures* (New York: Watchtower Bible and Tract Society, 1985), p. 175.

[32]Mary Baker Eddy, *Science and Health, with Key to the Scriptures* (Boston: First Church of Christ, Scientist, 1914), p. 266.

[33]Earnst Homes, *The Science of Mind* (New York: Dodd, Mead, 1938), p. 383.

[34]*Metaphysical Bible Dictionary* (Lee's Summit, Mo.: Unity School of Christianity, 1962), p. 271.

[35]Shirley MacLaine, *Out on a Limb* (New York, Bantam, 1983), p. 205, quoted in Douglas Groothuis, *Confronting the New Age* (Downers Grove, Ill.: InterVarsity Press, 1988), p. 103.

[36]Joe Fisher, *The Case for Reincarnation*, quoted in *The New Age Catalog* (New York: Doubleday, 1988), p. 103.

[37]G. C. Huckaby, comp. *Louisiana Masonic Monitor of the Degrees of the Entered Apprentice, Fellow Craft and Master Mason,* 1941, p. 68.

[38]John Ankerberg and John Weldon, *The Secret Teachings of the Masonic Lodge* (Chicago: Moody Press, 1990), p. 153.

[39]See Norman Geisler, "Canonicity of Bible," *Baker Encyclopedia of Apologetics* (Grand Rapids: Baker, 1999), pp. 84-85.

[40]See "From the Council of Chalcedon to the Present," *Documents of the Christian Church,* ed. Henry Bettenson, 2nd ed. (New York: Oxford University Press, 1967), p. 91.

[41]Norman Geisler, "Origen," *Baker Encyclopedia of Apologetics* (Grand Rapids: Baker, 1999), p. 565. The following discussion relies on this source.

[42]"The Fifth Ecumenical Council; The Second Ecumenical Council of Constantinople, A.D. 553," *Nicene and Post-Nicene Fathers* series 2, vol. 14, ed. Philip Schaff, The Master Christian Library, AGES Digital Library Collection 6 (1998).

[43]Jonathan Edwards, *The Works of Jonathan Edwards* (New York: Garland, 1987), 2.87.

[44]Ibid., 2.884, quoted in Geisler, *Baker Encyclopedia of Christian Apologetics,* p. 315.

Chapter 12: Onward Christian Soldiers

[1]Some of the material in this chapter is taken from H. Wayne House, "What Is the Best Way to Protect Myself from Spiritual Counterfeits?" *Kindred Spirit,* summer 1987, pp. 1, 14.

SELECTED BIBLIOGRAPHY

General References

Beckwith, Francis J., and Stephen E. Parish. *See the Gods Fall: Four Rivals to Christianity.* Joplin, Mo.: College Press, 1997.

Bettenson, Henry, ed. *Documents of the Christian Church.* 2nd ed. New York: Oxford University Press, 1967.

Bray, Gerald. *Creeds, Councils and Christ.* Downers Grove, Ill.: InterVarsity Press, 1984.

Bruce, F. F. *The New Testament Documents: Are They Reliable?* 5th ed. Downers Grove, Ill.: InterVarsity Press, 1960.

Craig, William Lane. *Reasonable Faith: Christian Truth and Apologetics.* Rev. ed. Wheaton, Ill.: Crossway, 1994.

Cross, F. L., and E. A. Livingstone, eds. *The Oxford Dictionary of the Christian Church.* New York: Oxford University Press, 1997.

Edwards, Paul, ed. *The Encyclopedia of Philosophy.* New York: Macmillan, 1967.

Elwell, Walter, ed. *Evangelical Dictionary of Theology.* Grand Rapids: Baker, 1984.

Erickson, Millard J. *Christian Theology.* Grand Rapids: Baker, 1992.

Ferguson, Sinclair B., David F. Wright and J. I. Packer, eds. *New Dictionary of Theology.* Downers Grove, Ill.: InterVarsity Press, 1988.

Geisler, Norman. *Baker Encyclopedia of Christian Apologetics.* Grand Rapids: Baker, 1999.

Geisler, Norman L., and William E. Nix. *A General Introduction to the Bible.* Chicago: Moody Press, 1986.

Grudem, Wayne. *Systematic Theology: An Introduction to Biblical Doctrine.* Grand Rapids: Zondervan, 1994.

Harris, Murray J. *Jesus as God.* Grand Rapids: Baker, 1992.

Harris, R. Laird. *Inspiration and Canonicity of the Bible: Contemporary Evangelical Perspectives.* Grand Rapids: Zondervan, 1984.

Henry, Carl F. H. *God, Revelation and Authority.* 6 vols. Waco, Tex.: Word, 1976.

Kelly, J. N. D. *Early Christian Doctrines.* Rev. ed. San Francisco: HarperSanFrancisco, 1978.

Martin, Walter. *The Kingdom of the Cults.* 4th ed. Edited by Hank Hanegraaff. Minneapolis: Bethany House, 1997.

Radmacher, Earl D., and Robert D. Preus, eds. *Hermeneutics, Inerrancy and the Bible.* Grand Rapids: Zondervan, 1984.

Ramsay, William Mitchell. *St. Paul, the Traveller and the Roman Citizen.* 14th ed. London: Hodder & Stoughton, 1925.

Rosten, Leo. *A Guide to the Religions of America.* New York: Simon & Schuster, 1963.

Sire, James. *Scripture Twisting: Twenty Ways Cults Misread the Bible.* Downers Grove, Ill.: InterVarsity Press, 1980.

REFERENCES TO SPECIFIC RELIGIOUS GROUPS

Christadelphians

Answering Your Questions About the Christadelphians. Privately published, n.d.

A Course in Miracles

Shucman, Helen. *A Course in Miracles,* vol. 1, *Text.* Tiburon, Calif.: Foundation for Inner Peace, 1975.

———. *A Course in Miracles,* vol. 2, *Workbook for Students.* Tiburon, Calif.: Foundation for Inner Peace, 1975.

Freemasonry

Ankerberg, John, and John Weldon. *The Secret Teachings of the Masonic Lodge.* Chicago: Moody Press, 1990.

Newton, Joseph Fort. *The Builders: A Story and Study of Freemasonry.* New York: Macoy, 1951.

Jehovah's Witnesses

Insight on the Scriptures. 2 vols. New York: Watchtower Bible and Tract Society, 1988.

Jehovah's Witnesses in the 20th Century. New York: Watchtower Bible and Tract Society, 1989.

"Let God Be True." Rev. ed. New York: Watchtower Bible and Tract Society, 1952.

Reasoning from the Scriptures. New York: Watchtower Bible and Tract Society, 1985.

Should You Believe in the Trinity? New York: Watchtower Bible and Tract Society, 1977.

You Can Live Forever in Paradise on Earth. New York: Watchtower Bible and Tract Society, 1982.

Mind Science Groups

Christian Science

Eddy, Mary Baker. *Science and Health with Key to the Scriptures.* Boston: Trustees Under the Will of Mary Baker G. Eddy, 1934.

———. *Miscellaneous Writings, 1883-1896.* Boston: J. Armstrong, 1897.

Religious Science

Holmes, Ernest, and Fenwicke L. Holmes. *What Religious Science Teaches.* Los Angeles: Institute of Religious Sciences, 1944.

Holmes, Ernest, with Maude Allison Lathem. *The Science of the Mind.* Los Angeles: Institute of Religious Science, 1944.

Mormonism

Articles of Faith. Salt Lake City: Church of Jesus Christ of Latter-day Saints, 1952.

Compton, Todd M., and Stephen D. Ricks, eds. *Mormonism and Early Christianity: The Collected Words of Hugh Nibley.* Vol. 4. Salt Lake City: Deseret, 1987.

Hunter, Milton R. *The Gospel Through the Ages.* Salt Lake City: Stevens and Wallis, 1945.

McConkie, Bruce R. *Mormon Doctrine*. Salt Lake City: Bookcraft, 1977.

Smith, Joseph. *The Doctrines & Covenants of the Church of Jesus Christ of Latter-day Saints*. Salt Lake City: Church of Jesus Christ of Latter-day Saints, 1986.

Smith, Joseph Fielding. *Doctrines of Salvation*. Salt Lake City: Bookcraft, 1954.

Talmage, James. *A Study of the Articles of Faith*. 26th ed. Salt Lake City: Church of Jesus Christ of Latter-day Saints, 1948.

What the Mormons Think of Christ. Salt Lake City: Deseret, 1873.

New Age

Fisher, Joe. *The Case for Reincarnation*. New York: Bantam, 1985.

Rosicrucianism

The Rosicrucian Cosmo-Conception, or Mystic Christianity. 1929. Reprint, Oceanside, Calif.: Rosicrucian Fellowship, 1974.

The Rosicrucian Philosophy in Questions and Answers. 2nd ed. Oceanside, Calif.: Rosicrucian Fellowship, 1910.

Seventh-day Adventist

Questions on Doctrine. Washington, D.C.: Review and Herald Publishing Association, 1957.

Seventh-day Adventists Believe: A Biblical Exposition of Twenty-Seven Foundational Doctrines. Washington, D.C.: Ministerial Association, General Conference of Seventh-day Adventists, 1988.

White, Ellen G. *The Great Controversy Between Christ and Satan: The Conflict of the Ages in the Christian Dispensation*. 1888. Reprint, Mountain View, Calif.: Pacific Press, 1950.

United Pentecostals

Bernard, David. K. *The Oneness of God: Series in Pentecostal Theology*. Vol. 1. Hazelwood, Mo.: Word Aflame, 1983.

The New Birth Series: Series in Pentecostal Theology. Hazelwood, Mo.: Word Aflame, 1984.

The P.A.S.T.O.R.S. Course: Theology. 5 vols.

Unity School of Christianity

Fillmore, Charles. *Christian Healing.* Kansas City, Mo.: Unity School of Christianity, 1909.

Metaphysical Bible Dictionary. Unity Village, Mo.: Unity School of Christianity, 1931.

Unity Statement of Faith. Article 24.

What Unity Teaches. Lee's Summit, Mo.: Unity School of Christianity, n.d.

Urantia Foundation

The Urantia Book. Chicago: Urantia Foundation, 1955.

The Way International

Wierwille, Victor P. *Power for Abundant Living.* New Knoxville, Ohio: American Christian Press, 1971.

For a more extensive bibliography, visit the Doctrine Twisting *book page of the IVP website: <www.gospelcom.net/cgi-ivpress/book.pl/code=1369>.*

Names Index

New Religious Movements and Beliefs Index

Scripture Index